THE TEACHINGS FOR
VICTORY

LEARNING FROM NICHIREN'S WRITINGS

THE TEACHINGS FOR
VICTORY

VOLUME 2

DAISAKU IKEDA

World Tribune
Press

The Teachings for Victory, Volume 2

Published by

World Tribune Press
606 Wilshire Blvd.
Santa Monica, CA 90401

Design by Lightbourne, Inc.
Source artwork: www.iStockphoto.com

ISBN: 978-1-935523-63-5
LCCN: 2013946892

10 9 8 7 6 5 4 3 2 1

CONTENTS

Editor's Note   vii

"ON PRACTICING THE BUDDHA'S TEACHINGS"

1   Part 1 of 3—Striving for Kosen-rufu in the Spirit of the
Oneness of Mentor and Disciple Is the Key to True "Peace
and Security in This Existence"   1

2   Part 2 of 3—The Compassionate Practice of Shakubuku   19

3   Part 3 of 3—Encountering Great Obstacles Is Proof of Propagating
the Correct Teaching for Attaining Buddhahood in the Latter Day
of the Law   35

"THE PROOF OF THE LOTUS SUTRA"

4   The Prayers of a Votary of the Lotus Sutra Triumph Over Illness   53

"THE HERO OF THE WORLD"

5   The Victory of the Disciples Is the Victory of the Mentor and the
Victory of Buddhism   69

"THE BLESSINGS OF THE LOTUS SUTRA"

6   Personal Initiative Is the Soka Gakkai's Founding Spirit   85

"THE SUTRA OF TRUE REQUITAL"

7   Nichiren Daishonin's Vow and Tireless Struggle for the
Enlightenment of Women   105

"KING RINDA"

8   Vibrant Chanting Opens the Great Path to Absolute Victory   123

"THE KALPA OF DECREASE"

9   Nichiren Daishonin's Buddhism: Wisdom for Realizing
Happiness for All Humanity   141

Index   159

EDITOR'S NOTE

This series of lectures by SGI President Daisaku Ikeda was published in SGI-USA's *Living Buddhism* magazine from the November–December 2010 issue through the January–February 2011 issue, and from the May–June 2011 issue through the November 2011 issue.

Please also see *The Writings of Nichiren Daishonin*, vol. 1, as follows:

"On Practicing the Buddha's Teachings," pp. 391–96
"The Proof of the Lotus Sutra," pp. 1108–09
"The Hero of the World," pp. 835–39
"The Blessings of the Lotus Sutra," pp. 667–73
"The Sutra of True Requital," pp. 928–34
"King Rinda," pp. 983–90
"The Kalpa of Decrease," pp. 1120–22

- GZ, page number(s)—refers to the *Gosho zenshu*, the Japanese-language compilation of letters, treatises, essays, and oral teachings of Nichiren Daishonin (Tokyo: Soka Gakkai, 1952).

- LSOC, page number(s)—refers to *The Lotus Sutra and Its Opening and Closing Sutras*, translated by Burton Watson (Tokyo: Soka Gakkai, 2009).

- OTT, page number(s)—refers to *The Record of the Orally Transmitted Teachings*, translated by Burton Watson (Tokyo: Soka Gakkai, 2004).

- WND, page number(s)—refers to *The Writings of Nichiren Daishonin*, vol. 1 (WND-1) (Tokyo: Soka Gakkai, 1999) and vol. 2 (WND-2) (Tokyo: Soka Gakkai, 2006).

References to dates in *The Writings of Nichiren Daishonin* are from the lunisolar calendar that was used in thirteenth-century Japan, which differs from the current Gregorian calendar commonly used in the West.

"ON PRACTICING THE BUDDHA'S TEACHINGS"—PART 1 OF 3

STRIVING FOR KOSEN-RUFU IN THE SPIRIT OF THE ONENESS OF MENTOR AND DISCIPLE IS THE KEY TO TRUE "PEACE AND SECURITY IN THIS EXISTENCE"

The Passage for Study in This Lecture

On examination [of the Lotus Sutra], we find that those who are born in this land and believe in this sutra when it is propagated in the Latter Day of the Law will be subjected to hatred and jealousy even greater than that which arose in the lifetime of the Thus Come One.

What is more, once you become a disciple or lay supporter of the votary who practices the true Lotus Sutra in accord with the Buddha's teachings, you are bound to face the three types of enemies. Therefore, from the very day you listen to [and take faith in] this sutra, you should be fully prepared to face the great persecutions of the three types of enemies that are certain to be more horrible now after the Buddha's passing. Although my disciples had already heard this, when both great and small persecutions confronted us, some were so astounded and terrified that they even forsook their faith. Did I not warn you in advance? I have been teaching you day and night directly from the sutra, which says, "Since hatred and jealousy toward this sutra abound even when the Thus Come One is in the world, how much more will this be so after his passing?"

This is indeed an accursed time to live in this land! However, the Buddha has commanded me to be born in this age, and it is impossible for me to go against the decree of the Dharma King. And so, as the sutra dictates, I have launched the battle between the provisional and the true teachings. Donning the armor of endurance and girding myself with the sword of the wonderful teaching, I have raised the banner of the five characters of Myoho-renge-kyo, the heart of the entire eight volumes of the Lotus Sutra. Then, drawing the bow of the Buddha's declaration, "I have not yet revealed the truth,"[1] and notching the arrow of "honestly discarding the provisional teachings,"[2] I have mounted the carriage drawn by the great white ox[3] and battered down the gates of the provisional teachings. Attacking first one and then another, I have refuted opponents from the eight and ten schools,[4] such as the Nembutsu, True Word, Zen, and Precepts. Some have fled headlong while others have retreated, and still others have been captured to become my disciples. I continue to repulse their attacks and to defeat them, but legions of enemies exist who oppose the single Dharma King and the handful who follow him. So the battle goes on even today.

"The Lotus Sutra is the teaching of shakubuku, the refutation of the provisional doctrines."[5] True to the letter of this golden saying, in the end, every last one of the believers of the provisional teachings and schools will be defeated and join the retinue of the Dharma King. The time will come when all people will abandon the various kinds of vehicles and take up the single vehicle of Buddhahood, and the Mystic Law alone will flourish throughout the land. When the people all chant Nam-myoho-renge-kyo, the wind will no longer buffet the branches, and the rain will no longer break the clods of soil. The world will become as it was in the ages of Fu Hsi and Shen Nung.[6] In their present existence the people will be freed from misfortune and disasters and learn the art of living long. Realize that the time will come when the truth will be revealed that both the person and the Law are unaging and eternal. There cannot be the slightest doubt about the sutra's promise of "peace and security in their present existence." (WND-1, 391–92)

LECTURE

The Chinese character *myo* of *myoho*, or Mystic Law, has the meaning of "to open."

Open the way with prayer based on the shared commitment of mentor and disciple!

Open the way with the courage to forge ahead bravely and vigorously!

Open the way with the wisdom to perceive the essential truth amid changing circumstances!

Open the way with self-assured and confident action!

Since the time of its first president, Tsunesaburo Makiguchi, the Soka Gakkai has grown and developed by pioneering new frontiers for kosen-rufu, always maintaining a direct connection to Nichiren Daishonin and basing everything on his writings. This will remain the Soka Gakkai's fundamental spirit for all time. This is also the key to faith for absolute victory, and it is highlighted in

Nichiren's writing "On Practicing the Buddha's Teachings."

The title of this letter literally translates as "On Practicing as the Buddha Teaches." Here, "as the Buddha teaches" can also be interpreted to mean "as the teacher expounds." Nichiren set an example for his disciples by reading the correct teaching of the Lotus Sutra with his life and practicing as the Buddha teaches. He waged a confrontation of words to "refute the erroneous and reveal the true," holding high the banner of universal enlightenment.[7]

And he did so in the Latter Day of the Law, an age of conflict,[8] when people lose sight of the Buddha's correct teaching and grow confused in their thinking and direction, which results in an environment of incessant strife. Nichiren's great struggle of refutation, or *shakubuku*, provoked attacks by the three powerful enemies,[9] just as the sutra predicts. But by boldly confronting and triumphing over these devilish functions, he proved the veracity of the Lotus Sutra. For us of modern times, practicing as the Buddha teaches means practicing in accord with the teachings of Nichiren.

The final chapter of Mr. Makiguchi's *Kachi ron* (Theory of Value), which second Soka Gakkai President Josei Toda revised, concludes with the following words, including some famous lines from "On Practicing the Buddha's Teachings":

Only when the correct teaching of Buddhism that elucidates the very essence of human existence comes to be widely disseminated will it be possible to truly

create a Land of Tranquil Light[10] that brings unsurpassed happiness to all people.

As the Daishonin writes: "'The Lotus Sutra is the teaching of shakubuku, the refutation of the provisional doctrines.'[11] . . . There cannot be the slightest doubt about the sutra's promise of 'peace and security in their present existence.'"[12]

Creating a Land of Tranquil Light that actualizes the sutra's promise of true peace and security in this existence was the ardent wish of the first and second presidents and the conclusion of Mr. Makiguchi's treatise on value. Mr. Makiguchi gave his life to the struggle to realize this ideal, refusing to submit to the unjust persecution of Japan's wartime militarist authorities. He practiced in exact accord with Nichiren's teachings.

Mr. Toda made a large double circle in red next to the title "On Practicing the Buddha's Teachings" in his copy of Nichiren's writings to indicate the special importance of this writing. As his loyal and devoted disciple, I also read this letter countless times, engraving in my heart Nichiren's spirit to refute error in the realm of Buddhism.

I fondly recall studying "On Practicing the Buddha's Teachings" with members who gathered at my apartment when I was the young men's division First Corps leader. Many years later, I lectured on this writing for high school division representatives. Nothing gives me greater joy than studying Nichiren's writings and putting them into practice together with the youth who will shoulder the future. I hope that today's youth division members will seriously study Nichiren's sublime philosophy and, in so doing, strengthen their conviction in faith and develop their ability to speak to others articulately about their Buddhist practice.

"On Practicing the Buddha's Teachings" outlines how genuine disciples strive to realize Buddhism's lofty ideals, unafraid of hardships, just as their teacher instructs. It is an important writing that contains the essence of the oneness of mentor and disciple. Let us engrave it deeply in our lives for the continuing development of kosen-rufu and the SGI's enduring victory into the eternal future of the Latter Day of the Law.

The Challenges of Propagating the Mystic Law in the Latter Day

On examination [of the Lotus Sutra], we find that those who are born in this land and believe in this sutra when it is propagated in the Latter Day of the Law will be subjected to hatred and jealousy even greater than that which arose in the lifetime of the Thus Come One. (WND-1, 391)

Dated the fifth month of 1273, "On Practicing the Buddha's Teachings" was composed at Ichinosawa on Sado Island during Nichiren Daishonin's exile. As the postscript indicates, it is addressed "To all my followers,"

along with the instruction, "Keep this letter with you at all times and read it over and over" (WND-1, 396). In this writing, Nichiren encourages his disciples to emulate his example of practicing the Lotus Sutra as the Buddha teaches and to diligently uphold their faith.

In his day, exile to Sado was tantamount to a death sentence; most people condemned to this remote isle never returned alive. During his time there, Nichiren's life was in constant danger. In "On the Buddha's Prophecy," dated one month later, he writes, "The chances are one in ten thousand that I will survive the year or even the month" (WND-1, 402).

Undaunted by indescribable hardships and privations, Nichiren proclaimed his struggle as the Buddha of the Latter Day of the Law to illuminate the darkness shrouding humankind with the light of universal enlightenment. The previous year, in the second month of 1272, he had composed "The Opening of the Eyes," which reveals the object of devotion in terms of the Person.[13] This was followed in the fourth month of 1273, just one month prior to "On Practicing the Buddha's Teachings," with "The Object of Devotion for Observing the Mind," which reveals the object of devotion in terms of the Law.[14] With the completion of these two important treatises, Nichiren had established the doctrinal framework for his teaching for the enlightenment of all people into the eternal future.

The rest was now up to his disciples. He knew that everything would hinge

5

on individuals genuinely committed to the correct teaching. If such dedicated disciples rose to action, kosen-rufu could be achieved without fail. His conviction is vividly conveyed in "On Practicing the Buddha's Teachings" and "On the Buddha's Prophecy." These two writings could be viewed as his enduring guidance for all his disciples.

"On Practicing the Buddha's Teachings" represents an impassioned call to his disciples who devote themselves selflessly to the Law. He urges them that now is the time to stand up and undertake the practice to refute the erroneous teachings rampant in the realm of Buddhism.

"On the Buddha's Prophecy," by contrast, is about actualizing the ideal of the westward transmission of the correct Buddhist teaching and its widespread propagation throughout the world in the distant future.

In other words, the grand vision of Nichiren's Buddhism of the people, a teaching for the enlightenment of all humanity, can only be realized when there are genuine disciples who strive for kosen-rufu "like Nichiren" or "with the same mind as Nichiren." That is why he calls on his disciples to take on the noble task of advancing kosen-rufu in the Latter Day without begrudging their lives.

At the beginning of this writing, Nichiren states, "Those who are born in this land and believe in this sutra when it is propagated in the Latter Day of the Law will be subjected to hatred and jealousy even greater than that which arose in the lifetime of the Thus Come One." This is based on the Lotus Sutra passage "Since hatred and jealousy toward this sutra abound even when the Thus Come One is in the world, how much more will this be so after his passing?" (LSOC, 203).

His purpose in making this statement is to deepen his followers' awareness of their mission to propagate the Mystic Law in this latter age and to prepare them for the opposition they are bound to incur along the way. Those fainthearted and afraid of hardship cannot realize the momentous undertaking of kosen-rufu. True disciples are those who stand up with the same ardent commitment as Nichiren to guide people to enlightenment and who have the dauntless strength to face obstacles head-on with selfless dedication. The joy of struggling together with one's mentor, sharing the same purpose, is also a source of boundless strength that helps one rise above all manner of hardships.

In the next passage, Nichiren explains why Lotus Sutra practitioners are destined to encounter far more intense opposition in the evil age of the Latter Day than during Shakyamuni's time. There are significant differences between the two ages. First, the person expounding the Law in Shakyamuni's day was the Buddha, whereas the person expounding the Law in the Latter Day is an ordinary practitioner. Also, the disciples in Shakyamuni's time were great bodhisattvas and arhats,[15] while the disciples in the Latter Day "come from among evil people defiled by the three poisons"[16] (WND-1, 391). Even during the time when the Buddha preached the Law and his teachings were practiced by outstanding disciples, many hated and were jealous of him and his community of believers. Nichiren notes that it is only natural, therefore, that even greater hostility and resentment should arise in the Latter Day when the Law is being expounded by a teacher who is ostensibly an ordinary practitioner and his disciples are people whose lives are steeped in the three poisons—greed, anger, and foolishness.

He therefore notes, "People shun the good teacher and associate with evil teachers" (WND-1, 391). Even though people may have the fortune to encounter the good teacher, Nichiren Daishonin, their inability to properly distinguish between good and evil, true and false, causes them to distance themselves from him in favor of erroneous teachers. That is the sad reality of the Latter Day.

"No Matter What Happens, Be Fearless!"

What is more, once you become a disciple or lay supporter of the votary who practices the true Lotus Sutra in accord with the Buddha's teachings, you are bound to face the three types of enemies. Therefore, from the very day you listen to [and take faith in] this sutra, you should be fully prepared to face the great persecutions of the three types of enemies that are certain to be more horrible now after the Buddha's passing. Although my disciples had already heard this, when both great and small persecutions confronted

us, some were so astounded and terrified that they even forsook their faith. Did I not warn you in advance? I have been teaching you day and night directly from the sutra, which says, "Since hatred and jealousy toward this sutra abound even when the Thus Come One is in the world, how much more will this be so after his passing?" (WND-1, 391)

This passage has become an unforgettable point of reference for me. Shortly after having my fateful encounter with Mr. Toda and embarking on the path of faith as a Soka Gakkai member, I took these golden words to heart and engraved them in my life.

Nichiren clearly states that those who practice as the Buddha teaches are bound to be assailed by the three powerful enemies and meet with persecutions even more severe than those during Shakyamuni's lifetime. As a young man, I accepted this and resolved to dedicate myself to kosen-rufu with the spirit of a revolutionary ready to give his life for the cause if need be. I was the disciple of Mr. Toda, a great leader of kosen-rufu who had gone to prison for his beliefs and had waged a heroic spiritual struggle. I knew that casting my lot with such a mentor would most certainly mean facing great persecutions on the path ahead. And I fervently vowed that I would remain fearless at such times.

In this passage, Nichiren rebukes the inner weakness of those disciples who foolishly allow themselves to be defeated by fear and cowardice and abandon their faith when persecutions large and small appear.

Mr. Toda was incredibly strict when he lectured on this passage. I recall one such instance at a study session he led in a small room at his company offices in Tokyo's Ichigaya area. He spoke with great passion, determined to impress upon his truehearted disciples the rigorous path of practicing Nichiren Buddhism. "No matter what happens, be fearless! Never retreat even a single step!" he said. His guidance was so strict because he had faithfully inherited Nichiren's spirit.

I remember being intensely struck and inspired by his words, learning for the first time the rigor and commitment of genuine faith and how the true purpose of Soka Gakkai activities perfectly accords with Nichiren's teachings.

At the end of this passage, Nichiren says that he has been telling his followers day and night about the sutra's warning: "Since hatred and jealousy toward this sutra abound even when the Thus Come One is in the world, how much more will this be so after his passing?" It is solely out of the wish for his disciples to remain fearless in the face of persecution that he has repeatedly done so.

As for the three powerful enemies, these are manifestations of the workings of the devil king of the sixth heaven,[17] or heavenly devil—the most fearful of the three obstacles and four devils.[18] As the teacher waging an unremitting battle against the onslaughts of these enemies, Nichiren constantly warned his followers that they were certain to encounter obstacles far worse than those experienced during Shakyamuni's time.

Nevertheless, some grew fainthearted and stopped practicing. It got to the point, writes Nichiren, where "999 out of 1,000 people . . . gave up their faith" ("Reply to Niiama," WND-1, 469).

Whether disciples triumph over devilish functions or are defeated by them will have a decisive impact on the spread of the Mystic Law in the Latter Day. Nothing is more painful for the teacher than to see disciples defeated by such obstacles.

In "The Opening of the Eyes," Nichiren writes:

Although I and my disciples may encounter various difficulties, if we do not harbor doubts in our hearts, we will as a matter of course attain Buddhahood. Do not have doubts simply because heaven does not lend you protection. Do not be discouraged because you do not enjoy an easy and secure existence in this life. This is what I have taught my disciples morning and evening, and yet they begin to harbor doubts and abandon their faith. Foolish men are likely to forget the promises they have made when the crucial moment comes. (WND-1, 283)

This passage describes how easy it is for people to grow fainthearted when actually faced with hardship or persecution. When such difficulties arise, that is the "crucial moment"—when our faith is put to the test.

The True Nature of the "Battle Between the Provisional and the True Teachings"

This is indeed an accursed time to live in this land! However, the Buddha has commanded me to be born in this age, and it is impossible for me to go against the decree of the Dharma King. And so, as the sutra dictates, I have launched the battle between the provisional and the true teachings. Donning the armor of endurance and girding myself with the sword of the wonderful teaching, I have raised the banner of the five characters of Myoho-renge-kyo, the heart of the entire eight volumes of the Lotus Sutra. Then, drawing the bow of the Buddha's declaration, "I have not yet revealed the truth," and notching the arrow of "honestly discarding the provisional teachings," I have mounted the carriage drawn by the great white ox and battered down the gates of the provisional teachings. Attacking first one and then another, I have refuted opponents from the eight and ten schools, such as the Nembutsu, True Word, Zen, and Precepts. Some have fled headlong while others have retreated, and still others have been captured to become my disciples. I continue to repulse their attacks and to defeat them, but legions of enemies exist who oppose the single Dharma King and the handful who follow him. So the battle goes on even today. (WND-1, 392)

Nichiren Daishonin declares that he has set in motion the battle between the provisional teachings[19] and the true teaching. Earlier, he proposes an answer to the question held by many, including some of his followers—namely, why those who practice the Lotus Sutra as the Buddha teaches should face fierce opposition from the three powerful enemies, even though the sutra assures them of peace and security in this existence. He offers the following three perspectives:

First, he cites the examples of Buddhist practitioners of the past such as Shakyamuni, Bodhisattva Never Disparaging (who represents Shakyamuni in a previous lifetime),[20] the Chinese priest Chu Tao-sheng,[21] the Tripitaka Master Fa-tao,[22] the Venerable Aryasimha,[23] the Great Teacher T'ien-t'ai[24] of China, the Great Teacher Dengyo[25] of Japan and others. Though all were votaries of the Lotus Sutra who practiced according to the Buddha's teachings, he notes, they each encountered harsh persecution (see WND-1, 391–92).

Second, Nichiren explains a true votary of the Lotus Sutra in the Latter Day undertakes the "battle between the provisional and the true teachings" in accord with the Buddha's decree and carries out extensive activities to propagate the Mystic Law. This is in the passage we are presently discussing.

Third, he declares that a genuine votary of the Lotus Sutra in the Latter Day aspires for the realization of an ideal society embodying the principle that "both the person and the Law are unaging and eternal" (WND-1, 392). He further clarifies that this ideal society will perfectly match the Lotus Sutra's description of peace and security in this existence.

The passage we are currently considering, which presents the second perspective, elucidates the essence of Nichiren's own struggles as the sutra's votary. He indicates that, far from simply waiting to be subjected to hardships, he has actively embarked on the "battle between the provisional and the true teachings."

The Latter Day is summed up by the line "This is the age of conflict in which the pure Law has been lost" (WND-1, 392). In other words, the Latter Day is a time when Buddhism falls into serious decline and all but perishes. Confusion reigns as to what constitutes the Buddha's correct teaching, with rival schools incessantly quarreling and disputing the validity of the different teachings they advocate. In addition to this confusion and disorder in the realm of Buddhism, people also become confused and disordered, and the land is imperiled as a result.

In such an age when the Law is on the brink of disappearing from society, the Lotus Sutra's votaries take on the challenge of refuting error in the realm of Buddhism and upholding the correct teaching in order to prevent it from being lost forever. They also uphold the ideal of establishing the correct teaching for the peace of the land in order to free people from suffering and put a halt to the country's ruin.

This is what it means to "practice as the Buddha teaches." In the Lotus Sutra, Shakyamuni addresses his bodhisattva disciples and urges them to undertake this struggle after his passing. Hence, Nichiren refers above to the command of the Buddha and the decree of the Dharma King (see WND-1, 392).

In the Lotus Sutra, Shakyamuni states that among his teachings there are those he expounded as expedient means (the provisional teachings, or the three vehicles) and one that contains his true intent (the true teaching, or the one vehicle).[26] He then instructs that, after his passing, his disciples should honestly discard the expedient teachings and spread the one vehicle of the Lotus Sutra. It is, therefore, the duty of votaries of the Lotus Sutra who appear in the Latter Day, when the Law is in danger of disappearing, to carry on the "battle between the provisional and true teachings" so as to make a clear distinction between them. The purpose of this battle is solely to prevent the correct Buddhist teaching from perishing.

Those who clarify the differences between the provisional teachings and the true teaching in the Latter Day, when the Buddha's teachings are in complete disarray, are certain to incur resentment and hostility from the established Buddhist schools, whose religious authority is based on the claimed supremacy of various provisional sutras. It is sure to unleash a storm of criticism, misunderstanding, and persecution. Consequently, those who wage this battle must do so with the recognition that this is "an accursed time" and don the "armor of endurance" so that they can withstand the inevitable fierce onslaughts.

The most powerful weapon in this battle is the Lotus Sutra itself, in which the Buddha clearly distinguished between the provisional teachings and the true teaching. Hence, Nichiren uses the expression, the "sword of the wonderful teaching." Nothing can cut through or refute error as incisively as the Buddha's own words. The practice of refuting erroneous teachings in the realm of Buddhism is ultimately a struggle of compassion fought with the force of reason. If it were to be waged with anything other than reason—for example, authority or brute force—then it would not be the battle of ideas commanded by the Buddha. Resorting to such means would be a negation of Buddhism itself, indicative of the most deplorable decline of the Law in the Latter Day.

The "banner of the five characters of Myoho-renge-kyo, the heart of the entire eight volumes of the Lotus Sutra" refers to Nam-myoho-renge-kyo, the essence of the Lotus Sutra. It is the banner of the forces who champion the correct teaching. It is the "banner of propagation of the Lotus Sutra" ("The Real Aspect of the Gohonzon," WND-1, 831), carried by the practitioners who widely proclaim the Mystic Law—a teaching of universal enlightenment—and refute error that plunges people into suffering.

The "five characters of Myoho-renge-kyo" constitute the name of the Buddha nature of all living beings,[27] and chanting Nam-myoho-renge-kyo is the practice that makes it possible for both ourselves and others to manifest this Buddha nature from within. This means that each of us has the power to unfurl the banner of victory in our lives. Ultimately, the "battle between the provisional and the true

teachings" is a struggle for human victory, one in which we aim—through chanting Nam-myoho-renge-kyo based on strong faith in the Mystic Law—to overcome all suffering and misfortune and open the way to happiness for everyone.

The votary who holds aloft the "banner of the five characters of Myoho-renge-kyo" can shoot down the workings of devilish functions by employing the "bow and arrow" of the Buddha's words "I have not yet revealed the truth" and "honestly discarding the provisional teachings."

Also, the "carriage drawn by the great white ox" signifies the one vehicle of the Lotus Sutra that can carry all people to the destination of enlightenment. It is a vehicle magnificent in size and grandeur, imparting boundless peace of mind to all who ride in it. It can travel freely anywhere, unrestrictedly, in order to free people from suffering.[28]

Nichiren says: "I have mounted the carriage drawn by the great white ox and battered down the gates of the provisional teachings. Attacking first one and then another, I have refuted opponents. . . . So the battle goes on even today." This passage conveys his dynamism and boundless vigor. It brims with his unrestrained passion and energy to fight tirelessly for kosen-rufu. His words are meant to sweep away all doubt regarding why those who practice the Lotus Sutra as the Buddha teaches do not enjoy peace and security in their present existence. SGI members' activities since the pioneering days of our movement reflect the same vigor and strength Nichiren conveys here.

Discussing this passage, Mr. Toda said: "We mustn't let harmful errors go unchallenged. We must stay on the offensive against them, continuing to press forward and thoroughly refuting them." Mr. Toda was a leader dedicated to guiding all people to true and lasting happiness. He was also a great warrior determined to refute the erroneous and reveal the true in the realm of Buddhism. He always brimmed with this spirit, the spirit of refutation, to do battle against error and wrongdoing.

In this passage, Nichiren also speaks of repulsing the attacks of enemies and defeating them. I would especially like our youth division members to emulate this spirit and have the unflagging determination to eradicate all roots of evil that cause people suffering and misery. To achieve kosen-rufu, we need to defeat the devilish nature or negativity that resides and proliferates in the human heart.

At the end of this passage, Nichiren writes: "Legions of enemies exist who oppose the single Dharma King and the handful who follow him. So the battle goes on even today." The first three Soka Gakkai presidents, connected by the bonds of mentor and disciple, have always taken action with the unwavering resolve to keep fighting for kosen-rufu. Amid rising Japanese militarism, Mr. Makiguchi boldly stood up alone to revive Nichiren Buddhism in modern times. Mr. Toda also stood up alone amid the devastation of postwar Japan to rebuild the Soka Gakkai and achieve the membership goal of 750,000 households. And I, the third president, stood up alone as Mr. Toda's disciple

and embarked on a momentous journey for worldwide kosen-rufu.

Kosen-rufu is a continuous struggle between the forces of the Buddha and devilish functions. Indeed, "the battle goes on even today." The true brilliance of the life state of Buddhahood shines in this spirit of unceasing challenge, as clearly illustrated by those who practice in accord with the Buddha's teaching.

Tenacious Dialogue and Shining Humanity

"The Lotus Sutra is the teaching of shakubuku, the refutation of the provisional doctrines." True to the letter of this golden saying, in the end, every last one of the believers of the provisional teachings and schools will be defeated and join the retinue of the Dharma King. The time will come when all people will abandon the various kinds of vehicles and take up the single vehicle of Buddhahood, and the Mystic Law alone will flourish throughout the land. When the people all chant Nam-myoho-renge-kyo, the wind will no longer buffet the branches, and the rain will no longer break the clods of soil. The world will become as it was in the ages of Fu Hsi and Shen Nung. In their present existence the people will be freed from misfortune and disasters and learn the art of living long. Realize that the time will come when the truth will be revealed that

both the person and the Law are unaging and eternal. There cannot be the slightest doubt about the sutra's promise of "peace and security in their present existence." (WND-1, 392)

This passage clarifies in terms of both reason and the Buddha's intent that the Lotus Sutra's promise of peace and security in this existence is definitely not false. "The Lotus Sutra is the teaching of shakubuku, the refutation of the provisional doctrines"—this is a well-known passage from T'ien-t'ai's *The Profound Meaning of the Lotus Sutra*. It means that shakubuku in the context of the Lotus Sutra refers to refuting the doctrines of the provisional teachings.

In the Lotus Sutra, Shakyamuni himself refutes these teachings; so, in the battle between the provisional and the true, those attached to the provisional are ultimately refuted by the Buddha himself. If they are sincere disciples, when they realize this fact they will be moved to follow the Buddha's true intent.

In the above passage, the image of all believers of the provisional teachings coming to correctly abide by the Buddha's intent is described as "joining the retinue of the Dharma King," while the concept of all the provisional teachings being integrated into the one vehicle of the Lotus Sutra is described as "all vehicles becoming the one Buddha vehicle."[29]

"The time when . . . the Mystic Law alone will flourish throughout the land" indicates the period in which the Mystic Law—the ultimate Law for attaining Buddhahood to which the Buddha became enlightened—is duly accepted and upheld as the correct Buddhist teaching. It is a time when slander and disbelief in the Mystic Law are swept away and Buddhism based on this supreme Law of life comes to prosper and flourish.

Nichiren Daishonin is not saying here that one school of Buddhism will gain dominance over all the other schools—even though he noted that the "eight and ten schools"[30] of the day were in disarray and quarreled endlessly among themselves, a defining feature of an age of conflict. What he means is that the Mystic Law—the ultimate essence of the Buddha's enlightenment, which is also the original source of the various Buddhist schools—will come to function as the fundamental guiding principle of society without opposition or impediment.

The passage "When the people all chant Nam-myoho-renge-kyo" describes the establishment of a spiritual framework supportive of kosen-rufu. It refers to a situation where people readily accept the correct teaching upon hearing it, without slander or opposition. It is a time when the benefit of this teaching—the Law for the enlightenment of all people that the Buddha demonstrated with his life and taught to others—spreads widely among the people. This also signifies "establishing the correct teaching" in terms of Nichiren's principle of "establishing the correct teaching for the peace of the land."

Mr. Makiguchi referred to "major good" as an aspect of the spiritual value that would be realized through spreading the Mystic Law.

Mr. Toda, meanwhile, espoused "human revolution" for all humankind. Inheriting their legacy, I have taken the further step of emphasizing the "dignity and sanctity of life" as the spiritual value to be shared and toward which all humanity should aspire.

Kosen-rufu is the most difficult of undertakings. It involves an inner transformation in people's lives. Faith in the Mystic Law is a self-motivating force. Steadfast efforts in one-to-one dialogue are indispensable to nurturing that faith, giving each person confidence in his or her potential to change from within.

Nichiren speaks of all people abandoning the various other vehicles and taking up the single vehicle of Buddhahood. The Law does not spread through coercion. As such, the ideal described in the aforementioned quote will only be realized when the humanism of Nichiren Buddhism gains widespread acceptance, becomes the philosophical current of society and develops into humankind's shared value. Kosen-rufu cannot be accomplished without tenacious dialogue and the shining humanity of those who spread the Law.

The great dialogue movement built by the SGI based on Buddhist humanism could rightly then be called a miracle of the present day. We are the sole organization carrying out the Buddha's decree in the modern world and faithfully practicing Nichiren Buddhism just as he taught. As a result, we have triumphed over countless adversities and vigorously advanced kosen-rufu.

The SGI's humanistic network, based on Nichiren Buddhism, has grown to encompass 192 countries and territories. In Japan and around the globe, many new SGI facilities are under construction, and increasing numbers of community leaders and friends in countless areas enjoy participating in SGI events. This is all due to the trust that members in each country have won through their tireless efforts to reach out to others through dialogue and to foster friendships in their communities and neighborhoods. Such actions truly embody Nichiren's conviction that "the Mystic Law alone will flourish." He declares that when the Mystic Law widely prevails, an age of peace and security in this existence will be realized without fail.

He then offers an image of what the world could be like when kosen-rufu is achieved. He writes, "The wind will no longer buffet the branches, and the rain will no longer break the clods of soil." When we believe in the Mystic Law, which provides a fundamental basis for the sanctity of life, and chant Nam-myoho-renge-kyo, then we can achieve a world of peace and security in the present existence that is apparent to all. As in the ages of the legendary Chinese rulers Fu Hsi and Shen Nung, peace, prosperity, and happiness will come to permeate the land.

Nichiren also says, "The time will come when the truth will be revealed that both the person and the Law are unaging and eternal." That the law is "unaging and eternal" means that the workings of the Mystic Law—which encompass, give rise to, and sustain all phenomena—neither decline nor cease to operate. On one level, this could be taken to mean that all things are harmonized and function to create value amid diversity. That the person is "unaging and eternal," on the other hand, does not mean, of course, that we do not grow old or die; but rather, through faith in the Mystic Law, we can establish a state of life pervaded by the four noble virtues—eternity, happiness, true self, and purity. In this state of life, we are neither perturbed nor defeated by the sufferings of aging or death. As Shakyamuni clarified, these sufferings arise from illusion, or ignorance of the true nature of life. In an age when the Mystic Law's power is freely manifested, people will naturally gain confidence in it and break through ignorance or darkness.

In this way, the struggle for kosen-rufu by those who correctly practice the Buddha's teachings will give rise to an ideal society in which all people enjoy peace and security in this existence. This goal of peace and security, however, is not to be found merely in some ideal future society. It describes the life state of those who faithfully practice the correct Lotus Sutra teaching with which to realize happiness and actualize a secure and peaceful land. This is clear from the preceding passages that describe Nichiren's own struggles. His dynamic stance in fighting for kosen-rufu undefeated by hardship is a shining example of genuine peace and security in this existence. This is the true meaning of this concept in Nichiren Buddhism.

When we exert ourselves in our Buddhist practice, our Buddhahood is powerfully activated. Our lives come to brim with supreme joy. There is no tragic self-sacrifice in the Nichiren Buddhist spirit of "selfless dedication" or "not begrudging one's life." When we vigorously challenge ourselves, joy always pulses vibrantly in our lives.

Nichiren concludes "On Practicing the Buddha's Teachings" with: "How can such joy possibly be described!" (WND-1, 396). And in the closing passage of "The Opening of the Eyes"—a writing in which he embarks on a still more detailed discussion of practicing as the Buddha teaches—he expresses his tremendous inner joy, saying: "For what I have done, I have been condemned to exile, but it is a small suffering to undergo in this present life and not one worth lamenting. In future lives I will enjoy immense happiness, a thought that gives me great joy" (WND-1, 287).

The struggle for kosen-rufu is a succession of hardships. These very efforts, however, also enable us to manifest the life state of Buddhahood, which is accompanied by unsurpassed joy. Those who strive all-out for kosen-rufu always savor such deep happiness and fulfillment. There is no greater peace and security in this existence than that found in the life state of one who truly understands the Buddhist principle that "great obstacles lead to enlightenment."

A steadfast commitment to striving for kosen-rufu as Nichiren teaches, firmly grounded in his writings, is the key to achieving a life of enduring happiness and hope.

This lecture was originally published in the January 2010 issue of the Daibyakurenge, *the Soka Gakkai's monthly study journal.*

NOTES

1. This is a line from the Immeasurable Meanings Sutra. Shakyamuni says, "In these more than forty years, I have not yet revealed the truth" (LSOC, 15), indicating that all of the teachings he expounded in the preceding period of more than forty years were expedient and provisional teachings and that he had not yet revealed the truth.

2. Nichiren cites the phrase "honestly discarding expedient means" (LSOC, 79) from "Expedient Means," the second chapter of the Lotus Sutra, with a slight alteration. With these words, Shakyamuni indicates that the teachings he expounded in the preceding period of more than forty years are provisional and, as such, should be discarded.

3. The carriage drawn by the great white ox symbolizes the supreme vehicle of Buddhahood, described in the parable of the three carts and the burning house that appears in "Simile and Parable," the third chapter of the Lotus Sutra.

4. Eight and ten schools: The eight schools are the eight major schools of Buddhism in Japan before the Kamakura period (1185–1333). They are the Dharma Analysis Treasury, Establishment of Truth, Precepts, Dharma Characteristics, Three Treatises, Flower Garland, Tendai, and True Word schools. The addition of the Pure Land (Nembutsu) and Zen schools, which emerged early in the Kamakura period, produces the ten schools, as they are often referred to collectively in Japanese Buddhist works.

5. From *The Supplement to the Meanings of the Commentaries on the Lotus Sutra*, a document attributed to Chih-tu, a disciple of the Great Teacher Miao-lo (711–82) of China.

6. Fu Hsi and Shen Nung: Legendary kings who constructed ideal societies in ancient China. It was said that during their reigns people's hearts were at peace, agriculture was abundant, and there were no disasters.

7. This is a reference to the fact that the Lotus Sutra opened the way to the enlightenment of all people, whereas the provisional pre-Lotus Sutra teachings had denied the possibility of attaining enlightenment in this lifetime to persons of the two vehicles (voice-hearers and cause-awakened ones), as well as to women and to evil people.

8. Age of conflict: An age of quarrels and disputes. A reference to a description of the fifth five-hundred-year period in the Great Collection Sutra, which says that, in this age—which corresponds to the Latter Day of the Law—rival Buddhist schools will quarrel endlessly among themselves and Shakyamuni's correct teaching will be obscured and lost.

9. Three powerful enemies: Three types of arrogant people who persecute those who propagate the Lotus Sutra in the evil age after Shakyamuni's death, described in a twenty-line verse section of "Encouraging Devotion," the thirteenth chapter of the Lotus Sutra. Miao-lo summarizes them as arrogant lay people, arrogant priests, and arrogant false sages.

10. Land of Tranquil Light: Also, Land of Eternally Tranquil Light. The Buddha land, which is free from impermanence and impurity. In many sutras, the actual saha world in which human beings dwell is described as an impure land filled with delusions and sufferings, while the Buddha land is described as a pure land free from these and far removed from this saha world. In contrast, the Lotus Sutra reveals the saha world to be the Buddha land, or the Land of Eternally Tranquil Light, and explains that the nature of a land is determined by the minds of its inhabitants.

11. From T'ien-t'ai's *The Profound Meaning of the Lotus Sutra*.

12. Translated from Japanese. Tsunesaburo Makiguchi, *Kachi ron* (Theory of Value), ed. Josei Toda (Tokyo: Daisanbunmei-sha, 1979), 192–93.

13. The object of devotion in terms of the Person: Nichiren clarifies that he is the Buddha of the Latter Day of the Law who possesses the three virtues—sovereign, teacher, and parent—and who will lead the people of the Latter Day to enlightenment.

14. The object of devotion in terms of the Law: Nichiren explains that Nam-myoho-renge-kyo is the fundamental Law for attaining Buddhahood that all people of the Latter Day should revere.

15. Arhat: One who has attained the highest of the four stages that voice-hearers aim to achieve through the practice of the Hinayana teachings, that is, the highest stage of Hinayana enlightenment.

16. Three poisons: Greed, anger, and foolishness. The fundamental evils inherent in life that give rise to human suffering. In Nagarjuna's *Treatise on the Great Perfection of Wisdom,* the three poisons are regarded as the source of all illusions and earthly desires. The three poisons are so called because they pollute people's lives and work to prevent them from turning their hearts and minds to goodness.

17. Devil king of the sixth heaven: Also, devil king or heavenly devil. This is a personification of the negative tendency to force others to one's will at any cost. The king of devils, who dwells in the highest or the sixth heaven of the world of desire. He is also named Freely Enjoying Things Conjured by Others, the king who makes free use of the fruits of others' efforts for his own pleasure. Served by innumerable minions, he obstructs Buddhist practice and delights in sapping the life force of other beings. The devil king is a personification of the negative tendency to force others to one's will at any cost.

18. Three obstacles and four devils: Various obstacles and hindrances to the practice of Buddhism. The three obstacles are (1) the obstacle of earthly desires, (2) the obstacle of karma, and (3) the obstacle of retribution. The four devils are (1) the hindrance of the five components, (2) the hindrance of earthly desires, (3) the hindrance of death, and (4) the hindrance of the devil king.

19. The provisional teachings are the teachings that Shakyamuni expounded as expedient means to lead people to the true teaching. According to T'ien-t'ai's doctrine, they include all the teachings expounded before the Lotus Sutra. The provisional teachings reveal only partial aspects of the truth that the Buddha attained. In contrast, the true teaching is the teaching in which Shakyamuni directly revealed his enlightenment, expounding the truth he attained in its entirety. T'ien-t'ai defined the true teaching as the Lotus Sutra.

20. Bodhisattva Never Disparaging: A bodhisattva described in "Bodhisattva Never Disparaging," the twentieth chapter of the Lotus Sutra. This bodhisattva—Shakyamuni in a previous lifetime—would bow in reverence to everyone he met. However, he was attacked by arrogant people, who beat him with sticks and staves, and threw stones at him. The sutra explains that his practice of respecting others' Buddha nature became the cause for him to attain Buddhahood.

21. Chu Tao-sheng (d. 434): Also known as Tao-sheng. A disciple of Kumarajiva in China. He argued that all people possess the Buddha nature and that even *icchantikas*, people of incorrigible disbelief, can attain Buddhahood. The elder priests attacked him for these views and expelled him from the community of priests. He retired to a mountain in Su-chou (modern-day Suzhou Province in China).

22. Fa-tao (1086–1147): A priest who remonstrated with Emperor Hui-tsung of China's Sung dynasty when the emperor supported Taoism and attempted to suppress Buddhism. He was branded on the face and exiled.

23. Aryasimha (n.d.): The last of Shakyamuni's twenty-three or twenty-four successors, who lived in central India during the sixth century. When Aryasimha was propagating Buddhism in Kashmir in ancient India, King Mirakutsu, who was hostile to Buddhism, destroyed many Buddhist temples and stupas, and executed a number of monks. Aryasimha was among those beheaded by the king.

24. T'ien-t'ai (538–97): Also known as Chih-i. The founder of the T'ien-t'ai school in China. Commonly referred to as the Great Teacher T'ien-t'ai. His lectures were compiled in such works as *The Profound Meaning of the Lotus Sutra*, *The Words and Phrases of the Lotus Sutra*, and *Great Concentration and Insight*. He spread the Lotus Sutra in China and established the doctrine of "three thousand realms in a single moment of life."

25. Dengyo (767–822): Also known as Saicho. The founder of the Tendai (T'ien-t'ai) school in Japan. Often referred to as the Great Teacher Dengyo. He refuted the errors of the six schools of Nara—the established Buddhist schools of the day—elevated the Lotus Sutra and dedicated himself to the establishment of a Mahayana ordination center on Mount Hiei.

26. The three vehicles are the teachings expounded for voice-hearers, cause-awakened ones, and bodhisattvas, respectively. The one vehicle of Buddhahood means the teaching that enables all people to attain Buddhahood and corresponds to the Lotus Sutra.

27. In "Conversation between a Sage and an Unenlightened Man," Nichiren writes: "Myoho-renge-kyo is the Buddha nature of all living beings. The Buddha nature is the Dharma nature, and the Dharma nature is enlightenment. . . . The Buddha nature that all these beings possess is called by the name Myoho-renge-kyo. Therefore, if you recite these words of the daimoku once, then the Buddha nature of all living beings will be summoned and gather around you. At that time the three bodies of the Dharma nature within you—the Dharma body, the reward body, and the manifested body—will be drawn forth and become manifest. This is called attaining Buddhahood" (WND-1, 131).

28. Nichiren writes: "These large carriages drawn by white oxen are able to fly at will through the sky of the essential nature of phenomena" ("On the Large Carriages Drawn by White Oxen," WND-2, 976).

29. "All vehicles" is a reference to the three vehicles, which comprise the two vehicles—voice-hearers and cause-awakened ones—plus the vehicle of bodhisattvas. The "one Buddha vehicle" means the Lotus Sutra, the one teaching that can enable all people to attain Buddhahood. "Expedient Means," the second chapter of the Lotus Sutra, explains: "In the Buddha lands of the ten directions there is only the Law of the one vehicle, there are not two, there are not three, except when the Buddha preaches so as an expedient means" (LSOC, 69).

30. Eight and ten schools: See note 4.

CHAPTER

2

"ON PRACTICING THE BUDDHA'S TEACHINGS"—PART 2 OF 3

THE COMPASSIONATE PRACTICE OF SHAKUBUKU

The Passage for Study in This Lecture

I insist that this is wrong. The most important thing in practicing the Buddhist teachings is to follow and uphold the Buddha's golden words, not the opinions of others.

The Buddha himself concluded that one's practice accords with the Buddha's teachings only when one bases one's faith firmly on the standard of these sutra passages, believing fully that "there is only the Law of the one vehicle."

Anyone who practices Buddhism should first understand the two types of practice—shoju and shakubuku.[1] All the sutras and treatises fall into one or the other of these two categories. Though scholars in this country may have studied Buddhism extensively, they do not know which practice accords with the time. . . .

The two millennia of the Former and Middle Days of the Law required the spread of the Hinayana and provisional Mahayana teachings, but the first five hundred years of the Latter Day call for only the Lotus Sutra, the pure and perfect teaching of the one vehicle of Buddhahood, to be spread abroad widely. As predicted by the Buddha, now is the age of quarrels and disputes when the pure Law becomes obscured and lost, and the provisional and true teachings are hopelessly confused.

When one must face enemies, one needs a sword, a stick, or a bow and arrows. When one has no enemies, however, such weapons are of no use at all. In this age, the provisional teachings have turned into enemies of the true teaching. When the time is right to propagate the teaching of the one vehicle, the provisional teachings become enemies. When they are a source of confusion, they must be thoroughly refuted from the standpoint of the true teaching. Of the two types of practice, this is shakubuku, the practice of the Lotus Sutra. With good reason T'ien-t'ai stated, "The Lotus Sutra is the teaching of shakubuku, the refutation of the provisional doctrines."

The four peaceful practices[2] [in the "Peaceful Practices" chapter] correspond to shoju. To carry them out in this age would be as foolish as sowing seeds in winter and expecting to reap the harvest in spring. It is natural for a rooster to crow at dawn, but strange for him to crow at dusk. Now, when the true and the provisional teachings are utterly confused, it would be equally unnatural for one to seclude oneself in the mountain forests and carry out the peaceful practice of shoju without refuting the enemies of the Lotus Sutra. One would lose the chance to practice the Lotus Sutra. (WND-1, 393–94)

Toward the end of January 1952, at a kickoff for the now famous February Campaign,[3] I called out to my fellow Kamata Chapter members, with whom I shared a profound connection, "Let's celebrate the month of Mr. Toda's birth with a brilliant victory!"

February is the month in which Nichiren Daishonin was born and the month of second Soka Gakkai president Josei Toda's birth as well. We can practice Nichiren Buddhism today because the Daishonin appeared in the Latter Day and propagated the Mystic Law for the enlightenment of all people. And we can practice correctly as SGI members because Mr. Toda courageously embarked on the solitary struggle to rebuild the Soka Gakkai after World War II and make kosen-rufu a reality, carrying on the vision of his mentor, Tsunesaburo Makiguchi, who died in prison for his beliefs. Thus, we threw ourselves into the February Campaign of 1952 with deep appreciation and the desire to repay our gratitude to these great leaders and teachers of kosen-rufu.

Kosen-rufu, or the widespread propagation of the Law, is the "practice of Buddhas" arising out of the profound compassion Buddhas have for all living beings, and it is also the "practice of bodhisattvas" undertaken by disciples who make this compassionate spirit of Buddhas their own.

The true power for spreading the Mystic Law is born when all of us, as practitioners, directly connect our lives to the correct teacher of the Law and the true mentors of kosen-rufu.

Mr. Toda's monumental vow to accomplish a membership of 750,000 households galvanized and reinvigorated the Soka Gakkai. All of us owe him an immeasurable debt. As his young disciple, I rose to action with the single-minded wish to realize his cherished dream.

The February Campaign was the Soka Gakkai's first full-fledged effort to actively expand the kosen-rufu movement. For me, having up to then dedicated all my energies to supporting Mr. Toda during his business difficulties, it was also effectively the first kosen-rufu campaign I led on the front lines of our organization at my mentor's direct behest. My sole thought was to make Mr. Toda's pledge to achieve a membership of 750,000 households a reality. I worked tirelessly, giving my all to actualize his vision. Practicing as my mentor instructed also meant that I was acting in accord with the Buddha's teachings, thereby embodying the very essence of Buddhism.

If we faithfully exert ourselves as the Buddha teaches, we can break through any obstacle. Practicing in accord with the Buddha's teachings means disciples challenging themselves in the same spirit as their teacher or mentor. When we unerringly walk the path of mentor and disciple, we can bring forth unlimited power. The mentor's lofty and expansive life state can inspire us to win in our own struggles.

I learned from Mr. Toda the essence of faith and practice based on staunchly adhering to the Buddha's teachings. One particularly instructive time was when he resigned as general director (in 1950), not wanting to let his business difficulties affect the Soka Gakkai. I alone stood by Mr. Toda, who I recognized was the one and only leader of our kosen-rufu movement, and devoted myself tirelessly to supporting and assisting him in any way I could. In a journal entry (dated November 17, 1950), I wrote:

> Read "On Practicing the Buddha's Teachings."
>
> Deeply realized the necessity of courageous faith. . . .
>
> In the end, our powers of faith and practice determine everything. The Gohonzon possesses the powers of the Buddha and the Law. Only by our own faith can we prove, test, and acquire the great power of the supreme Law embodied in the Gohonzon.[4]

When we bring forth the powers of courageous faith and practice that accord with the Buddha's teachings, the infinite powers of the Buddha and the Law will manifest without fail. To deepen our understanding of this essential Nichiren Buddhist teaching, let us continue studying "On Practicing the Buddha's Teachings" in this chapter, focusing on the way of faith and practice for advancing with the same spirit as our mentor.

The "One Buddha Vehicle" as the Correct Basis of Faith

I insist that this is wrong. The most important thing in practicing the Buddhist teachings is to follow and uphold the Buddha's golden words, not the opinions of others.

The Buddha himself concluded that one's practice accords with the Buddha's teachings only when one bases one's faith firmly on the standard of these sutra passages, believing fully that "there is only the Law of the one vehicle." (WND-1, 393)

Just before this section, Nichiren Daishonin poses the question: "How should one practice if one is to be faithful to the Buddha's teachings?" (WND-1, 392). He then explains the correct way of faith in the Lotus Sutra in the Latter Day of the Law.

The true intent of the Buddha, Shakyamuni, is revealed in the Lotus Sutra. His aim is to clarify that all vehicles are contained in the one Buddha vehicle[5] (see WND-1, 392) and that all people have the potential to attain enlightenment. "All vehicles" indicates the teachings other than the Lotus Sutra expounded by Shakyamuni in accord with the different capacities of the people. They specifically refer to the "three vehicles," the teachings expounded for the voice-hearers, cause-awakened ones, and bodhisattvas, respectively. But Shakyamuni's true purpose in expounding these teachings was to cultivate the people's capacity so that he could ultimately teach them the "one Buddha vehicle"—the sole vehicle by which people can attain the state of Buddhahood. As such, it is the only teaching in the Buddha's vast body of sutras that can lead all humanity to enlightenment in the Latter Day. And it is fully and clearly revealed by Shakyamuni in the Lotus Sutra.

The Lotus Sutra not only discloses the Buddha's true intent of helping all people attain Buddhahood but also reveals the name of the great Law that is the key to enlightenment: Myoho-renge-kyo—the wonderful Law, or Mystic Law. It also expounds the principle of the "true aspect of all phenomena,"[6] which serves as the theoretical basis for the universal attainment of Buddhahood.

In addition, it illuminates the ultimate causality at work in Shakyamuni's fundamental enlightenment in the remote past in terms of the doctrine of "true cause and true effect."[7] It also enumerates the countless benefits of practicing the Lotus Sutra, including the "blessings to be gained through one instance of belief and understanding in the Lotus Sutra,"[8] the "purification of the six sense organs,"[9] the "eradication of one's offenses"[10] and the "attainment of Buddhahood in one's present form."[11]

The Lotus Sutra also elucidates the great vow of kosen-rufu—the vow to widely spread the correct teaching to enable all living beings to attain Buddhahood. It asserts that devoting one's life to this great vow or aspiration is the true and eternal bodhisattva way.

The Lotus Sutra thus teaches from a variety of angles that the one vehicle of Buddhahood represents the Buddha's true intent. In fact, it showcases this supreme teaching from beginning to end. Further, the sutra describes how those who hear and embrace the Lotus Sutra arouse faith in the one vehicle of Buddhahood and cast off the delusion that prevents them from attaining enlightenment. The causality of attaining Buddhahood is thus engraved in their lives, enabling them to manifest the supreme benefit of enlightenment in this lifetime. The Lotus Sutra is the sole sutra that not only provides a concrete teaching but also explains how it should be practiced and the benefit that will ensue from such a practice.

It is imperative, therefore, that those who would practice the Lotus Sutra in accord with the Buddha's teachings embrace faith solely in that sutra. If they fail to comprehend the Buddha's true intent and place greater importance on earlier teachings, which the Buddha expounded as expedient means, it could cause them to veer from the path of faith in the one vehicle of Buddhahood.

Many Buddhist scholars in Japan of Nichiren's day misunderstood the concept that "all vehicles are contained in the one Buddha vehicle" and persisted in advocating erroneous views of faith. In "On Practicing the Buddha's Teachings," the Daishonin summarizes their misguided stance as follows:

Since all vehicles are opened up and incorporated in the one vehicle of Buddhahood, no teaching is superior or inferior, shallow or profound, but all are equal to the Lotus Sutra. Hence the belief that chanting the Nembutsu, embracing the True Word teaching, practicing Zen meditation, or professing and reciting any sutra or the name of any Buddha or bodhisattva equals following the Lotus Sutra. (WND-1, 392–93)

This points to a grave misapprehension of the concept of "opened up and incorporated." Its true meaning is to clarify the ultimate truth and integrate the various expedient teachings in relation to that truth. The ultimate truth, or the one Buddha vehicle, that integrates these various teachings is revealed in the Lotus Sutra alone. In other words, the expedient teachings are simply a means by which to approach the ultimate truth expounded in the Lotus Sutra. It thus follows that while the expedient teachings are "opened up and incorporated" in the one Buddha vehicle, they can only be considered teachings that express a partial aspect of the truth expounded therein. The value of the various expedient teachings only comes to life when viewed based on the Lotus Sutra, the teaching of the one Buddha vehicle.

Ignorant of the Lotus Sutra's true significance, the priests of the established Buddhist schools of Nichiren's day espoused incorrect ways of faith. But in the Lotus Sutra, Shakyamuni himself elucidates the correct way of faith. Accordingly, in this section of "On Practicing the Buddha's Teachings," seeking to help people realize their error and establish correct faith, Nichiren says that, in practicing Buddhist teachings, we should "uphold the Buddha's golden words, not the opinions of others." To illustrate, he cites several passages of "the Buddha's golden words" from the Immeasurable Meanings Sutra and Lotus Sutra (see WND-1, 393).

First from the Immeasurable Meanings Sutra—which serves as an introduction to the Lotus Sutra—is a passage indicating that one should clearly distinguish between the provisional teachings (expedient means) and the true teaching (the truth): "Preaching the Law in various different ways, I made use of the power of expedient means. But in these more than forty years, I have not yet revealed the truth" (LSOC, 15). Second is a passage asserting that one can never hope to attain Buddhahood through the earlier provisional teachings that call for countless kalpas[12] of practice: "[One] will in the end fail to gain unsurpassed enlightenment" (LSOC, 20–21).

From the Lotus Sutra, meanwhile, various passages indicate how Shakyamuni himself discards the expedient teachings and preaches the true teaching of the one vehicle of Buddhahood:

The World-Honored One has long expounded his doctrines and now must reveal the truth. (LSOC, 59)

In the Buddha lands of the ten directions there is only the Law of the one vehicle, there are not two, there are not three, except when the Buddha preaches so as an expedient means. (LSOC, 69)

Honestly discarding expedient means. (LSOC, 79)

Also cited is a passage emphasizing that practitioners of the correct teaching of Buddhism should believe solely in the Lotus Sutra: "Not accepting a single verse of the other sutras" (LSOC, 115). There is also a passage warning against slander of the Lotus Sutra: "If a person fails to have faith but instead slanders this sutra, immediately he will destroy all the seeds for becoming a Buddha in any world. . . . When his life comes to an end he will enter the Avichi hell" (LSOC, 110). And finally, citing the passage "There is only the Law of the one vehicle" (LSOC, 69), Nichiren observes that those who uphold this firm conviction in faith are truly practicing as the Buddha teaches.

It is important to note here, however, that these quotes should not be misinterpreted to indicate intolerance. Nichiren was simply committed to abiding by the Buddha's intent and therefore called on his followers to establish faith in the one vehicle of Buddhahood.

The Latter Day is described as an "age of quarrels and disputes when the pure Law becomes obscured and lost."[13] In other words, it is a time when people have grown ignorant of the Buddha's true teaching of the one vehicle of Buddhahood, when the standard for integrating all Buddhist teachings into an organic whole has been lost, and when

conflict among different Buddhist schools prevails. It is an age in which the future of Buddhism itself is imperiled.

The schism in Japanese Buddhism during Nichiren's time—as characterized by the reference to the "eight or ten schools"[14]—highlighted the danger of the Law's decline as a result of people losing sight of the one Buddha vehicle. To overcome this danger, Nichiren called on people to embrace faith in the Lotus Sutra—the only sutra that fully expounds the supreme sanctity of life and respect for all people in both principle and practice, thereby opening the way to universal enlightenment.

The decline of the Law also directly threatened the people's happiness and welfare; it could lead to conditions that would bring about conflict and war (for instance, the calamities of internal strife and foreign invasion that the Daishonin predicted would occur), thus destroying the peace and tranquillity of the land and society.

To overcome this danger, the mission of Nichiren's disciples awakened to the Lotus Sutra's true teaching is to foster active, self-motivated individuals possessing steadfast faith in the one Buddha vehicle.

The Two Types of Practice— Shoju and Shakubuku

Anyone who practices Buddhism should first understand the two types of practice—shoju and shakubuku. All the sutras

and treatises fall into one or the other of these two categories. **Though scholars in this country may have studied Buddhism extensively, they do not know which practice accords with the time. . . . The two millennia of the Former and Middle Days of the Law required the spread of the Hinayana and provisional Mahayana teachings, but the first five hundred years of the Latter Day call for only the Lotus Sutra, the pure and perfect teaching of the one vehicle of Buddhahood, to be spread abroad widely. (WND-1, 394)**

In the previous section, Nichiren Daishonin discussed practicing the Buddha's teachings in the Latter Day in terms of faith. Now, he discusses this in terms of practice.

Immediately before this section, he takes up the question of whether those who believe only in the Lotus Sutra and carry out the five practices it teaches or follow the four practices, described in "Peaceful Practices," the fourteenth chapter, can be considered to be practicing in accord with the Buddha's teachings (see WND-1, 393).

The five practices are taught in "Teacher of the Law," the tenth chapter; they are to embrace, read, recite, expound, and transcribe the Lotus Sutra. In contrast, Nichiren sets forth the single practice of embracing the "five characters of Myoho-renge-kyo"[15] (accepting and upholding the Gohonzon) as the fundamental practice of the Lotus Sutra in the Latter Day of the Law.

Furthermore, the "Peaceful Practices" chapter teaches *shoju* as the means by which

those in the early stages of practice can attain the fruit of Buddhahood by practicing the Lotus Sutra without discomfort or trouble in the evil age after Shakyamuni's passing. It is a method of practicing with quiet tranquillity and without ever criticizing others, as indicated by the sutra passage "He should not delight in speaking of the faults of other people or scriptures" (LSOC, 240).

The question taken up by Nichiren expresses the doubts people had regarding his emphasis on shakubuku—or rigorously refuting error in the realm of Buddhism and clarifying the correct teaching—as the appropriate method of practice for those who uphold the Lotus Sutra in the Latter Day of the Law. It was a question raised not only by followers of other Buddhist schools but also by his disciples.

In response, Nichiren first says, "Anyone who practices Buddhism should first understand the two types of practice—shoju and shakubuku." Shoju, here, as indicated in several of the teachings, refers to a practice of solitary and quiet devotion. The Lotus Sutra expounds both shoju, as seen in the "Peaceful Practices" chapter, and shakubuku—that of asserting the truth of the supreme teaching to all people—as seen in "Bodhisattva Never Disparaging," the twentieth chapter. Fundamentally, both types of practice—shoju and shakubuku—are necessary, depending on the time. When the time calls for shoju, we should judge the situation calmly and practice shoju as necessary, and when the time calls for shakubuku, we should summon up our courage and practice shakubuku. We shouldn't decide that one is correct to the exclusion of the other. That's why the Lotus Sutra teaches both practices.

Accordingly, strict adherence to shoju that rejects shakubuku or strict adherence to shakubuku that rejects shoju runs counter to the original teaching of there being two ways of practice. The Daishonin discusses shoju and shakubuku at length in "The Opening of the Eyes" and "Letter from Sado," both written in 1272, the year before "On Practicing the Buddha's Teachings."

In "The Opening of the Eyes," Nichiren states: "In the Latter Day of the Law . . . both shoju and shakubuku are to be used" (WND-1, 285). He explains this by saying: "When the country is full of evil people without wisdom, then shoju is the primary method to be applied. . . . But at a time when there are many people of perverse views who slander the Law, then shakubuku should come first" (WND-1, 285). And in "Letter from Sado," he writes, "Buddhism should be spread by the method of either shoju or shakubuku, depending on the age" (WND-1, 301). In other words, Nichiren maintains that the method should be chosen as deemed appropriate to the particular time. In the section of "On Practicing the Buddha's Teachings" we are presently studying, he refers to this as knowing "which practice accords with the time."

But the priests of the various Buddhist schools in the Daishonin's day, though having studied Buddhism extensively, were unaware of this standard. As a result, they were biased in favor of shoju—which had been the main method of practice used throughout the Former Day and Middle Day of the Law— and criticized the Daishonin's advocacy of shakubuku as antithetical to Buddhism. This was a reflection of their deplorable ignorance regarding the basic tenets of Buddhism.

In this writing, Nichiren illustrates the importance of the time, noting that even in such endeavors as farming, a clear recognition of the time or season is crucial. In the realm of Buddhism, too, there are appropriate times, respectively, for the Hinayana, the provisional Mahayana, or the true Mahayana (Lotus Sutra) teachings to be disseminated for the benefit of humanity (see WND-1, 393).

Time, here, does not simply mean the passage of time. It indicates clearly delineated eras characterized by significant shifts in people's receptivity to the Law after Shakyamuni's passing—in other words, it refers to the three time periods known as the Former Day, Middle Day, and Latter Day of the Law.[16] It is also a comprehensive recognition of the time that takes into account the spiritual condition of the people, the state of society and of the country, the teachings and beliefs that prevail there, and so on.

Nichiren clarifies that the two millennia of the Former Day and the Middle Day of the Law marked the time for the spread of the Hinayana and provisional Mahayana teachings (see WND-1, 394). During these periods, many people had the capacity to understand the Buddha's teachings. There were also those who, having cultivated sufficiently deep connections with the Lotus Sutra in past lifetimes, could readily attain enlightenment through the Hinayana or provisional Mahayana teachings. And as a general tendency, in the Former Day and Middle Day, if even a few individuals attained enlightenment through these teachings, their character and conduct could have a positive impact on society.

In contrast to this, the Daishonin explains that in the Latter Day of the Law only "the Lotus Sutra, the pure and perfect teaching of the one vehicle of Buddhahood," should be spread widely. "Pure and perfect" means that it elucidates only the pure and perfect teaching for attaining enlightenment, unalloyed by expedient teachings. "One vehicle" means that it is the teaching of the ultimate truth, or the one Buddha vehicle, as I discussed earlier.

The Latter Day is an age when the correct Buddhist teaching is in danger of being lost; it is an evil age defiled by the five impurities,[17] teeming with negative influences that confuse people's minds. At such a time, none of the Buddha's pre-Lotus Sutra teachings has the power to guide the people and the age in the direction of lasting happiness.

The Latter Day is also an age when the devilish nature that slanders the Law and denigrates the one Buddha vehicle is rampant. The Daishonin inscribed the object of devotion, the Gohonzon, which represents the ultimate revelation of the Law (Nam-myoho-renge-kyo) in which we should place our faith in order to attain Buddhahood. He also set forth the practice of chanting Nam-myoho-renge-kyo as a regular practice designed to help us maintain steadfast faith. In this way, he established the Buddhism of sowing that

directly activates the innate Buddha nature of people in the Latter Day. Furthermore, he demonstrated through his own actions that the practice of shakubuku is vital in terms of refuting slander of the Law and, as such, constitutes a crucial aspect of Nichiren Buddhism.

A Lofty Spiritual Struggle To Refute the Erroneous and Reveal the True

As predicted by the Buddha, now is the age of quarrels and disputes when the pure Law becomes obscured and lost, and the provisional and true teachings are hopelessly confused.

When one must face enemies, one needs a sword, a stick, or a bow and arrows. When one has no enemies, however, such weapons are of no use at all. In this age, the provisional teachings have turned into enemies of the true teaching. When the time is right to propagate the teaching of the one vehicle, the provisional teachings become enemies. When they are a source of confusion, they must be thoroughly refuted from the standpoint of the true teaching. Of the two types of practice, this is shakubuku, the practice of the Lotus Sutra. With good reason T'ien-t'ai stated, "The Lotus Sutra is the teaching of shakubuku, the refutation of the provisional doctrines." (WND-1, 394)

Here Nichiren Daishonin states that the Latter Day is an "age of quarrels and disputes when the pure Law becomes obscured and lost." I discussed this designation of the Latter Day earlier. He also refers to the disarray within the realm of Buddhism, noting that the provisional teachings and true teaching are "hopelessly confused."

In light of their function in the Buddha's teachings, the provisional sutras were expounded as expedient means to cultivate people's capacity for understanding and ultimately guide them to the one Buddha vehicle of the Lotus Sutra. In the defiled Latter Day, however, influential Buddhist schools based themselves on different provisional teachings and proclaimed them to be the Buddha's ultimate teaching. Some even openly slandered the Lotus Sutra and were so blinded by delusion that they instructed others to discard faith in it. In that sense, Nichiren says, the provisional teachings have turned into "enemies of the true teaching," "enemies of the Lotus Sutra."

In such an age and land, if one wishes to lead all people to enlightenment through practicing the Lotus Sutra, it is essential, Nichiren declares, to thoroughly refute the error of those who adhere to the provisional teachings and who are influenced by devilish functions to slander the Lotus Sutra. This is the essence of Nichiren's commitment to shakubuku. He writes, "[The provisional teachings] must be thoroughly refuted from the standpoint of the true teaching." To assert the supremacy of the provisional teachings (partial teachings of the truth) over the

true teaching (the one Buddha vehicle that is the Buddha's intent) is a serious error. Shakubuku, therefore, is a philosophical struggle to address such errors from the standpoint of the correct teaching.

As we saw in the previous chapter, Nichiren called this struggle the "battle between the provisional teachings and the true teaching" (see WND-1, 392). From start to finish, it is a "battle of dialogue" and a "battle of reason"—a struggle to help people understand and to convey the Buddha's true intent.

Here again, Nichiren cites the words of the Great Teacher T'ien-t'ai: "The Lotus Sutra is the teaching of shakubuku, the refutation of the provisional doctrines."[18] To make it possible for people to attain enlightenment, the Buddha expounded the Lotus Sutra, clarifying that his earlier teachings were merely expedient means and refuting the provisional doctrines he had previously taught. This struggle powered by compassion and reason is the essence of the Lotus Sutra's practice of shakubuku.

It is also clear in light of the sutras that one who dares point out the errors of the other Buddhist schools of the day and propagate the Mystic Law is certain to be assailed by the three obstacles and four devils[19] and face opposition from the three powerful enemies.[20] But Nichiren could not ignore the misfortune and suffering that loomed over the people, nor could he turn a blind eye to the correct Buddhist teaching being obliterated. Driven by an irrepressible impulse, he waged a powerful struggle for the happiness of all people, practicing with selfless devotion and valuing the Law more than his own life. This is the true significance of the Daishonin's shakubuku spirit.

Indeed, the practice of shakubuku as taught in the Lotus Sutra overflows with the original all-embracing spirit of Buddhism, which is dedicated to helping all people attain enlightenment. It was Mr. Makiguchi's firm conviction that "rejecting evil and embracing good are two sides of the same coin."[21] Expressing genuine concern for all people means upholding a philosophy of respect for others and battling negative functions that cause people suffering, while refusing to condone violence or oppression that threatens human dignity or equality. If we observe views that justify using human lives as a means to an end or that divides and discriminates against people, then we must vigorously denounce the misguided teachings or ideas that form the spiritual soil for such thought. It is a battle against the fundamental darkness or ignorance that plunges people's lives into suffering and misery. This is the essence of the "battle between the provisional teachings and the true teaching" and the crux of the shakubuku spirit in Nichiren Buddhism.

In essence, this means firmly believing in one's own Buddha nature and that of others and therefore respecting all people. The heart of shakubuku is compassion. And because it also involves resolutely battling the devilish nature or fundamental darkness that derides human dignity, it constitutes fearless refutation in which compassion gives rise to courage.

We of the SGI have been able to carry out dialogues with leaders of world religions about issues between different civilizations precisely because of our commitment to humanism. This commitment is guided by the compassion to speak out against evils that trample on human dignity and fundamental human rights. It is possible for us to join together with other religions and philosophies that share the values of respecting human beings and the dignity of life in what Mr. Makiguchi termed "humanistic competition" channeled toward eradicating human misery and suffering. Indeed, it is an indispensable requirement of religion in the twenty-first century to denounce all abuses of human dignity.

As SGI members, we engage in a lofty spiritual struggle to refute the erroneous and reveal the true through our daily efforts—respectful conduct toward all people like that epitomized by Bodhisattva Never Disparaging; a strong commitment unshaken by opposition or obstacle; a readiness to stand up against inhumanity and injustice; a wonderful example of winning trust in our immediate environment and promoting understanding of Nichiren Buddhism. I wish to declare that such efforts constitute the practice of shakubuku in modern times.

Fulfilling the Mission to Realize the Buddha's Intent and Decree

The four peaceful practices [in the "Peaceful Practices" chapter] correspond to shoju. To carry them out in this age would be as foolish as sowing seeds in winter and expecting to reap the harvest in spring. It is natural for a rooster to crow at dawn, but strange for him to crow at dusk. Now, when the true and the provisional teachings are utterly confused, it would be equally unnatural for one to seclude oneself in the mountain forests and carry out the peaceful practice of shoju without refuting the enemies of the Lotus Sutra. One would lose the chance to practice the Lotus Sutra. (WND-1, 394)

Here Nichiren Daishonin issues a scathing refutation of the priests of the established Buddhist schools who adhere to the practice of shoju. At a time when the provisional teachings and true teaching are in dire confusion, these priests seclude themselves in mountain forests, gaining prestige and authority by standing aloof from the world. He declares that their behavior is as strange and unnatural as a rooster crowing at dusk instead of dawn.

As I mentioned earlier, the Latter Day of the Law is a time when the provisional teachings and true teaching become "hopelessly confused" as a result of the workings of devilish functions. To make matters even worse, priests of the Tendai school,[22] a school that had originally espoused the supremacy of the Lotus Sutra, failed to challenge or refute error in the realm of Buddhism and instead devoted themselves to carrying out shoju in mountain forests far removed from society.

Failing to fight for truth when the time demands, standing by idly when grave error is committed in the realm of Buddhism—such conduct is tantamount to abetting evil. This is because, ultimately, it contributes to the very destruction of Buddhism itself.

In the Daishonin's day, because the rigor and intent of the Buddha's teaching were lost or confused, many priests grew corrupt and degenerate. Becoming lazy and remiss in their Buddhist practice, they grew spiritually weak and were concerned only with protecting their own interests. This caused them to align with the ruling authorities and marked the start of growing authoritarianism among the established Buddhist schools. At the root of this development was the exclusive reliance on the practice of shoju. Because the Buddhist teachings that sustained the beliefs and values forming the bedrock of society were confused and misguided, practicing shakubuku to refute error and transform the spiritual climate of society accorded with the Buddha's true intent.

The Nichiren Shoshu priesthood today is every bit as misguided as the various schools that persecuted Nichiren in his time. During World War II, Mr. Makiguchi and Mr. Toda of the Soka Gakkai opposed the demands of the Japanese militarist authorities and stood up for peace and the happiness of the people, undaunted by persecution. The priesthood, fearful of the authorities, suspended publication of Nichiren's collected writings and excised lines from certain passages, committing an unpardonable offense as Nichiren's disciples. Not only that, but as soon as Mr. Makiguchi and Mr. Toda were arrested, the priesthood had them banned from visiting the head temple, even though these two leaders were practicing exactly as the Daishonin had taught.

After the war, too, it was the Soka Gakkai and not the priesthood that practiced shakubuku—actively propagating the Mystic Law just as Nichiren instructed. In more recent times, the priesthood plotted to destroy the Soka Gakkai, the organization dedicated to realizing the Buddha's noble decree of kosen-rufu. Who is practicing in accord with the Buddha's teachings, keeping the Daishonin's shakubuku spirit alive, and walking the correct path of faith? The answer is perfectly clear.

To fight for truth when the time demands—both Mr. Makiguchi and Mr. Toda walked this path of true champions. The SGI is a harmonious community of practitioners striving to actualize kosen-rufu in accord with the Buddha's teachings. Making Nichiren's spirit our own, we are committed to realizing happiness for ourselves and others and spreading the humanistic ideals and principles of Nichiren Buddhism for the peace and prosperity of our countries. The Soka Gakkai organization has appeared in accord with the time

for kosen-rufu, endowed with the mission to realize the Buddha's intent and decree. This is the true significance of the Soka Gakkai's appearance in this world.

There is something truly wondrous and unfathomable in the fact that Mr. Makiguchi and Mr. Toda, Buddhist leaders of extraordinary caliber, appeared in Japan at a time of war when the correct teaching of Buddhism was on the brink of being obliterated.

Mr. Makiguchi, speaking out against the mistaken ideology that had plunged the country into war, articulated the concept of punishment based on the Gohonzon[23]—on the law of cause and effect (Nam-myoho-renge-kyo). Mr. Toda stood up alone in the wasteland of postwar Japan and embarked on propagating Nichiren Buddhism to free people from misery, emphasizing benefit based on devoting one's life to the Mystic Law. Carrying on their spirit, I launched a global kosen-rufu movement amid the turmoil of the postwar world, emphasizing the importance—as taught in Nichiren Buddhism—of showing actual proof based on one's behavior as a human being.

This is also the wisdom of value creation born of a readiness to rise up to defend the correct Buddhist teaching and the people's happiness, in accord with the principles found in "On Practicing the Buddha's Teachings."

I will always remember these words that Mr. Toda addressed to Soka Gakkai leaders:

As leaders, you must have the courage to fight against injustice when the time comes to do so. It would be irresponsible, otherwise. You can't protect our precious members unless you do. . . . Once you embark on a struggle for kosen-rufu, it's vital to win. To initiate a struggle and not see it through is a disgrace.

Because I have faithfully followed my mentor's guidance, I have won in every struggle. I hope the youth division members, in particular, will bravely carry on this spirit, which is the cause for certain victory.

This lecture was originally published in the February 2010 issue of the Daibyakurenge, *the Soka Gakkai's monthly study journal.*

NOTES

1. *Shoju* is a way of practice that gradually leads others to the correct teaching according to their capacity and without refuting their attachment to mistaken views. *Shakubuku*, meanwhile, is a way of practice that directly awakens others to the correct teaching by refuting their mistaken views.

2. Four peaceful practices: Also, four easy practices, four comfortable practices, or four peaceful ways of practice. The practices for bodhisattvas in the evil age after Shakyamuni's death, set forth in "Peaceful Practices," the fourteenth chapter of the Lotus Sutra. While the descriptions of these practices in the sutra text are lengthy, T'ien-t'ai categorized these as the four peaceful practices. They are: (1) the peaceful practice of the body, which means avoiding temptations and meditating in a quiet and secluded place; (2) the peaceful practice of the mouth, or to teach the Lotus Sutra without despising or speaking of the faults of other people or scriptures; (3) the peaceful practice of the mind, or to discard a mind of jealousy or contention toward other sutras or those who embrace them; and (4) the peaceful practice of vows, which means to vow to save all people through great compassion. "Encouraging Devotion," the thirteenth chapter, which precedes "Peaceful Practices," sets forth a more difficult bodhisattva practice in which bodhisattvas are required to endure all hardships and persecutions, to propagate the sutra without begrudging their lives. When contrasted with this kind of practice, T'ien-t'ai viewed the four peaceful practices set forth in

the "Peaceful Practices" chapter as passive and less difficult and therefore as disciplines for bodhisattvas still in the early stages of practice.

3. February Campaign: In February 1952, President Ikeda, then an adviser to Tokyo's Kamata Chapter, initiated a dynamic propagation campaign. Together with the Kamata members, he broke through the previous monthly record of some 100 new households by introducing Nichiren Buddhism to 201 new households.

4. Daisaku Ikeda, *A Youthful Diary: One Man's Journey from the Beginning of Faith to Worldwide Leadership for Peace* (Santa Monica, CA: World Tribune Press, 2001), 62.

5. The Buddha's teaching is compared to a vehicle (Skt *yana*) that carries one to a particular state of enlightenment. In accordance with people's capacities, the pre-Lotus Sutra teachings expound and emphasize the three vehicles—namely, the vehicle of voice-hearers (*shravaka-yana*), which leads to the state of arhat; the vehicle of cause-awakened ones (*pratyekabuddha-yana*), which leads to the state of pratyekabuddha; and the vehicle of bodhisattvas (*bodhisattva-yana*), which after many kalpas of practice leads one to Buddhahood. The Lotus Sutra teaches that these three vehicles are not ends in themselves but expedient means designed to guide people to the one Buddha vehicle, which leads to the attainment of Buddhahood.

6. True aspect of all phenomena: The ultimate truth or reality that permeates all phenomena and is in no way separate from them. Through the explanation of the ten factors, "Expedient Means," the second chapter of the Lotus Sutra, clarifies that all people are inherently endowed with the potential to become Buddhas and the truth that they can tap and manifest this potential.

7. True cause and true effect: True cause refers to the practice that Shakyamuni carried out countless kalpas in the past in order to attain his original enlightenment, long before his enlightenment in India. True effect refers to the original enlightenment Shakyamuni achieved. They are revealed in "Life Span," the sixteenth chapter of the Lotus Sutra.

8. Blessings to be gained through one instance of belief and understanding of the Lotus Sutra: The first of the four stages of practice for those who embrace the sutra during Shakyamuni's lifetime. It is described as having boundless and immeasurable benefit in "Distinctions in Benefits," the seventeenth chapter of the Lotus Sutra.

9. Purification of the six sense organs: The five sense organs of eyes, ears, nose, tongue, and body (skin), along with the mind (which processes the information gathered by the sense organs) becoming pure, making it possible to apprehend all things correctly. "Benefits of the Teacher of the Law," the nineteenth chapter of the Lotus Sutra, explains that those who uphold and practice the sutra acquire eight hundred benefits of the eyes, nose, and body, and twelve hundred benefits of the ears, tongue, and mind and that through these benefits the sense organs become refined and pure.

10. Eradication of one's offenses: Refers to the benefit of changing one's karma. This principle is explained in the

Lotus Sutra through the example of Bodhisattva Never Disparaging in "Bodhisattva Never Disparaging," the twentieth chapter. The sutra states that through his practice of venerating others and undergoing persecution as a result, he was able to wipe out all his past offenses of slander of the Law.

11. Attainment of Buddhahood in one's present form: To attain Buddhahood just as one is, without discarding the body of an ordinary person or having to perform austere practices for countless kalpas. This principle is often illustrated by the example of the dragon king's daughter who, according to "Devadatta," the twelfth chapter of the Lotus Sutra, attained Buddhahood in a single moment without changing her dragon form, through the beneficial power of the Mystic Law.

12. Kalpa: In ancient Indian cosmology, an extremely long period of time.

13. This description originally appears in the Great Collection Sutra. During the Latter Day of the Law, quarrels and disputes arise among the followers of the Buddha's teachings, causing the pure Law to become lost and obscured.

14. Eight and ten schools: The eight schools are the eight major schools of Buddhism in Japan before the Kamakura period (1185–1333). They are the Dharma Analysis Treasury, Establishment of Truth, Precepts, Dharma Characteristics, Three Treatises, Flower Garland, Tendai, and True Word schools. The addition of the Pure Land (Nembutsu) and Zen schools, which emerged early in the Kamakura period, produces the ten schools, as they are often referred to collectively in Japanese Buddhist works.

15. Five characters of Myoho-renge-kyo: Myoho-renge-kyo is written with five Chinese characters, while Nam-myoho-renge-kyo is written with seven (nam, or namu, being composed of two characters). Nichiren, however, often uses Myoho-renge-kyo synonymously with Nam-myoho-renge-kyo in his writings.

16. Three periods: The Former Day, Middle Day, and Latter Day of the Law. Three consecutive periods or stages into which the time following a Buddha's death is divided. During the Former Day of the Law, the spirit of Buddhism prevails and people can attain enlightenment through its practice. During the Middle Day of the Law, although Buddhism becomes firmly established in society, it grows increasingly formalized, and fewer people benefit from it. In the Latter Day of the Law, people are tainted by the three poisons—greed, anger, and foolishness—and lose their aspiration for enlightenment; Buddhism itself loses the power to lead them to Buddhahood.

17. Five impurities: Also, five defilements. Impurity of the age, of desire, of living beings, of thought (or view), and of life span. This term appears in "Expedient Means," the second chapter of the Lotus Sutra. The five impurities are: (1) impurity of the age includes repeated disruptions of the social or natural environment; (2) impurity of desire is the tendency to be ruled by the five delusive inclinations: greed, anger, foolishness, arrogance, and doubt; (3) impurity of living beings is the physical and spiritual decline of human beings; (4) impurity of thought, or impurity of view, which is the prevalence of wrong views such as the five false views; and (5) impurity of life span, which is the shortening of the life spans of living beings.

18. T'ien-t'ai's The Profound Meaning of the Lotus Sutra.

19. Three obstacles and four devils: Various obstacles and hindrances to the practice of Buddhism. The three obstacles are: (1) the obstacle of earthly desires, (2) the obstacle of karma, and (3) the obstacle of retribution. The four devils are: (1) the hindrance of the five components, (2) the hindrance of earthly desires, (3) the hindrance of death, and (4) the hindrance of the devil king.

20. Three powerful enemies: Three types of arrogant people who persecute those who propagate the Lotus Sutra in the evil age after Shakyamuni Buddha's death, described in a twenty-line verse section of "Encouraging Devotion," the thirteenth chapter of the Lotus Sutra. The Great Teacher Miao-lo (711–82) of China summarizes them as arrogant lay people, arrogant priests, and arrogant false sages.

21. Translated from Japanese. Tsunesaburo Makiguchi, "Zen'aku-kan to aisho-kan to no konmei" (The Confusion in Views of Good and Evil, Great and Small), in Makiguchi Tsunesaburo zenshu (Collected Writings of Tsunesaburo Makiguchi) (Tokyo: Daisanbunmei-sha, 1988), 9:97.

22. Tendai school: The Japanese counterpart of the Chinese T'ien-t'ai (Jpn Tendai) school of Buddhism, founded in the early ninth century by the Japanese priest Dengyo (767–822), also known as Saicho. Because of a permissive attitude toward the erroneous teachings of other schools, however, including the True Word, Pure Land (Nembutsu), and Zen, by the time of Nichiren, it had lost the stance of strictly basing itself on the Lotus Sutra.

23. President Ikeda writes: "'Buddhism expounds the law of cause and effect that governs all life; it teaches us the formula for becoming happy. If we reject this causal law of life and try to go against it, then before long we will find ourselves deadlocked. It is natural, therefore, that a valid and effective religious teaching is certain to generate two types of clear-cut actual proof: benefit and punishment. . . . The "benefit" of our practice is eradicating the evil in our lives and cultivating good. . . . Propagating the Mystic Law is an act that extinguishes evil and cultivates good in others' lives. Our activities to teach people about Buddhism simultaneously open the path of benefit for them and for ourselves. This is the Buddhism of Nichiren Daishonin'" (The New Human Revolution (Santa Monica, CA: World Tribune Press, 1996), 4:103–04).

"ON PRACTICING THE BUDDHA'S TEACHINGS"—PART 3 OF 3

ENCOUNTERING GREAT OBSTACLES IS PROOF OF PROPAGATING THE CORRECT TEACHING FOR ATTAINING BUDDHAHOOD IN THE LATTER DAY OF THE LAW

The Passage for Study in This Lecture

Now, in the Latter Day of the Law, who is carrying out the practice of shakubuku in strict accordance with the Lotus Sutra? Suppose someone, no matter who, should unrelentingly proclaim that the Lotus Sutra alone can lead people to Buddhahood, and that all other sutras, far from enabling them to attain the way, only drive them into hell. Observe what happens should that person thus try to refute the teachers and the doctrines of all the other schools [that base themselves on these provisional teachings]. The three powerful enemies[1] will arise without fail.

Our teacher, the Thus Come One Shakyamuni, practiced shakubuku during the last eight years of his lifetime, the Great Teacher T'ien-t'ai[2] for more than thirty years, and the Great Teacher Dengyo[3] for more than twenty. I have been refuting the provisional doctrines for more than twenty years, and the great persecutions I have suffered during this period are beyond number. I do not know whether they are equal to the nine great persecutions[4] suffered by the Buddha, but surely neither T'ien-t'ai nor Dengyo ever faced persecutions as great as mine for the sake of the Lotus Sutra. They encountered only hatred, envy, and slander, whereas I twice incurred the wrath of the rulers and was exiled to remote provinces. Furthermore, I was nearly beheaded at Tatsunokuchi,[5] wounded on the forehead [at Komatsubara],[6] and slandered time and again. My disciples have also been exiled and thrown into prison, and my lay supporters have been evicted and had their fiefs confiscated. How can the persecutions faced by Nagarjuna,[7] T'ien-t'ai, or Dengyo possibly compare with these? Understand then that the votary who practices the Lotus Sutra exactly as the Buddha teaches will without fail be attacked by the three powerful enemies.

In the more than two thousand years that have passed since the Buddha's advent, Shakyamuni himself, T'ien-t'ai, and Dengyo were the only three who perfectly carried out the Buddha's teachings. Now in the Latter Day of the Law, Nichiren and his disciples and lay believers are just such practitioners. If we cannot be called votaries faithful to the Buddha's teachings, then neither can Shakyamuni, T'ien-t'ai, or Dengyo. (WND-1, 394–95)

Life flashes by in but a moment. No matter how many terrible enemies you may encounter, banish all fears and never think of backsliding. Even if someone were to cut off our heads with a saw, impale our bodies with lances, or shackle our feet and bore them through with a gimlet, as long as we are alive, we must keep chanting Nam-myoho-renge-kyo, Nam-myoho-renge-kyo. Then, if we chant until the very moment of death, Shakyamuni, Many Treasures,[8] and the Buddhas of the ten directions will come to us instantly, exactly as they promised during the ceremony at Eagle Peak.[9] Taking our hands and bearing us on their shoulders, they will carry us to Eagle Peak. The two sages, the two heavenly kings, and the ten demon daughters[10] will guard us, while all the heavenly gods and benevolent deities will raise a canopy over our heads and unfurl banners on high. They will escort us under their protection to the treasure land of Tranquil Light.[11] How can such joy possibly be described! (WND-1, 395–96)

LECTURE

"The Soka Gakkai is the king of the religious world!" declared second Soka Gakkai president Josei Toda, addressing the six thousand high-spirited youth who had assembled for a historic gathering on March 16, 1958. His powerful cry still resonates in my heart to this day. It was an expression of the towering conviction of our mentor, who had undergone a profound spiritual awakening to the essence of the Mystic Law while in prison and struggled selflessly to realize kosen-rufu in accord with Nichiren Daishonin's decree. It was a proclamation of victory by a champion of faith who gave his life to practicing as the

Buddha teaches—a great leader, who had launched a solitary struggle for kosen-rufu amid postwar Japan's devastation and who surmounted countless obstacles. Above all, it was a lion's roar infused with the invincible Soka Gakkai spirit—an impassioned cry that would endure for all time.

We, the youth gathered on that occasion, were deeply inspired by his triumphant declaration. His words drove home to each of us anew our lofty mission, and we trembled with emotion to be practicing Nichiren Buddhism. It was a ceremony in which the baton of kosen-rufu was passed on from the mentor to the disciples—with each of us inheriting Mr. Toda's great confidence in the correct teaching and the nobility of our cause.

That was more than fifty years ago. Repeating my mentor's declaration throughout these many decades—in the spirit of the disciple's voice joining the teacher's in unison to create a powerful lion's roar (see OTT, 111)—I have proclaimed Mr. Toda's greatness far and wide and have spread the Mystic Law throughout Japan and the entire world. I have done so with the unshakable conviction that we are champions of thought and philosophy; champions of peace, culture, and education; and champions of a new humanism.

The time has now come for the present generation of youth to inherit the spiritual baton of the Soka Gakkai. It is time for you, my young friends, to take on full responsibility for kosen-rufu and its ongoing development into the eternal future of the Latter Day of the Law. It is your mission to forge a solidarity of peace and humanism throughout the world. People everywhere await your endeavors. It is now time to take your place on the main stage of our movement, with the wonderful victories you have already achieved so far.

Indeed, one reason I chose to discuss "On Practicing the Buddha's Teachings" at this time is because I wish to entrust the future of our movement to the youth.

In this chapter, we will look at the concluding section of this writing, which is infused with Nichiren Daishonin's solemn hopes for the appearance of disciples who will practice the Buddha's teachings with his same spirit.

Propagating the Correct Teaching Rouses Opposition From the Three Powerful Enemies

Now, in the Latter Day of the Law, who is carrying out the practice of shakubuku in strict accordance with the Lotus Sutra? Suppose someone, no matter who, should unrelentingly proclaim that the Lotus Sutra alone can lead people to Buddhahood, and that all other sutras, far from enabling them to attain the way, only drive them into hell. Observe what happens should that person thus try to refute the teachers and the doctrines of all the other schools [that base themselves on these provisional teachings]. The three powerful enemies will arise without fail. (WND-1, 394)

Prior to this section, Nichiren Daishonin explained the way of faith and practice for those who wish to correctly carry out the Buddha's teachings in the Latter Day of the Law. He clarified that the way of faith true to the Buddha's intent is to believe only in the Lotus Sutra—the one Buddha vehicle that enables all people to attain enlightenment. He also explained that the practice appropriate for the Latter Day of the Law is the practice of shakubuku as taught in the Lotus Sutra—the staunch refuting of those forces that slander the Lotus Sutra and seek to obstruct people's happiness.

Having affirmed these essential points, Nichiren identifies the votaries who practice the Buddha's teachings with correct faith and in a manner appropriate to this evil latter age.

First, in this section, he asks, "Now, in the Latter Day of the Law, who is carrying out the practice of shakubuku in strict accordance with the Lotus Sutra?" "Now, in the Latter Day of the Law" indicates a time "when the true and the provisional teachings are utterly confused" (WND-1, 394), as was mentioned in the preceding passage. Unless this confusion is rectified, it will give rise to an age when "quarrels and disputes prevail, and the pure Law is obscured and lost."[12] That is why the practice of shakubuku is crucial. It is necessary to clarify that the Lotus Sutra (the true teaching) alone can lead all people to enlightenment, whereas the other sutras (the provisional teachings) not only fail to do so but ultimately cause people to fall into a state of inner hell or suffering.

The pre-Lotus Sutra teachings, though intended for people's enlightenment, do not actually provide a way to achieve that goal in this lifetime. This is because they do not contain the all-important principles of "mutual possession of the Ten Worlds"[13] and "three thousand realms in a single moment of life."[14] Of course, if people are led via these provisional sutras to the Lotus Sutra and awaken to the Mystic Law of the mutual possession of the Ten Worlds and three thousand realms in a single moment of life, it is possible for them to attain Buddhahood as a result. But during Nichiren's time, which

marked the start of the Latter Day of the Law, a wide assortment of Buddhist schools proliferated, with each asserting that the different provisional teachings on which they based their respective doctrines were the Buddha's ultimate teaching. Consequently, far from guiding people to an understanding of the true Lotus Sutra teaching, these schools propounded doctrines that denigrated it. There was, as Nichiren noted, utter confusion among the provisional and true teachings. Therefore, it was necessary to refute the provisional sutras, clarifying that they do not lead to enlightenment and that only the Lotus Sutra does.

Nichiren says that when anyone—no matter who—carries out shakubuku, the three powerful enemies are sure to appear. The practice of shakubuku as taught in the Lotus Sutra indicates the kind of refutation I have just described, which is based on the correct teaching for attaining Buddhahood; it is not by any means motivated by intolerance or self-righteousness. As we also confirmed in the last chapter, shakubuku in Nichiren Buddhism is grounded in a deep commitment to the correct teaching and the compassion to help guide people to genuine, lasting happiness. The spirit of refuting error in the realm of Buddhism, valuing the Law more highly than one's own life, means courageously battling the workings of the devilish nature inherent in life that slander the correct teaching and plunge people into misery. When such compassion and altruism underlies our actions, we can vanquish all error or evil.

Because carrying out shakubuku as taught in the Lotus Sutra is the correct way of practice in the Latter Day—serving to both protect the Law and free people from suffering—it is inevitable that opposition and resistance will arise from arrogant forces. Unless we grasp this principle, we will not understand the true nature of the great obstacles that befall the votaries of the Lotus Sutra.

The Characteristics of the Three Powerful Enemies

To further clarify this point, let's review the concept of the three powerful enemies once again.

At the start of "Encouraging Devotion," the thirteenth chapter of the Lotus Sutra, it says regarding the Latter Day of the Law:

> Living beings in the evil age to come will have fewer and fewer good roots. Many will be overbearingly arrogant and greedy for offerings and other forms of gain, increasing the roots that are not good and moving farther away than ever from emancipation. (LSOC, 229)

Clearly, whoever should attempt to preach the correct teaching of the Lotus Sutra amid such arrogant multitudes is bound to encounter opposition. In this chapter, the bodhisattvas gathered at the assembly of the Lotus Sutra vow to propagate it in the saha world[15] in the evil age after the Buddha's passing, no matter the daunting obstacles. The chapter's concluding verse section[16] describes the vows these bodhisattvas make and the nature of the obstacles and persecutions that will await them. Three types of people who will persecute the Lotus Sutra practitioners are identified. These are the three powerful enemies—arrogant lay people, arrogant priests, and arrogant false sages.

According to the description in the sutra, arrogant lay people are characterized as "ignorant"; arrogant priests are characterized by "perverse wisdom and hearts that are fawning and crooked"; and arrogant false sages are characterized as "despising and looking down on all humankind," being "greedy for profit and support," "with evil in their hearts" (see LSOC, 232).

The arrogance of these ignorant, perverse, and evil people, respectively, arises from the workings of the inherent darkness or ignorance in their lives. This inner darkness is the source of earthly desires and other deluded impulses, leading people to unhappiness and misery. The fundamental form of this darkness is ignorance to the truth that all things and phenomena are entities of the Mystic Law. It is this fundamental darkness or ignorance, for instance, that prevents a person from believing or understanding the correct teaching when they hear it and that creates tendencies to reject it or even seek to destroy it. Here, we see the fearfulness of ignorance.

The fundamental darkness inherent in human life gives rise to the ultimate devilish function—what Buddhism refers to as the "devil king of the sixth heaven."[17] Those who oppose and attack the votary of the Lotus Sutra are ruled by this insidious negative function.

In "Letter to Misawa," Nichiren explains that when an ordinary person in the Latter Day practices the correct teaching with the aim of attaining Buddhahood, the devil king of the sixth heaven will set various functions into motion to sabotage their efforts. In other words, one person attaining Buddhahood will lead many others to become Buddhas too, until eventually this saha world will be transformed into a pure land. Because the devil king, who rules over the saha world, fears being robbed of his domain, he orders his retainers to obstruct the Buddhist practice of the votary of the Lotus Sutra. If this fails, he will have those retainers enter the bodies of the votary's disciples and followers or the people of the land and scheme to deter the votary through admonishments or threats. And if that too should fail, then the devil king will himself possess the mind and body of the country's ruler and use intimidation to prevent the votary from attaining Buddhahood.[18]

In discussing the three obstacles (the obstacles of earthly desires, karma, and retribution) and four devils (the hindrances of earthly desires, our own physical and mental functions, death, and the devil king) that beset practitioners of Buddhism, President Toda often used to say, "You may be able to triumph over the three obstacles and the first three devils or hindrances, which includes even death, but the last one—the devil king—is truly formidable."

As we also see in other writings of Nichiren,[19] the devil king manipulates the minds of arrogant lay people and arrogant priests and possesses the bodies of arrogant false sages who in turn influence the ruling authorities to harass and persecute the votary of the Lotus Sutra.

Elsewhere, Nichiren states: "The single word 'belief' is the sharp sword with which one confronts and overcomes fundamental darkness or ignorance" (OTT, 119–20). Mr. Toda also frequently emphasized that "the sharp sword of faith is the only means for defeating the devil king of the sixth heaven." When we vanquish fundamental darkness or ignorance through faith in the Mystic Law, the fundamental nature of enlightenment, or Dharma nature,[20] with which our lives are inherently endowed, will well forth. The Dharma nature is the ultimate truth of all phenomena to which the Buddha became awakened in his own life.

Attaining Buddhahood, in a sense, means winning in this struggle between darkness and enlightenment. Through the practice of shakubuku, those who uphold the Lotus Sutra can bring forth the fundamental nature of enlightenment in their own lives and help others do the same.

The Lotus Sutra Is the Teaching That Activates the Buddha Nature

Viewed afresh from the perspective of darkness and enlightenment, the reason Nichiren Daishonin passionately refutes the provisional sutras, declaring them ineffectual in leading people to Buddhahood, is that their doctrines only add to the darkness or ignorance of those who embrace faith in them.

Essentially, attaining Buddhahood in one's present form rests on the principle of the mutual possession of the Ten Worlds, which is revealed in the Lotus Sutra. In the provisional teachings, however, the nine worlds and the world of Buddhahood are taught as being completely separate from one another. This position of rejecting the nine worlds of delusion and aspiring for the enlightened world of Buddhahood may have seemed reasonable to ordinary people and been easy to understand. The provisional sutras were thus expounded by the Buddha "in accordance with others' minds"—that is, taking into account people's capacity for understanding.

If people truly wish to attain Buddhahood, however, they should rightfully discard these teachings that have been expounded merely as expedient means and turn their attention to the true teaching, which was preached "in accordance with the Buddha's mind"—that is, revealing the ultimate truth just as it is. This, of course, is the Lotus Sutra, which elucidates the true causality for attaining Buddhahood. Should people adhere to the provisional teachings and reject the Lotus Sutra, they will follow an erroneous path that will merely increase the darkness or ignorance that pervades their lives.

The workings of darkness or ignorance give rise to attachment to these provisional teachings, whose partial or incomplete nature in turn produces even greater darkness. This cycle of ever-deepening darkness leads Nichiren to conclude that the provisional sutras only drive people into hell (see WND-1, 394).

The Lotus Sutra, in contrast, directly expresses the Buddha's true intent, revealing the ultimate essence of attaining Buddhahood based on the mutual possession of the Ten Worlds. Of the Buddha's many teachings, it alone has the power to activate the Buddha nature of all people. Hence, the Daishonin says, "The Lotus Sutra alone can lead people to Buddhahood."

To lead all people of the Latter Day to enlightenment, therefore, it is necessary to refute the provisional sutras, which aggravate darkness or ignorance, and spread the Lotus Sutra, which activates the fundamental nature of enlightenment or Dharma nature inherent in people's lives. This also means, however, that the devil king's opposition to those who practice the Lotus Sutra will intensify and that the three powerful enemies are sure to appear. Therefore, the Daishonin states, "The three powerful enemies will arise without fail."

❧

Waging a Struggle of Profound Compassion Amid Great Obstacles

Our teacher, the Thus Come One Shakyamuni, practiced shakubuku during the last eight years of his lifetime, the Great Teacher T'ien-t'ai for more than thirty years, and the Great Teacher Dengyo for more than twenty. I have been refuting the provisional doctrines for more than twenty years, and the great persecutions I have suffered during this period are beyond number. I do not know whether they are equal to the nine great persecutions suffered by the Buddha, but surely neither T'ien-t'ai nor Dengyo ever faced persecutions as great as mine for the sake of the Lotus Sutra. They encountered only hatred, envy, and slander, whereas I twice incurred the wrath of the rulers and was exiled to remote provinces. Furthermore, I was nearly beheaded at Tatsunokuchi, wounded on the forehead [at Komatsubara], and slandered time and again. My disciples have also been exiled and thrown into prison, and my lay supporters have been evicted and had their fiefs confiscated. How can the persecutions faced by Nagarjuna, T'ien-t'ai, or Dengyo possibly compare with these? Understand then that the votary who practices the Lotus Sutra exactly as the Buddha teaches will without fail be attacked by the three powerful enemies. (WND-1, 394–95)

Here Nichiren Daishonin looks at the kinds of persecutions that befell Shakyamuni and votaries of the Lotus Sutra of later ages, such as the great teachers T'ien-t'ai and Dengyo. All three encountered fierce opposition through proclaiming the correct teaching of the Lotus Sutra and refuting erroneous teachings. Shakyamuni's nine great persecutions or ordeals are well known. But when it comes to T'ien-t'ai and Dengyo, Nichiren says, their persecutions effectively took the form of only "hatred, envy, and slander" and were not of the same magnitude as the persecutions he himself experienced.

The Daishonin underwent a series of life-threatening persecutions that included two exiles by the government; near execution at Tatsunokuchi; and the Komatsubara Persecution, during which he sustained a wound to his forehead and had his left hand broken. He also writes that several of his disciples also suffered persecution, such as exile, imprisonment, land confiscation, or eviction.

He most likely compares his own persecutions with those of T'ien-t'ai and Dengyo to underscore the close correlation between the depth of the teaching propagated and the severity of resistance it meets. In "The Treatment of Illness," the Daishonin discusses the three obstacles and four devils, which invariably arise to hinder Lotus Sutra practitioners, and declares: "Now each and every one has risen to confront me. They are even more powerful than the three obstacles and four devils that T'ien-t'ai, Dengyo, and others had to face" (WND-1, 1114). And with regard to the difference in the depth of the teachings and the persecutions practitioners encounter, he says:

There are two ways of perceiving the three thousand realms in a single moment of life. One is theoretical, and the other, actual. What T'ien-t'ai and Dengyo practiced was theoretical, but what I practice now is actual. Because what I practice is superior, the difficulties attending it are that much greater. ("The Treatment of Illness," WND-1, 1114–15)

The teaching of "actual three thousand realms in a single moment of life"[21] represents the great Law of the Buddhism of sowing that directly activates the fundamental nature of enlightenment or Dharma nature. This is the Law of Nam-myoho-renge-kyo that is the key to the immediate attainment of enlightenment.[22] It has the power to sever darkness and awaken the Buddha nature in all people. At the same time, it has the power to cause people to question their assumptions and doubt their misguided beliefs so that they can awaken to and embrace the correct teaching,[23] a development that stirs up the fundamental darkness inherent in life and calls forth the three obstacles and four devils—especially, the devil king of the sixth heaven.

Because Nichiren Daishonin, the votary of the Lotus Sutra in the Latter Day, spread the Law of sowing (Nam-myoho-renge-kyo), which is the fundamental cause for attaining Buddhahood, he encountered far more intense persecution than that faced by T'ien-t'ai and Dengyo during the Middle

Day of the Law. The crucial point is that overcoming adversity in the course of propagating the correct teaching is what marks one as a genuine votary of the Lotus Sutra. By triumphing over daunting obstacles, one can prove the power of the Law.

Even amid great persecutions, Nichiren demonstrates an invincible state of life brimming with the "boundless joy of the Law."[24] For example, during the Izu Exile,[25] he declares: "I feel immense joy" ("The Four Debts of Gratitude," WND-1, 41), and "For anyone born human, what greater joy could there be?" (WND-1, 43). And at the time of the Sado Exile,[26] he says, "I, Nichiren, am the richest man in all of present-day Japan" ("The Opening of the Eyes," WND-1, 268). Nichiren triumphed over every ordeal. Speaking of his greatest crisis, he states: "I survived even the Tatsunokuchi Persecution.[27] . . . By now, the devil king must be thoroughly discouraged" (GZ, 843).[28] These words reveal his triumphant state of life in having overcome all adversity and vanquished the devil king of the sixth heaven.

Mr. Toda often remarked on this: "While weathering every imaginable kind of persecution, the Daishonin waged a struggle of profound compassion for the enlightenment of all people. And he triumphed over every onslaught. This is indisputable proof that he is the Buddha of the Latter Day of the Law."

Buddhism is a struggle to be victorious. By defeating the three obstacles and four devils and the three powerful enemies, we prove ourselves genuine votaries of the Lotus Sutra.

In "The Opening of the Eyes," Nichiren writes, "As regards my ability to endure persecution and the wealth of my compassion for others, I believe [T'ien-t'ai and Dengyo] would hold me in awe" (WND-1, 242).

Because of his compassionate wish to lead people of the Latter Day to enlightenment, he dauntlessly propagated the Lotus Sutra, ready to face the most terrible persecution. He stood up alone and bore the full brunt of all obstacles and attacks—like a roof protecting the people from harm or a pillar supporting the nation amid disorder and confusion. He did so to create an enduring solidarity of good that would forever be dedicated to realizing individual and collective happiness. His efforts were coupled with his keen ability and wisdom to discern the invisible roots of evil and misfortune and to encourage suffering people in a way that would inspire them or revitalize their lives. No obstacles or powerful enemies could sway this towering spirit in which compassion and wisdom were one and inseparable. Indeed, because his life and actions exemplified supreme compassion for all humanity into the eternal future, we regard Nichiren Daishonin as the Buddha of the Latter Day of the Law.

The Shared Commitment of Mentor and Disciple to Practice as the Buddha Teaches

In the more than two thousand years that have passed since the Buddha's advent, Shakyamuni himself, T'ien-t'ai, and Dengyo were the only three who perfectly carried out the Buddha's teachings. Now in the Latter Day of the Law, Nichiren and his disciples and lay believers are just such practitioners. If we cannot be called votaries faithful to the Buddha's teachings, then neither can Shakyamuni, T'ien-t'ai, or Dengyo. (WND-1, 395)

This is Nichiren Daishonin's important conclusion to this writing. He clearly identifies the votaries or practitioners faithful to the Buddha's teachings. With absolute conviction, he declares that after Shakyamuni's passing—aside from T'ien-t'ai and Dengyo during the Middle Day of the Law—only "Nichiren and his disciples and lay believers" fit this description in the Latter Day.

The essential point here is that Nichiren does not say that it is him alone. He uses the word *we*, which includes all his disciples—priests and laity—clarifying that those who exert themselves in Buddhist practice with his same selfless and altruistic spirit to propagate the Law are also votaries acting in perfect accord with the Buddha's teachings. Here, we can see the boundless compassion of the Buddha of the Latter Day.

The oneness of mentor and disciple is the cornerstone of Nichiren Buddhism. And true attainment of Buddhahood is found in the shared struggle of mentor and disciple to practice as the Buddha teaches.

Nichikan, a great restorer of Nichiren Buddhism, wrote a commentary on this writing. Discussing the meaning of "practicing as the Buddha teaches," he says:

"As the Buddha teaches" means "as the teacher instructs." "Practice" refers to the actions of the disciple. The disciple practicing as the teacher instructs is therefore the essence of "practicing in accord with the Buddha's teaching."[29]

In other words, practicing as the Buddha teaches is identical to teacher and disciple striving with the same spirit, and such Buddhist practice is the foundation for everything.

As the teacher, Nichiren Daishonin has but one wish and that is for dedicated disciples—a multitude of Bodhisattvas of the Earth—to appear and take action in all spheres with his same aspiration. Because he seeks genuine disciples, he urges his followers to pursue his same obstacle-fraught path. And being genuine disciples, they regard all hardships and trials for the sake of the Law as a source of pride. There is profound significance in the Daishonin identifying the votaries of the Latter Day as "Nichiren and his disciples and lay believers." Doubtless, these words also arose from his immense compassion for those who had been striving alongside him through great adversities in a spirit of shared commitment to propagating the correct teaching. We can easily imagine the Daishonin's disciples reading this passage and being deeply inspired to emulate his dauntless spirit all the more.

Putting the Buddha's teachings into practice requires that genuine disciples stand up and take earnest action. From there, the great river of kosen-rufu flows powerfully. We of the SGI have inherited this great river of universal enlightenment and, in the present age, have continued to propagate the correct teaching in the same spirit as Nichiren, while battling various obstacles.

Mr. Makiguchi, Mr. Toda, and I—the first three Soka Gakkai presidents—have all confronted and triumphed over fierce onslaughts by the three powerful enemies and the three obstacles and four devils. The first two presidents faced wartime persecution by the Japanese militarist authorities. I also became the target of unjust attack by authorities in the Osaka Incident.[30] In the wake of that incident, Mr. Toda declared:

It is important to speak out and refute what needs to be refuted. If we remain silent, the public will accept such falsehoods as true. . . . We can't afford to let justice be beaten by a pack of lies! . . . We speak of justice triumphing, but it's not always a foregone conclusion that justice will prevail. Without a struggle, justice will be lost. Because our cause is just, we mustn't be defeated. We have to win. That's why it's so important that we stand up for justice.

Because we champion the highest good, we must keep fighting and win without fail. This is the Soka Gakkai spirit pulsing in the hearts of the first three presidents; the spirit of practicing as the Buddha teaches is the pride of the Soka Gakkai, the "king of the religious world." In a letter to the lay nun Sennichi, Nichiren writes: "Let them say what they will. Entrust yourself to the golden teachings of the Lotus Sutra, Shakyamuni Buddha, T'ien-t'ai, Miao-lo,[31] Dengyo, and Chang-an.[32] This is what is signified by the expression, 'practicing according to the Buddha's teachings'" ("The Embankments of Faith," WND-1, 626). Thus, to his women followers as well, Nichiren stresses the vital importance of practicing in accord with the Buddha's teachings, just as he did.

We must never forget that the Soka Gakkai has been built through the prayers, efforts, and unity of our members practicing as the Buddha teaches—not least our women's division and young women's division members.

Establishing the Eternal Life State of Buddhahood

Life flashes by in but a moment. No matter how many terrible enemies you may encounter, banish all fears and never think of backsliding. Even if someone were to cut off our heads with a saw, impale our bodies with lances, or shackle our feet and bore them through with a gimlet, as long as we are alive, we must keep chanting Nam-myoho-renge-kyo, Nam-myoho-renge-kyo. Then, if we chant until the very moment of death, Shakyamuni, Many Treasures, and the Buddhas of the ten directions will come to us instantly, exactly as they promised during the ceremony at Eagle Peak. Taking our hands and bearing us on their shoulders, they will carry us to Eagle Peak. The two sages, the two heavenly kings, and the ten demon daughters will guard us, while all the heavenly gods and benevolent deities will raise a canopy over our heads and unfurl banners on high. They will escort us under their protection to the treasure land of Tranquil Light. How can such joy possibly be described! (WND-1, 395–96)

"Banish all fears and never think of backsliding," like the lion king admonishing his cubs, Nichiren Daishonin exhorts his disciples who are experiencing immense trials as a result of the onslaught of the three powerful enemies.

In my youth, I heard Mr. Toda lecture on the passage in which these words appear. At that time, he said, "Without this kind of resolve, you can't be called a genuine leader in faith." He also commented on the rest of the passage that begins, "Even if someone were to cut off our heads," which highlights the spirit of selfless dedication to propagating the Law. "This is the essence of faith," Mr. Toda declared. My mentor's insightful and pointed guidance is still burned into my memory.

Given the reality of the persecutions that already confronted Nichiren and his disciples, this passage's descriptions of ordeals they might have to endure were by no means excessive or outlandish.

Of course, Nichiren Buddhism is not a teaching of reckless self-sacrifice or martyrdom that places little value on life. The Daishonin writes, "As long as we are alive, we must keep chanting Nam-myoho-renge-kyo . . . until the very moment of death." He thus teaches that we should strive to live to the very end, steadfastly practicing the correct teaching. Truly practicing with selfless devotion to spreading the Mystic Law means that we strive wholeheartedly for the sake of the Law and our mentor, giving our all to help others to the last moment of our lives.

That said, should some situation arise that would cause us to lose our lives on account of our Buddhist practice, death itself would definitely not be wretched or miserable. Mr. Toda solemnly stated: "If we should lose our lives in the course of upholding the Mystic Law, then we will attain Buddhahood without fail. Death in that case would be something like having a brief dream shortly after drifting off to sleep and then falling into a deep, peaceful slumber afterward." Also, while sometimes members may meet untimely accidental death, in light of the Mystic Law's great beneficial power, there is absolutely nothing to fear.

As Nichiren ensures us in this passage, the lives of those who have sincerely chanted Nam-myoho-renge-kyo will, at the moment of death, enter the boundless state of Buddhahood and be pervaded by absolute happiness throughout eternity. He describes this in terms of the Buddhas Shakyamuni and Many Treasures and all Buddhas in the ten directions immediately coming forth to take us by the hand and carry us on their shoulders to Eagle Peak. And indeed, he says, the protective forces of the universe—all Buddhist gods and heavenly deities, including the two sages, the two heavenly kings, and the ten demon daughters—will guard us, the Lotus Sutra practitioners, as they escort us to the Land of Tranquil Light, a Buddha land brimming with benefit. What comfort his words must have given his disciples!

In another writing, he says: "Should you depart from this life before I do, you must report to Brahma, Shakra, the four heavenly kings, and King Yama.[33] Declare yourself to be a disciple of the priest Nichiren, the foremost votary of the Lotus Sutra in Japan. Then they cannot possibly treat you discourteously" ("Encouragement to a Sick Person," WND-1, 82).[34] And in still another letter, he writes: "No matter what may happen on the road between this life and the next, he should declare himself to be a disciple of Nichiren. . . . With regard to believing in the Lotus Sutra, I am the foremost sage in Jambudvipa. My name resounds throughout the pure lands of the ten directions, and heaven and earth no doubt know it. If your husband declares that he is Nichiren's disciple, I do not think that evil demons of any kind can claim ignorance of my name" ("The Good Medicine for All Ills," WND-1, 938).[35]

Faith based on the shared commitment of mentor and disciple assures peace and happiness in both life and death. In other words, we can savor joy throughout both of the two phases, life and death.

When Nichiren's disciples dedicate themselves to the Mystic Law with the same spirit as their teacher, who is the foremost votary of the Lotus Sutra, then, together with him, they will attain a state of absolute happiness over the three existences, guaranteeing victory as well as peace and security in both life and death. In "On Practicing the Buddha's Teachings," Nichiren thus declares, "When our prayers for Buddhahood are answered and we are dwelling in the true land of Tranquil Light, we will experience the boundless joy of the Law." He promises that those who base their lives on the Mystic Law can achieve this state of absolute happiness. Therefore, at the end of this passage, he writes, "How can such joy possibly be described!"

As disciples, there is nothing more honorable than steadfastly walking the path of faith we have vowed to our mentor we will follow. Nichiren assures his followers that their prayers for Buddhahood will be fulfilled and they will come to dwell in the "true land of Tranquil Light," enjoying immense peace of mind. Therefore, no matter what great obstacles may arise, they have absolutely nothing to worry about or fear. From the eternal viewpoint of the Buddha of the Latter Day, he assures them that they will "experience the boundless joy of the Law." There is no greater happiness than this.

As indicated by the line "If we chant until the very moment of death," it all depends on whether we continue chanting wholeheartedly for the happiness of ourselves and others until the end of our lives. This is the essence of faith based on practicing the Buddha's teachings in a spirit of oneness with our mentor.

A passage we discussed earlier comes vividly to mind: "Suppose someone, no matter who, should unrelentingly proclaim that the Lotus Sutra alone can lead people to Buddhahood." Using our voices, declaring the truth, could be said to express the cornerstone of practicing as the Buddha teaches. Elsewhere, too, Nichiren describes himself as having "never spared his voice" (OTT, 57), and as not "hesitating to speak out" ("The Teaching That Accords with the Buddha's Mind," WND-1, 970), and so forth. He also cites the passage "The voice carries out the work of the Buddha" (OTT, 4).

Unhesitatingly saying what needs to be said, not leaving unspoken anything that needs to be communicated—this is the spirit of shakubuku in Nichiren Buddhism. As long as we always forge ahead with this spirit, we will continually make great strides in our kosen-rufu movement. This is the Daishonin's unshakable conviction; it is also the Soka Gakkai spirit.

Mr. Makiguchi said, "Fainthearted individuals who cannot say what must be said will not qualify as disciples of the Daishonin."

At the end of this writing, Nichiren says, "Keep this letter with you at all times and read it over and over" (WND-1, 396). We, too, must never forget this spirit of cherishing his writings. As honorable disciples of Nichiren, let's earnestly carry out one-to-one dialogue based on the compassionate spirit to lead people to the Mystic Law, aiming to realize an inner transformation in our own lives and help others do the same. This is the Soka Gakkai's most fundamental activity.

While steadfastly chanting Nam-myoho-renge-kyo and tirelessly conducting dialogue, let's write a brilliant history of growth and development for our movement by practicing the Buddha's teachings in accord with the Buddha's decree and win the applause and praise of all Buddhas and heavenly deities throughout the universe.

This concludes the three-part lecture on "On Practicing the Buddha's Teachings."

—With my prayers for the victory
of my genuine disciples.

This lecture was originally published in the March 2010 issue of the Daibyakurenge, *the Soka Gakkai's monthly study journal.*

NOTES

1. Three powerful enemies: Three types of arrogant people who persecute those who propagate the Lotus Sutra in the evil age after Shakyamuni Buddha's death, described in the concluding verse section of "Encouraging Devotion," the thirteenth chapter of the Lotus Sutra. The Great Teacher Miao-lo (711–82) of China summarizes them as arrogant lay people, arrogant priests, and arrogant false sages.

2. T'ien-t'ai (538–97): Also known as Chih-i. The founder of the T'ien-t'ai school in China. Commonly referred to as the Great Teacher T'ien-t'ai. His lectures were compiled in such works as *The Profound Meaning of the* *Lotus Sutra, The Words and Phrases of the Lotus Sutra,* and *Great Concentration and Insight.* He spread the Lotus Sutra in China and established the doctrine of three thousand realms in a single moment of life.

3. Dengyo (767–822): Also known as Saicho. The founder of the Tendai (T'ien-t'ai) school in Japan. Often referred to as the Great Teacher Dengyo. He refuted the errors of the six schools of Nara—the established Buddhist schools of the day—elevated the Lotus Sutra, and dedicated himself to the establishment of a Mahayana ordination center on Mount Hiei.

4. Nine great persecutions: Also, nine great ordeals. The major hardships that Shakyamuni Buddha underwent. They are listed in *The Treatise on the Great Perfection of Wisdom* by Nagarjuna and in other Buddhist works but differ slightly according to the source. They include such incidents as an assassination attempt by Devadatta, who pushed a boulder from a cliff hoping to crush Shakyamuni but succeeded only in injuring the latter's toe, and a group of Brahmans instigating a plot in which a beautiful woman named Sundari spread scandalous rumors about Shakyamuni to besmirch his reputation.

5. Tatsunokuchi Persecution: On September 12, 1271, powerful figures in the government unjustly arrested Nichiren. They led him off in the middle of the night to the execution grounds on the beach at Tatsunokuchi on the outskirts of Kamakura, the seat of government, where they tried to execute him under cover of darkness. The execution attempt failed, and about a month later, Nichiren was exiled to Sado Island.

6. Komatsubara Persecution: An attempt by Tojo Kagenobu, the steward of Tojo Village, to kill Nichiren at nearby Komatsubara in Awa Province on November 11, 1264. Nichiren suffered a sword cut on his forehead, and his left hand was broken; two of his followers were killed during the incident.

7. Nagarjuna (n.d.): A Mahayana scholar of southern India, thought to have lived between the years 150 and 250. Nagarjuna wrote many important treatises, including *The Treatise on the Middle Way,* and had a major impact on the development of Buddhist thought in China and Japan. Nichiren identifies Nagarjuna as a successor who correctly understood Shakyamuni's true intent.

8. Many Treasures: A Buddha who appeared, seated within the treasure tower at the Ceremony in the Air, in order to lend credence to Shakyamuni's teachings in the Lotus Sutra. According to "Treasure Tower," the eleventh chapter of the Lotus Sutra, he lives in the Land of Treasure Purity in the east. While still engaged in bodhisattva practice, he pledged that even after having entered nirvana he would appear in order to attest to the validity of the Lotus Sutra, wherever it might be taught.

9. Ceremony at Eagle Peak: The assembly on Eagle Peak, where Shakyamuni preached the Lotus Sutra. Eagle Peak, also known as Vulture Peak, is an actual mountain located to the northeast of Rajagriha, the capital of Magadha in ancient India. It also symbolizes the Buddha land or the state of Buddhahood, as is the meaning in the next sentence of this passage.

10. The two sages, the two heavenly kings, and the ten demon daughters: August beings who pledge in "Dharani," the twenty-sixth chapter of the Lotus Sutra, to protect the sutra's practitioners. The two sages are the bodhisattvas Medicine King and Brave Donor. The two heavenly kings are two of the so-called four heavenly kings, Hearer of Many Teachings and Upholder of the Nation. And the ten demon daughters are ten female protective deities who appear in the Lotus Sutra as the "daughters of *rakshasa* demons" or the "ten *rakshasa* daughters."

11. A reference to the land of Tranquil Light. Also, Land of Eternally Tranquil Light. The Buddha land, which is free from impermanence and impurity. It is often used interchangeably with Eagle Peak or the pure land of Eagle Peak.

12. This description originally appears in the Great Collection Sutra. During the Latter Day of the Law, quarrels and disputes arise among the followers of the Buddha's teachings, causing the pure Law to become lost and obscured.

13. Mutual possession of the Ten Worlds: The principle that each of the Ten Worlds possesses the potential for all ten within itself. "Mutual possession" means that life is not fixed in one or another of the Ten Worlds but can manifest any of the ten—from hell to the state of Buddhahood—at any given moment. The important point of this principle is that all beings in any of the nine worlds possess the Buddha nature. This means that every person has the potential to manifest Buddhahood, while a Buddha also possesses the nine worlds and in this sense is not separate or different from ordinary people.

14. Three thousand realms in a single moment of life: A doctrine developed by the Great Teacher T'ien-t'ai of China based on the Lotus Sutra. The principle that all phenomena are contained within a single moment of life and that a single moment of life permeates the three thousand realms of existence, or the entire phenomenal world.

15. Saha world: Our present world, which is filled with suffering. Often translated as the world of endurance. In Sanskrit, saha means the earth; it derives from a root meaning "to bear" or "to endure." In this context, the saha world indicates a world in which people must endure suffering. It is also defined as an impure land, a land defiled by earthly desires and illusion, in contrast with a pure land.

16. In the concluding verse section of "Encouraging Devotion," the thirteenth chapter of the Lotus Sutra, countless multitudes of bodhisattvas vow to Shakyamuni to propagate the sutra in the evil age after his death. This section is also often called the twenty-line verse section, because the original Chinese translation consists of twenty lines. It begins with the passage: "We beg you not to worry. After the Buddha has passed into extinction, in an age of fear and evil we will preach far and wide" (LSOC, 232). It then goes on to enumerate the persecutions that will occur in the evil age designated in the sutra. Based on this section, the Great Teacher

Miao-lo of China classified those who persecute practitioners of the Lotus Sutra into three types of powerful enemies.

17. Devil king of the sixth heaven: Also, devil king or heavenly devil. The king of devils who, in Buddhist mythology, dwells in the highest or the sixth heaven of the world of desire. He is also named Freely Enjoying Things Conjured by Others, the king who makes free use of the fruits of others' efforts for his own pleasure. Served by innumerable minions, he obstructs Buddhist practice and delights in sapping the life force of other beings. The devil king is a personification of the negative tendency to force others to one's will at any cost.

18. Nichiren writes: "When an ordinary person of the latter age is ready to attain Buddhahood, having realized the essence of all the sacred teachings of the Buddha's lifetime . . ., this devil is greatly surprised. He says to himself, 'This is most vexing. If I allow this person to remain in my domain, he not only will free himself from the sufferings of birth and death, but will lead others to enlightenment as well. Moreover, he will take over my realm and change it into a pure land. What shall I do?' The devil king then summons all his underlings from the threefold world of desire, form, and formlessness and tells them: 'Each of you now go and harass that votary, according to your respective skills. If you should fail to make him abandon his Buddhist practice, then enter into the minds of his disciples, lay supporters, and the people of his land and thus try to persuade or threaten him. If these attempts are also unsuccessful, I myself will go down and possess the mind and body of his sovereign to persecute that votary. Together, how can we fail to prevent him from attaining Buddhahood?'" ("Letter to Misawa," WND-1, 894–95).

19. For instance, "Reply to Sairen-bo" (WND-1, 309–13).

20. Fundamental nature of enlightenment, or Dharma nature: The unchanging nature inherent in all things and phenomena. It is identified with the fundamental Law itself, the essence of the Buddha's enlightenment, or ultimate truth.

21. Actual three thousand realms in a single moment of life: The doctrine of three thousand realms in a single moment of life, which is the fundamental teaching for attaining enlightenment, is classified into two as the theoretical principle and the actual embodiment of this principle. These are respectively termed "theoretical three thousand realms in a single moment of life" and "actual three thousand realms in a single moment of life." The theoretical principle is based on the theoretical teaching (first half) of the Lotus Sutra, while the actual principle is revealed in the essential teaching (latter half) of the sutra. But in the Latter Day of the Law, these are both theoretical, and Nam-myoho-renge-kyo that Nichiren revealed is the actual teaching of three thousand realms in a single moment of life.

22. Immediate attainment of Buddhahood based on the doctrine of three thousand realms in a single moment of life: This refers to beings in the nine words bringing forth their inherent Buddhahood and attaining

enlightenment. The term is used in contrast to attaining Buddhahood through transformation, that is, through devoting oneself ceaselessly to arduous Buddhist practice over countless lifetimes until gradually ascending to the highest stage of supreme enlightenment.

23. This refers to the principle of "upsetting attachments and arousing doubts," a way of instruction employed by the Buddha to lead people toward the correct teaching. It means to disturb the mind that is attached to inferior teachings, thereby arousing doubt in those attachments and causing the person to aspire for a deeper understanding of the correct teaching.

24. Boundless joy of the Law: The supreme and ultimate happiness of the Buddha, the benefit of the Mystic Law.

25. Izu Exile: A persecution in which Nichiren was exiled to Ito in Izu Province, from May 1261 through February 1263. In August 1260, a group of Nembutsu believers, infuriated at Nichiren's criticism of the Pure Land (Nembutsu) school in his treatise "On Establishing the Correct Teaching for the Peace of the Land," attacked his dwelling at Matsubagayatsu in Kamakura to assassinate him. Nichiren narrowly escaped and fled to Toki Jonin's house in Shimosa Province. When he reappeared in Kamakura in spring 1261 and resumed propagation activities, the government arrested him and, without due investigation, ordered him exiled to Ito. About two years after arriving in Izu, Nichiren was pardoned and returned to Kamakura.

26. Sado Exile: The exile of Nichiren to Sado Island in the Sea of Japan from 1271 through 1274. When the priest Ryokan of Gokuraku-ji, a temple in Kamakura, was defeated by Nichiren in a contest to pray for rain, he spread false rumors about the Daishonin, using his influence with the wives and widows of high government officials. This led to Nichiren's confrontation with Hei no Saemon, deputy chief of the Office of Military and Police Affairs, who arrested him and maneuvered to have him executed at Tatsunokuchi in September 1271. When the execution attempt failed, the authorities sentenced him the following month to exile on Sado Island, which was tantamount to a death sentence.

But when Nichiren's predictions of internal strife and foreign invasion were fulfilled, the government issued a pardon in March 1274, and he returned to Kamakura.

27. Tatsunokuchi Persecution: See note 5.

28. "Oko kikigaki" (The Recorded Lectures); not translated in WND, vols. 1 and 2.

29. Translated from Japanese. Nichikan, "Commentary on 'On Practicing the Buddha's Teaching,'" in *Nichikan Shonin mondanshu* (The Commentaries of Nichikan Shonin) (Tokyo: Seikyo Shimbunsha, 1980), 748.

30. Osaka Incident: The occasion when Daisaku Ikeda, then Soka Gakkai youth division chief of staff, was arrested and wrongfully charged with election law violations in a House of Councillor's by-election in Osaka in 1957. At the end of the court case, which dragged on for almost five years, he was exonerated of all charges.

31. Miao-lo (711–82): A patriarch of the T'ien-t'ai school in China. He is revered as the school's restorer. His commentaries on T'ien-t'ai's three major works are titled *The Annotations on "The Profound Meaning of the Lotus Sutra," The Annotations on "The Words and Phrases of the Lotus Sutra,"* and *The Annotations on "Great Concentration and Insight."*

32. Chang-an (561–632): T'ien-t'ai's disciple and successor. He recorded T'ien-t'ai's lectures and later compiled them as *The Profound Meaning of the Lotus Sutra, The Words and Phrases of the Lotus Sutra,* and *Great Concentration and Insight.* His own works include *The Annotations on the Nirvana Sutra* and *The Profound Meaning of the Nirvana Sutra.*

33. These are gods and kings depicted in Buddhist mythology. Brahma and Shakra are the two principal tutelary gods of Buddhism. The four heavenly kings serve Shakra and protect the four quarters of the world. King Yama is king of the world of the dead who judges and determines the rewards and punishments of the deceased.

34. This letter was addressed to the ailing Nanjo Hyoe Shichiro, the father of Nanjo Tokimitsu.

35. This letter was addressed to the lay nun Myoshin concerning her sick husband.

"THE PROOF OF THE LOTUS SUTRA"

THE PRAYERS OF A VOTARY OF THE LOTUS SUTRA TRIUMPH OVER ILLNESS

The Passage of Study for This Lecture

How does the mirror of the Lotus Sutra portray the people who, in the evil world of the latter age, believe in the teachings of the Lotus Sutra just as they are set forth in the sutra? Shakyamuni Buddha has left us words from his golden mouth revealing that such people have already made offerings to a hundred thousand million Buddhas in their past existences.[1] . . . (WND-1, 1108)

When ordinary people in the latter age believe in even one or two words of the Lotus Sutra, they are embracing the teaching to which the Buddhas of the ten directions have given credence. I wonder what karma we created in the past to have been born as such persons, and I am filled with joy. The words of Shakyamuni that I referred to above indicate that the blessings that come from having made offerings to a hundred thousand million Buddhas are so great that, even if one has believed in teachings other than the Lotus Sutra and as a result of this slander been born poor and lowly, one is still able to believe in this sutra in this lifetime. A T'ien-t'ai [school's] commentary states, "It is like the case of a person who falls to the ground, but who then pushes himself up from the ground and rises to his feet again."[2] One who has fallen to the ground recovers and rises up from the ground. Those who slander the Lotus Sutra will fall to the ground of the three evil paths, or of the human and heavenly realms, but in the end, through the help of the Lotus Sutra, they will attain Buddhahood.

Now since you, Ueno Shichiro Jiro,[3] are an ordinary person in the latter age and were born to a warrior family, you should by rights be called an evil man,[4] and yet your heart is that of a good man. I say this for a reason. Everyone, from the ruler on down to the common people, refuses to take faith in my teachings. They inflict harm on the few who do embrace them, heavily taxing or confiscating their estates and fields, or even in some cases putting them to death. So it is a difficult thing to believe in my teachings, and yet both your mother and your deceased father dared to accept them. Now you have succeeded your father as his heir, and without any prompting from others, you too have wholeheartedly embraced these teachings. Many people, both high and low, have admonished or threatened you, but you have refused to give up your faith. Since you now appear certain to attain Buddhahood, perhaps the heavenly devil[5] and evil spirits[6] are using illness to try to intimidate you. Life in this world is limited. Never be even the least bit afraid!

And you demons, by making this man suffer, are you trying to swallow a sword point first, or embrace a raging fire, or become the archenemy of the Buddhas of the ten directions in the three existences? How terrible this will be for you! Should you not cure this man's illness immediately, act rather as his protectors, and escape from the grievous sufferings that are the lot of demons? If you fail to do so, will you not have your heads broken into seven pieces in this life[7] and fall into the great hell of incessant suffering in your next life! Consider it deeply. Consider it. If you ignore my words, you will certainly regret it later. (WND-1, 1108–09)

LECTURE

Good health is the wish of all people. Long life is the desire of all humankind. From the time I became Soka Gakkai president (on May 3, 1960), I have earnestly prayed each day for the health, longevity, safety, and well-being of all my fellow members. For the last five decades, I have prayed fervently that all Buddhas and bodhisattvas, all heavenly deities—the positive forces throughout the universe—rigorously protect and safeguard my disciples without fail.

Nam-myoho-renge-kyo is the great beneficial medicine for good health and a long life; it is the fundamental rhythm of the universe and the wellspring of the immense life force of Buddhas. My sincerest wish, therefore, is that all who possess this wonderful medicine of the Mystic Law will lead supremely rewarding and deeply satisfying lives of mission, living out their lives to the fullest. Faith in the Mystic Law drives us to live life to the fullest.[8]

In this chapter, with my sincere prayers for the happiness and safety of all our members, I will discuss the writing "The Proof of the Lotus Sutra." In this letter, Nichiren Daishonin pours his life into encouraging a beloved disciple battling a life-threatening illness.

This letter is dated February 28, 1282. Nichiren himself had been suffering from ill health since the previous year. News had reached him that Nanjo Tokimitsu—who had been fighting valiantly under the leadership of Nikko Shonin against religious persecution in Suruga Province (present-day central Shizuoka Prefecture)—had fallen seriously ill. Tokimitsu was only twenty-four at the time.

Three days before writing this letter, Nichiren had dictated a note conveying his prayers for Tokimitsu's speedy recovery, which Nichiro, a principal disciple, had transcribed and delivered. But it appears that his deep concern for his beloved young follower prompted Nichiren to pick up his brush and write a letter of earnest encouragement. In this letter, he seeks to awaken in Tokimitsu the fighting spirit not to be defeated by the devil of illness, instructing him in the essence of faith for overcoming illness. This illustrates the incredible care and compassion of this great teacher.

One rather unusual feature of this writing is that it begins with Nichiren's signature, "Nichiren, the votary of the Lotus Sutra" (WND-1, 1108). In all his extant writings, "The Proof of the Lotus Sutra" is the only one he begins with this type of signature.

A votary of the Lotus Sutra is someone who works to establish the supreme teaching for the enlightenment of all people in the evil age of the Latter Day of the Law and selflessly propagates that teaching for the sake of worldwide kosen-rufu into the eternal future. "The Proof of the Lotus Sutra" is a letter in which Nichiren offers strict yet compassionate guidance as a votary of the Lotus Sutra to a young follower who will carry on the mission of propagating the Mystic Law. He urges Tokimitsu to battle and resolutely triumph over the devil of illness so that he may bring forth the victorious life state of Buddhahood for all to see.

In addition, Nichiren directly addresses the so-called demons, or negative workings in life. He sternly admonishes them for inflicting suffering on the disciple of a votary of the Lotus Sutra, warning that in doing so they risk making enemies of all the Buddhas throughout the ten directions and three existences. His words deeply and powerfully convey his towering spirit and conviction as a votary who has triumphed over great obstacles in his efforts to widely propagate the Mystic Law in the Latter Day.

At the end of the writing, we find the words "Delivered by Hoki-bo" (WND-1, 1109). This indicates that the letter was first sent to Hoki-bo—otherwise known as Nikko Shonin. We can well imagine Nichiren's trusted disciple going to see the ailing Tokimitsu with this heartfelt letter of encouragement and reading it to him at his bedside. Most certainly the ardent lion's roar of Nichiren contained therein penetrated Tokimitsu's life and made him deepen his resolve not to be defeated by the negative functions that were assailing him. In fact, he overcame his illness and lived for another fifty years.

When the disciple strives with the same spirit as the mentor, there is no obstacle or devilish function that cannot be surmounted, and there is no illness that cannot be positively transformed in accord with the principle of "changing poison into medicine."[9] "The Proof of the Lotus Sutra" highlights the key to good health and long life and conveys the victory of mentor and disciple.

Possessing a Profound Connection With the Lotus Sutra

How does the mirror of the Lotus Sutra portray the people who, in the evil world of the latter age, believe in the teachings of the Lotus Sutra just as they are set forth in the sutra? Shakyamuni Buddha has left us words from his golden mouth revealing that such people have already made offerings to a hundred thousand million Buddhas in their past existences. . . . (WND-1, 1108)

When ordinary people in the latter age believe in even one or two words of the Lotus Sutra, they are embracing the teaching to which the Buddhas of the ten directions have given credence. I wonder what karma we created in the past to have been born as such persons, and I am filled with joy. The words of Shakyamuni that I referred to above indicate that the blessings that come from having made offerings to a hundred thousand million Buddhas are so great that, even if one has believed in teachings other than the Lotus Sutra and as a result of this slander been born poor and lowly, one is still able to believe in this sutra in this lifetime. A T'ien-t'ai [school's] commentary states, "It is like the case of a person who falls to the ground, but who then pushes himself up from the ground and rises to his feet again." One who has fallen to the ground

recovers and rises up from the ground. Those who slander the Lotus Sutra will fall to the ground of the three evil paths, or of the human and heavenly realms, but in the end, through the help of the Lotus Sutra, they will attain Buddhahood. (WND-1, 1108)

In the first half of this writing, Nichiren Daishonin explains that those who believe in the Lotus Sutra in the Latter Day of the Law have an extremely profound karmic connection with Buddhism reaching back to previous existences. First, he emphasizes that they are people who have made offerings to "a hundred thousand million Buddhas" in the past. Not only does Shakyamuni Buddha tell us this, but Many Treasures Buddha and all the Buddhas of the ten directions also affirm it (see WND-1, 1108).

We are able to uphold the Lotus Sutra—the teaching of the highest truth—in the Latter Day because our lives are endowed with great good fortune and benefit beyond imagination. Shakyamuni, Many Treasures, and the Buddhas of the ten directions unanimously attest to this truth.

This prompts Nichiren to observe, "I wonder what karma we created in the past to have been born as such persons, and I am filled with joy." In the Latter Day, an age steeped in suffering and confusion, it is through immense good fortune and an extraordinary karmic connection that we can uphold the Lotus Sutra. The Daishonin teaches that if we practice the Lotus Sutra with this conviction, we will definitely overcome any hardship and attain the life state of absolute happiness that is Buddhahood.

Why, then, should those whose lives are endowed with vast good fortune and benefit gained from having made offerings to countless Buddhas be born into an evil age and experience sufferings and hardships? Nichiren explains that this is because of their slander of the Lotus Sutra in past existences. However, their immense good fortune and benefit of making offerings to untold Buddhas makes it possible for them—through their reverse relationship with the Lotus Sutra—to be born in this world as people who believe in the Lotus Sutra and have the potential to attain enlightenment through this sutra in this lifetime.

This is illustrated by the following passage in Miao-lo's *Annotations on "The Words and Phrases of the Lotus Sutra,"* "It is like the case of a person who falls to the ground, but who then pushes himself up from the ground and rises to his feet again." This passage offers a metaphor for people who, though falling into evil paths as a result of slander, form a connection with the correct teaching that will ultimately enable them to find their way to enlightenment through that teaching.

Those who fall to the ground get back on their feet by using the ground to push themselves up. In the same way, those who slander the Lotus Sutra will gain enlightenment through the Lotus Sutra. The Mystic Law embraces even those who form a reverse relationship with it, enabling all people to attain Buddhahood. Such is the unfathomable power of the "poison-drum relationship"[10] in Buddhism.

Seeing Illness as an Opportunity to Deepen One's Faith

Those who uphold the Mystic Law have the power to withstand any adversity. Nam-myoho-renge-kyo has the beneficial power to lessen karmic retribution and change poison into medicine.

Here, let us look at some of the encouragement and guidance that Nichiren Daishonin sent to other followers who were struggling with illness.

In "On Curing Karmic Disease," which is addressed to the lay priest Ota, he writes that even illnesses that result from karma and are the most difficult to cure can be healed by the good medicine of the Lotus Sutra, Myoho-renge-kyo (see WND-1, 632). And he cites a passage from the Great Teacher T'ien-t'ai's *Great Concentration and Insight* that explains: "Even if one has committed grave offenses . . . the retribution can be lessened in this life. Thus, illness occurs when evil karma is about to be dissipated" (WND-1, 631). This expresses the principle of "lessening karmic retribution."[11]

Nichiren explains that Ota is most surely experiencing his present illness so that he can avoid worse suffering that would appear as retribution for his past slander of the Law. He also assures him that he will definitely be healed and his life span extended (see WND-1, 634). He even goes so far as to say that should there fail to be signs of recovery, Ota should cry out: "The Buddha, the eye of the entire world, is a great liar, and the Lotus, the wonderful sutra of the single vehicle, is a scripture of clever flourishes. The World-Honored One should give me proof if he cares about his good name" (WND-1, 634). In these words of encouragement, Nichiren is voicing his wholehearted wish that Ota regain his health.

Elsewhere, he assures the lay nun Toki (Toki Jonin's wife), who was suffering from a protracted illness, that because Buddhism has the power to change even fixed karma,[12] it was definitely possible for her to extend her life. He tells her: "Sincere repentance will eradicate even fixed karma, to say nothing of karma that is unfixed" ("On Prolonging One's Life Span," WND-1, 954); and "Your illness is surely not due to karma, but even if it were, you could rely on the power of the Lotus Sutra to cure it" ("The Bow and Arrow," WND-1, 656).

Being gravely ill doesn't necessarily mean that one will die. Nichiren writes to the lay nun Myoshin, the wife of the ailing lay priest Takahashi, "A person's death is not determined by illness" ("The Good Medicine for All Ills," WND-1, 937). He continues: "Could not this illness of your husband's be the Buddha's design, because the Vimalakirti and Nirvana sutras both teach that sick people will surely attain Buddhahood? Illness gives rise to the resolve to attain the way" (WND-1, 937). If, as a result of falling ill, one deepens one's determination in faith, then the path to Buddhahood will definitely open. Illness then becomes "the Buddha's design."

No doubt Nichiren also wished to convey this powerful conviction to Tokimitsu. In "The Proof of the Lotus Sutra," he writes in a similar vein, "In the end, through the help of the Lotus Sutra, they will attain Buddhahood." Nichiren is urging Tokimitsu to have absolute confidence that he will gain the life state of Buddhahood.

Being Determined to Battle the Three Obstacles and Four Devils

Now since you, Ueno Shichiro Jiro, are an ordinary person in the latter age and were born to a warrior family, you should by rights be called an evil man, and yet your heart is that of a good man. I say this for a reason. Everyone, from the ruler on down to the common people, refuses to take faith in my teachings. They inflict harm on the few who do embrace them, heavily taxing or confiscating their estates and fields, or even in some cases putting them to death. So it is a difficult thing to believe in my teachings, and yet both your mother and your deceased father dared to accept them. Now you have succeeded your father as his heir, and without any prompting from others, you too have wholeheartedly embraced these

teachings. Many people, both high and low, have admonished or threatened you, but you have refused to give up your faith. Since you now appear certain to attain Buddhahood, perhaps the heavenly devil and evil spirits are using illness to try to intimidate you. Life in this world is limited. Never be even the least bit afraid! (WND-1, 1108–09)

Here Nichiren broadens the scope of his discussion from illness to life's various hardships and sufferings in general. He emphasizes that it is by fearlessly confronting and overcoming such challenges that we can establish a life of unshakable victory. He explains that the difficulties or trials that arise when we are earnestly persevering in our Buddhist practice are the workings of the three obstacles and four devils[13] that seek to prevent us from attaining Buddhahood.

First, Nichiren affirms how difficult it is to remain steadfast in faith in the evil age of the Latter Day. He specifically refers to the struggles faced by Tokimitsu's family, deeply commending the young man's parents on their strong faith. He also praises Tokimitsu, as his father's heir, for his staunch commitment to faith amid great adversity.

His circumstances had been far from easy or tranquil. In Suruga Province, where the Atsuhara Persecution[14] took place, Tokimitsu had striven tirelessly to protect his fellow practitioners and applied himself with unflagging devotion to his Buddhist practice. It must have seemed as though the negative forces were intensifying to make Tokimitsu,

a key figure among Nichiren's followers in the area, abandon his faith. Nichiren writes, "Many people, both high and low, have admonished or threatened you."

What makes Tokimitsu so admirable is that despite all the obstacles he faced, he continued to exert himself bravely and vigorously for the sake of the Law, refusing to discard his faith. Praising his sincere faith, Nichiren declares that Tokimitsu must be close to attaining Buddhahood. He explains that this is undoubtedly the reason why illness is now assailing his young disciple. In other words, devilish functions are seeking to intimidate Tokimitsu in the form of illness and prevent him from moving forward—it is a trial in which Tokimitsu's faith will be put to the test.

Allow me to clarify here that falling ill is not a sign of weak faith or defeat. No one can escape the four universal sufferings of birth, aging, sickness, and death. When we fall ill, if we can summon up powerful faith to battle the devil of illness, illness itself can become an opportunity for us to achieve a life imbued with eternity, happiness, true self, and purity—the four noble virtues of the Buddha. It can serve as a chance for us to strengthen our faith even more so that we can triumph over devilish functions. And when we have the strong, invincible faith to withstand any onslaught of the three obstacles and four devils, nothing can stop us from attaining the life state of Buddhahood.

The three obstacles and four devils descend in force when an ordinary person is close to attaining Buddhahood. Nichiren notes that when these obstructing forces appear, "the wise will rejoice while the foolish will retreat" ("The Three Obstacles and Four Devils," WND-1, 637). Are we wise in faith, pushing on with a dauntless fighting spirit? Or are we foolish in faith, our minds filled with alarm and doubt?

In the case of sickness, having the spirit to fight through to the end against the devil of illness is vital. It is a battle of whether we win over the devil of illness or allow ourselves to be defeated by it. When we encounter painful suffering such as illness, we stand at a crossroads of great spiritual growth and inner development.

Founding Soka Gakkai President Tsunesaburo Makiguchi said:

To live one's life based on the Mystic Law is to "change poison into medicine." As long as we live in society, there will be times when we encounter accidents or natural disasters or experience setbacks such as business failures. Such painful and unfortunate events could be described as "poison" or "karmic retribution." But no matter what situation we face, if we base our lives on faith, on the Mystic Law, and exert ourselves in our Buddhist practice without doubting the power of the Gohonzon, we can definitely turn poison into medicine—transforming a negative situation into something positive.

For example, if you fall ill and just spend your time worrying that your illness is karmic retribution, it won't

solve anything. The important thing is to persevere in faith with the strong conviction and determination to positively transform your illness and achieve the great good fortune and benefit of regaining your health. When you do so, not only will you overcome your illness but, when you make a complete recovery, you will be even healthier than before. This is the power of the Mystic Law, which can change poison into medicine.[15]

What is crucial is the absolute confidence that you can change poison into medicine, no matter what daunting obstacles you may face. This unshakable belief is the key to overcoming illness and other difficulties in life and to opening wide the path for attaining Buddhahood without fail. In *The Record of the Orally Transmitted Teachings*, Nichiren clarifies this, saying, "The single word 'belief' is the sharp sword with which one confronts and overcomes fundamental darkness or ignorance" (pp. 119–20).

In "The Proof of the Lotus Sutra," Nichiren's stance on illness is very clear. He says: "Life in this world is limited. Never be even the least bit afraid!" This is his essential guidance to Tokimitsu.

Making Our Limited Life in This World One of Victory

Our life in this world is limited. Death comes to us all. As Nichiren Daishonin says, "No one can escape death" ("The Dragon Gate," WND-1, 1003). That is why he urges Tokimitsu to devote his life unhesitatingly to the Lotus Sutra.[16]

There is nothing to fear when one dedicates one's limited life in this world to widely propagating the Mystic Law and establishing the correct teaching for the peace of the land. There is nothing to fear when one is determined to raise high the banner of supreme victory and glory and achieve happiness that will endure throughout the three existences.

In another letter to the lay nun Toki, Nichiren writes, "Take care of yourself, and do not burden your mind with grief" ("The Bow and Arrow," WND-1, 656). Because we are human, a serious or protracted illness may drain our strength or spirit, causing us to lament our situation or succumb to feelings of powerlessness or doubt without our even realizing it. But no matter what ails us, we should live with the resolve to not give in to grief or sorrow. Especially, in terms of faith, we should rouse a powerful spirit to battle the devil of illness and not be defeated by our sickness. The key to this is chanting Nam-myoho-renge-kyo, of which Nichiren declares, "Only the ship of Myoho-renge-kyo enables one to cross the sea of the sufferings of birth and death" ("A Ship to Cross the Sea of Suffering," WND-1, 33). The beneficial power of chanting Nam-myoho-renge-kyo

even once is boundless and immeasurable. All that matters is that we keep moving forward in our hearts each day, even if only a fraction of an inch, taking a step forward by continuing to "strengthen our faith day by day and month after month" (see "On Persecutions Befalling the Sage," WND-1, 997). Even if things don't always progress the way we'd hoped, we should remember that many fellow members are also chanting for us to get well. There is no greater source of strength and support than this.

When we steadfastly battle the devil of illness through faith, our illness in its entirety becomes an opportunity to transform our karma through the beneficial power of the Mystic Law to change poison into medicine. As Nichiren confidently declares: "There is nothing to lament when we consider that we will surely become Buddhas" (WND-1, 657). He is describing a state of absolute assurance, of absolute peace of mind.

The Noble Value of Life as a Human Being

We practice Nichiren Buddhism so that we can live out our lives to the fullest. The benefit of living even one day longer with faith in the Mystic Law is unfathomable. If we live even one day longer, we can spread the teachings of Buddhism that much more. This endows our lives with immeasurable good fortune and benefit. Through their examples, those who battle the devil of illness based on faith teach others of the noble value of life as a human being. As practitioners of Nichiren Buddhism, no matter what our circumstances, we are able to bring forth wisdom and compassion and make our own lives and those of others shine brightly. This is the way we of the SGI live our lives.

That is why using our wisdom to stay fit and healthy is also important. Faith means having both the wisdom to prevent illness and to deal with illness appropriately should it arise so we can continue creating value. For instance, when we have overcome a serious illness or are still in the early stages of recovery, we should take care not to overexert ourselves. This is also vital wisdom for regaining our health. When we fall ill, we shouldn't be impatient or forget to be careful. When we need to rest, we should listen to our bodies and not overdo things. Once we have fully regained our health, we can devote ourselves to SGI activities again as energetically as we like.

Learning that his disciple Sairen-bo wished to seclude himself in the mountains because of ill health, Nichiren responds by telling him to concentrate on treating his illness and to then return to making tireless efforts to propagate the Mystic Law when he has recovered (see "Letter Sent with the Prayer Sutra," WND-2, 460).

We cannot defeat the devil of illness with a weak resolve. If we forget the fighting spirit to struggle for kosen-rufu in the same spirit as our mentor in faith, "devils will take advantage" ("On Persecutions Befalling the Sage," WND-1, 997).

Using faith to battle illness has become firmly established in the SGI through the real-life struggles and actual proof of countless members. There are innumerable heroic individuals who have demonstrated the beneficial power of faith to change poison into medicine, inspiring those around them with their positive spirit and refusal to be defeated by the devil of illness.

Experiences of battling illness and enacting a joyful drama of victory, supported by the sincere prayer of family and fellow members, are themselves a great testimony to the power of Nichiren Buddhism.

A Towering State of Absolute Confidence

And you demons, by making this man suffer, are you trying to swallow a sword point first, or embrace a raging fire, or become the archenemy of the Buddhas of the ten directions in the three existences? How terrible this will be for you! Should you not cure this man's illness immediately, act rather as his protectors, and escape from the grievous sufferings that are the lot of demons? If you fail to do so, will you not have your heads broken into seven pieces in this life and fall into the great hell of incessant suffering in your next life! Consider it deeply. Consider it. If you ignore my words, you will certainly regret it later. (WND-1, 1109)

"And you demons!" cries Nichiren Daishonin in this passage, which constitutes an angry rebuke of the devilish functions bent on taking away the life of his young disciple. As I mentioned earlier, it also constitutes his refutation as a votary of the Lotus Sutra seeking to denounce error and clarify the truth. He warns that inflicting suffering on Tokimitsu, a disciple of the votary of the Lotus Sutra, is to alienate all the Buddhas throughout the ten directions and three existences.

Here, "demons" refers to the negative functions that seek to weaken people and rob them of their lives. Viewed from the perspective of traditional Buddhist cosmology, there are evil demons that trouble Buddhist practitioners and benevolent demons that protect Buddhism. In this passage, Nichiren demands the evil demons to immediately cure Tokimitsu's illness and become benevolent demons that will protect him instead of harming him.

"Should you not . . . escape from the grievous sufferings that are the lot of demons?," he asks. Demons represent beings that have fallen into the world of hungry spirits, a state that is filled with great suffering. Only the Lotus Sutra can free them from this realm of suffering. He urges the evil demons tormenting Tokimitsu to escape from their suffering by protecting this practitioner of the Lotus Sutra. Otherwise, he says, they will "have their heads broken into seven pieces in this life and fall into the great hell of incessant suffering in their next life." In this way, Nichiren sternly chastises the demons. He no doubt wished to show Tokimitsu his fearless conviction as a votary of the Lotus Sutra.

In light of this, let each of us, too, further strengthen our prayers as a votary of the Lotus Sutra, ready to courageously challenge the devil of illness head-on should it appear. Let us forge ahead with a firm resolve to turn even negative functions into positive influences that will support and assist us in our lives of great mission.

It is therefore important to chant Nam-myoho-renge-kyo that is like the roar of a lion. Nichiren writes:

Nam-myoho-renge-kyo is like the roar of a lion. What sickness can therefore be an obstacle? It is written that those who embrace the daimoku of the Lotus Sutra will be protected by the Mother of Demon Children[17] and by the ten demon daughters.[18] ("Reply to Kyo'o," WND-1, 412)

When faced with sickness, we need to summon the heart of a lion king from within and fearlessly take on the devil of illness. This kind of courageous faith is vital.

Nichiren also challenged his own illness with the heart of a lion king. At the time of writing "The Proof of the Lotus Sutra," he was suffering from prolonged ill health. In a letter written the previous year (1281), he says: "My body is worn out and my spirit suffers from the daily debates, monthly persecutions, and two exiles. That is why for the last seven or eight years illnesses of aging have assailed me yearly, though none has led to a crisis" ("The Reconstruction of Hachiman Shrine," WND-2, 949).

But no matter what his circumstances, Nichiren continued to offer encouragement to his followers and carry on his tireless struggle to propagate the correct teaching. We see a clear example of this in this letter, which Nichiren wrote despite his own debilitating illness for the sake of a youth to whom he wished to entrust the future.

In another letter toward the end of his life, expressing his appreciation for a disciple's visit and sincere offerings that had benefited his health, Nichiren writes exuberantly that he felt as though he were fit enough to catch a tiger or even ride a lion (see "On Three Seating Mats," WND-2, 991).

To encourage his followers, Nichiren gave vivid accounts of how he successfully repulsed the attacks of the three obstacles and four devils. In doing so, he left behind an inspiring example of a life undefeated by the innate sufferings of birth, aging, sickness, and death.

Life Itself Is a Joy

Mr. Makiguchi asserted: "The main requirement for happiness is good health. And to enjoy good health, we must put Soka Gakkai activities first." Good health means having a challenging spirit. There was no better way to stay fit and healthy, Mr. Makiguchi taught, than by actively exerting ourselves in activities for the sake of kosen-rufu.

At the same time, Mr. Makiguchi always warmly embraced those who were struggling with illness. In 1942, during World War II,

he traveled all the way to the home of a family living in the village of Shimotsuma in Ibaraki Prefecture to offer encouragement to their sick seven-year-old child. This was the year before he was imprisoned for his beliefs by the Japanese militarist authorities.

My mentor, second Soka Gakkai President Josei Toda, gave the following encouragement:

As a result of embracing the Gohonzon, even those who are worried or anxious about illness or other problems will be able to gain complete peace of mind. As they come to savor a deep inner confidence and assurance, life itself will be a source of joy.

Nevertheless, because we are living beings of the nine worlds, we will still encounter problems at times. We may also find that the nature of our problems can change. For instance, whereas before we were preoccupied with our own concerns, we are able to turn our attention to the problems and sufferings of others instead. Don't you think that finding life itself an absolute joy is what it means to be a Buddha?

He also said:

Outwardly at times we might look like a "Bodhisattva Poverty" or "Bodhisattva Sickness," but that is merely a role we're playing in the drama of life. We are in fact bonafide Bodhisattvas of the Earth! Since life is a grand drama, we should thoroughly enjoy playing the role we have undertaken and demonstrate the greatness of the Mystic Law. . . .

The sharp sword that sets us free from a life shackled in such suffering [as illness or financial hardship] is the Mystic Law. Freeing all people throughout the land from such shackles is the mission and spirit of the Soka Gakkai.

What is true health? It is not simply the absence of illness. It comes down to whether we vibrantly continue our endeavors to create value based on faith. Those who transform the karma of illness into mission and constantly strive for self-renewal have already triumphed over the devil of illness. True health in both body and mind is found in the midst of struggle. This is the teaching of Nichiren Buddhism.

In another letter to the ailing lay priest Ota, Nichiren Daishonin writes, "On the one hand, knowing that you are in agony grieves me, but on the other, I am delighted" ("On Curing Karmic Disease," WND-1, 631). He says this because, viewed from the perspective of Buddhism, illness serves as a means for us to deepen our faith, while also indicating that we are on the path to attaining Buddhahood. In this respect, illness can be viewed as fortuitous.

The fact that struggling against illness can enrich and deepen a person's life is something that many leading thinkers recognize. The Swiss philosopher Carl Hilty, for instance, writes: "Every illness leaves its mark, like the floodwaters of our rivers. One who correctly apprehends and endures illness becomes deeper, stronger, bigger; he gains insights and convictions that would previously never have occurred to him."[19]

In our case, we base our lives on the Mystic Law. When we do so, there is no suffering that we cannot transform into happiness. Those who are battling illness are climbing the lofty mountain of Buddhahood. When they reach the summit, they will be able to enjoy a vast and magnificent view. All their present hardship and suffering thus become a precious treasure for the purpose of constructing eternal happiness.

In this letter, Nichiren teaches the young Tokimitsu of this great beneficial power of Buddhism. A person who is never defeated, never discouraged, and who never gives up, no matter what happens, is a victor in life and a true champion of health and longevity.

My wife and I will continue to pray wholeheartedly for all our fellow members to enjoy long, healthy, fulfilling lives. Living lives overflowing with the brilliant actual proof of good health and longevity enables us to garner greater understanding for our movement and serve as a guiding light in creating a century of life.

I pray fervently
for our resounding victory, and for everyone
to enjoy good health
and lead long, fulfilling lives.

This lecture was originally published in the September 2010 issue of the Daibyakurenge, *the Soka Gakkai's monthly study journal.*

NOTES

1. See LSOC, 200.
2. Miao-lo's *Annotations on "The Words and Phrases of the Lotus Sutra."*
3. This is a reference to Nanjo Tokimitsu.
4. Nichiren says this because the work of a warrior involves killing.
5. Heavenly devil: Also, devil king of the sixth heaven. The devil king is a personification of the negative tendency to force others to one's will at any cost.
6. The word for "evil spirits" in the original Japanese passage is *gedo,* which literally means "out of the way" and usually indicates heretics and non-Buddhists. Here, the word means someone or something that brings about disasters.
7. Heads broken into seven pieces: This is punishment befalling those who slander the votary of the Lotus Sutra. "Dharani," the twenty-sixth chapter of the Lotus Sutra, states, "If there are those who fail to heed our spells and trouble and disrupt the preachers of the Law, their heads will split into seven pieces like the branches of the arjaka tree" (LSOC, 351).
8. A passage in "Life Span," the sixteenth chapter of the Lotus Sutra, reads, "We beg you to cure us and let us live out our lives!" (LSOC, 269). It appears in the parable of the outstanding physician, who imparts "good medicine" (which Nichiren equates with Myoho-renge-kyo) to his children who have "drunk poison" (succumbed to delusion) and implore him to cure their illness. This passage sets forth the principle of prolonging one's life through faith in the Mystic Law.
9. Changing poison into medicine: The principle that earthly desires and suffering can be transformed into benefit and enlightenment by virtue of the power of the Law.
10. Poison-drum relationship: A reverse relationship, or a relationship formed through rejection. A bond formed with the Lotus Sutra by opposing or slandering it. One who opposes the Lotus Sutra when it is preached will still form a relationship with it by virtue of opposition and will thereby attain Buddhahood eventually. A "poison drum" is a mythical drum daubed with poison; this is a reference to a statement in the Nirvana Sutra that once the poison drum is beaten, all those who hear it will die, even if they are not of the mind to listen to it. Similarly, when the correct teaching is preached, both those who embrace it and those who oppose it will equally receive the seeds of Buddhahood. In this analogy, the "death" that results from hearing the correct teaching is the death of illusion or earthly desires.
11. Lessening karmic retribution: This term, which literally means, "transforming the heavy and receiving it lightly," appears in the Nirvana Sutra. "Heavy" indicates negative karma accumulated over countless lifetimes in the past. As a benefit of protecting the correct teaching of Buddhism, we can experience relatively light karmic retribution in this lifetime, thereby expiating heavy karma that ordinarily would adversely affect us not only in this lifetime but over many lifetimes to come.
12. Fixed karma: Also, immutable karma. Karma that inevitably produces a fixed or set result, whether negative or positive. Fixed karma may also be interpreted as karma whose effects are destined to appear at a fixed time. It was held that one's life span was fixed as retribution for karma.
13. Three obstacles and four devils: Various obstacles and hindrances to the practice of Buddhism. The three obstacles are (1) the obstacle of earthly desires, (2) the obstacle of karma, and (3) the obstacle of retribution. The four devils are (1) the hindrance of the five components, (2) the hindrance of earthly desires, (3) the hindrance of death, and (4) the hindrance of the devil king.
14. Atsuhara Persecution: A series of threats and acts of violence against followers of Nichiren Daishonin in Atsuhara Village, in Fuji District of Suruga Province, starting around in 1275 and continuing until around 1283. In 1279, twenty farmers, all believers, were arrested on false charges. They were interrogated by Hei no Saemon, the deputy chief of the Office of Military and Police Affairs, who demanded that they renounce their faith. However, not one of them yielded. Hei no Saemon eventually had three of them executed. Nanjo Tokimitsu used his influence to protect other believers during this time, sheltering some in his home. Nichiren honored him for his courage and tireless efforts by calling him "Ueno the Worthy."
15. Translated from Japanese. Tsunesaburo Makiguchi, *Makiguchi Tsunesaburo shingenshu* (Selected Quotes of Tsunesaburo Makiguchi), ed. Takehisa Tsuji (Tokyo: Daisanbunmei-sha, 1979), 196–97.
16. Nichiren writes, "Since death is the same in either case, you should be willing to offer your life for the Lotus Sutra" ("The Dragon Gate," WND-1, 1003).
17. Mother of Demon Children: A demoness said to have fed the babies of others to her own children. In "Dharani," the twenty-sixth chapter of the Lotus Sutra, however, she pledges before the Buddha to safeguard the votaries of the Lotus Sutra.
18. Ten demon daughters: The ten female protective deities who appear in the "Dharani" chapter as the "daughters of *rakshasa* demons" or the "ten *rakshasa* daughters." They vow to the Buddha to guard and protect the sutra's votaries, saying that they will inflict punishment on any who trouble these votaries.
19. Translated from German. C. Hilty, *Neue briefe* (New Letters) (Leipzig: J.C. Hinrichs'sche Buchhandlung, 1906), 49.

5

"THE HERO OF THE WORLD"

THE VICTORY OF THE DISCIPLES IS THE VICTORY OF THE MENTOR AND THE VICTORY OF BUDDHISM

The Passage of Study for This Lecture

Having glanced through your letter, I feel as relieved as if the day had finally broken after a long night, or as if I had returned home after a long journey.

Buddhism primarily concerns itself with victory or defeat, while secular authority is based on the principle of reward and punishment. For this reason, a Buddha is looked up to as the Hero of the World,[1] while a king is called the one who rules at his will. India is called the Land of the Moon,[2] and our country, the Land of the Sun. Of the eighty thousand countries in the land of Jambudvipa, India is one of the largest, and Japan, one of the smallest. When it comes to the auspiciousness of their names, however, India ranks second and Japan first. Buddhism began in the Land of the Moon; it will reside in the Land of the Sun. It is in the natural course of events that the moon appears in the west[3] and travels eastward while the sun proceeds from east to west. This truth is as inalterable as the fact that a magnet attracts iron, or that the ivory plant is nourished by the sound of thunder.[4] Who could possibly deny it? (WND-1, 835)

꙳

If there are any among my followers who are weak in faith and go against what I, Nichiren, say, they will meet the same fate as did the Soga family. . . . (WND-1, 838)

꙳

Draw your own conclusions from what I said above. Those among my followers who fail to carry through their faith to the end will incur punishment even more severe. Even so, they should not harbor a grudge against me. Remember what fate Sho-bo, Noto-bo, and others met.

Be extremely cautious, and for the time being never submit yourself to writing a pledge, whatever it may concern. . . . Untempered iron quickly melts in a blazing fire, like ice put in hot water. But a sword, even when exposed to a great fire, withstands the heat for a while, because it has been well forged. In admonishing you in this way, I am trying to forge your faith.

Buddhism is reason. Reason will win over your lord. No matter how dearly you may love your wife and wish never to part from her, when you die, it will be to no avail. No matter how dearly you may cherish your estate, when you die, it will only fall into the hands of others. You have been prosperous enough for all these years. You must not give your estate a second thought. As I have said before, be millions of times more careful than ever.

> Since childhood, I, Nichiren, have never prayed for the secular things of this life but have single-mindedly sought to become a Buddha. Of late, however, I have been ceaselessly praying for your sake to the Lotus Sutra, Shakyamuni Buddha, and the god of the sun, for I am convinced that you are a person who can inherit the soul of the Lotus Sutra. (WND-1, 839)

LECTURE

Mentors always look forward to hearing about the victories and successes of their disciples. That certainly was the case with my mentor, second Soka Gakkai President Josei Toda. I always strove valiantly as his direct disciple, and nothing made me happier than being able to report my achievements to him. It is the same even now. I am especially proud today to be in a position to report to him that we have established a solid network of youth dedicated to advancing worldwide kosen-rufu into the future.

The development of our movement hinges on disciples striving and winning in their respective missions for kosen-rufu.

In Nichiren Daishonin's day, too, the period after he moved to Mount Minobu is marked by the earnest struggles of genuine disciples. Many of them battled and surmounted great obstacles, going on to achieve brilliant victories. Throughout,

Nichiren continued to encourage and guide these disciples. Among them was Shijo Kingo.

In 1277, Kingo faced his greatest adversity. In June of that year, a religious debate was held at Kuwagayatsu[5] in Kamakura. Afterward, Ema, the feudal lord whom Kingo served as a samurai retainer, was falsely informed that an armed group led by Kingo had burst in and disrupted the proceedings. This led Ema to order Kingo to write an oath renouncing his faith in the Lotus Sutra—failure to comply would result in his lands being confiscated.

Kingo sent the Daishonin a letter in which he voiced his resolve never to submit such an oath. In reply, Nichiren wrote "A Warning against Begrudging One's Fief,"[6] dated the following month. While praising Kingo for his determination, he affirmed in the letter, "However wretched a beggar you might become, never disgrace the Lotus Sutra" (WND-1, 824). He also composed "The Letter of Petition from Yorimoto"[7] on

Kingo's behalf to explain the true situation to Ema.

In addition, at the end of the writing titled "The Hero of the World"—which we will be studying in this chapter—Nichiren discusses the timing for submitting this letter of petition.[8] "The Hero of the World" is therefore thought to have been written not long after "A Warning against Begrudging One's Fief." The Daishonin's encouragement in this letter is imbued with his ardent wish to guide Kingo in the direction of victory.

Mentors invariably want their disciples to succeed.

The key point of Nichiren's guidance in "The Hero of the World" is that "Buddhism primarily concerns itself with victory or defeat."

Faith in the Mystic Law Is the Foundation for Victory

Having glanced through your letter, I feel as relieved as if the day had finally broken after a long night, or as if I had returned home after a long journey.

Buddhism primarily concerns itself with victory or defeat, while secular authority is based on the principle of reward and punishment. For this reason, a Buddha is looked up to as the Hero of the World, while a king is called the one who rules at his will. India is called the Land of the Moon, and our country, the Land of the Sun. Of the eighty thousand countries in the land of Jambudvipa, India is one of the largest, and Japan, one of the smallest. When it comes to the auspiciousness of their names, however, India ranks second and Japan first. Buddhism began in the Land of the Moon; it will reside in the Land of the Sun. It is in the natural course of events that the moon appears in the west and travels eastward while the sun proceeds from east to west. This truth is as inalterable as the fact that a magnet attracts iron, or that the ivory plant is nourished by the sound of thunder. Who could possibly deny it? (WND-1, 835)

The opening lines of this writing suggest that there may have been some positive development in Shijo Kingo's situation that had greatly reassured Nichiren Daishonin. He says, "I feel as relieved as if the day had finally broken after a long night." Or perhaps the source of his relief may simply have been due to the fact that Kingo, despite his difficult circumstances, had shown profound resolve. Another possibility may have been that Lord Ema had softened his stance somewhat and was willing to meet with Kingo. The words toward the end of this writing, "If your lord coaxes you with soft words" (WND-1, 839), could be taken as alluding to such an opportunity, with Nichiren telling Kingo that should the meeting happen, he must approach it with extreme caution and not let down his guard, no matter what. Still, the Daishonin remained apprehensive, as reflected in such lines as: "Never submit yourself to writing a pledge, whatever it may concern" and "You will certainly be deceived by others" (WND-1, 839). Whatever the case may be, Shijo Kingo's situation was still critical, and Nichiren must have felt it even more imperative that Kingo stand firm and tenaciously continue his struggle. At this crucial time, the Daishonin taught his disciple the principle that "Buddhism is about winning" so that he could achieve true victory in life.

In this opening section, the Daishonin addresses Buddhism and secular authority. This was undoubtedly a subject of vital relevance to Shijo Kingo, who was faced with two choices: (1) continuing his Buddhist practice and risking the loss of his estate; or (2) obeying his lord's directive and discarding his faith in the Lotus Sutra. Though he had already resolved not to write the oath sought by Ema, he nonetheless was still embroiled in a situation that pitted his faith against the decree of his lord.

Buddhism does not deny things of worldly or secular value. As practitioners, however, we will not be able to realize true happiness if we lose sight of the supreme teaching and highest value of Buddhism by allowing ourselves to become obsessed with ephemeral attainments such as wealth, status, and fame or intimidated by tyrannical secular authorities. All that will await us in the end is spiritual defeat.

That's why, amid the realities of daily life and society, we must always make Buddhism our fundamental guide and standard and continue challenging ourselves

tenaciously to secure ultimate victory. Making Buddhism our foundation means forging ahead with rock-solid faith that is not swayed by the reward or punishment of secular authority or the vicissitudes of worldly fortune.

"Buddhism primarily concerns itself with victory or defeat," says Nichiren. This fundamental tenet is at the heart of our commitment to keep striving based on the unsurpassed teaching of Buddhism, come what may. Our determination and actual efforts to show concrete proof of the power of faith, therefore, are crucial.

Next, the Daishonin refers to the Hero of the World, one of the titles of the Buddha, meaning a champion of peerless wisdom who has triumphed over suffering and delusion and acquired a state of indestructible happiness. He most likely mentions this title to underscore the importance of using the profound wisdom of Buddhism to discern what is of true value and to confidently build a life of genuine happiness and victory amid the realities of society.

He then notes that a king is called "one who rules at his will." In a general sense, this can be taken to refer to how a king in the secular realm rules his subjects, meting out reward and punishment as he pleases. But perhaps Nichiren also draws this distinction to indicate that the power of the Buddha—the Hero of the World and the king of the Law[9]—is exercised freely.[10]

In the Lotus Sutra, Shakyamuni states, "I am the Dharma king, free to do as I will with the Law" (LSOC, 109).

In the feudal society in which Shijo Kingo lived, the fortunes of a samurai retainer were determined by the evaluation and judgment of his lord—namely, the rewards and punishments he meted out. Here, however, Nichiren is showing Kingo how it is possible to ultimately triumph over any secular authority—no matter how powerful or oppressive—by basing oneself on the supreme teaching of Buddhism and freely exercising its power in one's life.

To clarify this point, the Daishonin turns to the history of Buddhism's transmission in China and Japan, noting how people in these two countries came to accept Buddhism and how people prospered at those times when they lived in accord with Buddhist principles.

Those Who Act to Destroy Buddhism Bring About Their Own Ruin

In "The Hero of the World," Nichiren Daishonin gives a detailed description of the transmission of Buddhism in Japan, citing *The Chronicles of Japan*.[11] He recounts the conflict between the pro-Buddhist Soga clan and the anti-Buddhist Mononobe clan. Of course, today this conflict is viewed in the context of a broader power struggle, rather than simply centering on the question of accepting Buddhist teachings. Nevertheless, the main point here is what the Daishonin seeks to impart based on the historical records of his day.

Nichiren outlines how Buddhism in Japan was denounced and repressed before it came to be widely respected in society. He gives examples of how, even among secular rulers, there were those who governed justly based on Buddhist principles and enjoyed prosperity and those who actively opposed and attacked Buddhism and brought ruin upon themselves. Further, he observes that there is evidence that when Buddhism first spread to China and Japan, people who venerated painted or wooden images of Shakyamuni Buddha prospered. In light of this, he says, "Thus Shakyamuni Buddha is perfectly just in administering reward and punishment" (WND-1, 838). What he means by this is that our actions, depending on whether they are in tune with or against the universal principles of Buddhism expounded by Shakyamuni Buddha, produce either positive or negative consequences—reward or punishment—in our lives, based on the inexorable workings of the law of cause and effect (see WND-1, 838).

Nichiren notes that even high and mighty secular powers of earlier times could not help falling into ruin as a result of their attempts to destroy Buddhism. In other words, the prosperity or decline of such powers came down to whether they chose a philosophy that made the people a means to an end or put the people first. In light of this truth, it was obvious that the forces persecuting Shijo Kingo—a practitioner of the correct teaching—would lose their strength and disappear. Nichiren therefore urges Kingo not to be defeated, however difficult his present circumstances might be.

The Daishonin's profound compassion is clearly discernible in the great lengths he goes in this writing to explain the history of Buddhism and key Buddhist principles in order to help Kingo fortify his conviction and emerge victorious.

Persevering With Unremitting Faith

If there are any among my followers who are weak in faith and go against what I, Nichiren, say, they will meet the same fate as did the Soga family. . . . (WND-1, 838)

Draw your own conclusions from what I said above. Those among my followers who fail to carry through their faith to the end will incur punishment even more severe. Even so, they should not harbor a grudge against me. Remember what fate Sho-bo, Noto-bo, and others met. (WND-1, 839)

Next Nichiren Daishonin relates that, though the once pro-Buddhist Soga clan rose to the height of power and influence, the subsequent tyranny and ruthless cruelty of its leaders led to the eventual downfall of the entire clan. These individuals who had grown so arrogant (see WND-1, 838), he notes, were ultimately defeated by forces who respected and venerated Shakyamuni Buddha. The ruined Sogas came to serve as an example of people who, though they had

made significant contributions to the cause of Buddhism in the past, ended their lives in defeat as a result of growing arrogant and departing from the caring and compassionate Buddhist spirit to guide others toward genuine happiness.

The Daishonin declared that should any of his disciples turn their backs on him—a teacher selflessly propagating the Law for the enlightenment of all people, just as the Lotus Sutra taught—they were bound to meet a fate similar to that of the Soga clan. Citing examples from history, he stressed the importance of always persevering in faith without being swayed by secular concerns. He said that those disciples who failed to carry through with their faith as a result of being defeated by their own inner weakness or preoccupied with immediate gain would incur negative consequences even more severe than those experienced by the Soga clan in times past. He exhorted them not to travel the same course as such former disciples of his as Sho-bo or Noto-bo, who abandoned their faith and betrayed their teacher and fellow believers.[12]

It is in times of adversity that the true measure of one's faith is revealed. When it comes to battling the three obstacles and four devils,[13] confronting the three powerful enemies[14] or waging a critical struggle to transform one's karma, unremitting faith is of paramount importance.

During the difficult period of his Sado Exile (1271–74), and also during times when Kingo himself faced great personal hardship, Nichiren consistently encouraged his loyal samurai disciple to remain steadfast in faith. For instance, he urged Kingo: "Carry through with your faith in the Lotus Sutra. You cannot strike fire from flint if you stop halfway" ("Earthly Desires Are Enlightenment," WND-1, 319). He also told him: "To accept is easy; to continue is difficult. But Buddhahood lies in continuing faith. Those who uphold this sutra should be prepared to meet difficulties" ("The Difficulty of Sustaining Faith," WND-1, 471).

Difficulties forge our faith and strengthen our character. They are inescapable obstacles that we have to surmount on the road to attaining Buddhahood in this lifetime. If we persevere in faith and overcome every obstacle, the laurels of victory will definitely await us. The important thing is that we never discard our faith. The Daishonin's strict compassion for Shijo Kingo is particularly evident in this section of "The Hero of the World."

Forging Inner Strength and Maintaining Resolute Faith

Be extremely cautious, and for the time being never submit yourself to writing a pledge, whatever it may concern. . . . Untempered iron quickly melts in a blazing fire, like ice put in hot water. But a sword, even when exposed to a great fire, withstands the heat for a while, because it has been well forged. In admonishing you in this way, I am trying to forge your faith.

Buddhism is reason. Reason will win over your lord. No matter how dearly you may love your wife and wish never to part from her, when you die, it will be to no avail. No matter how dearly you may cherish your estate, when you die, it will only fall into the hands of others. You have been prosperous enough for all these years. You must not give your estate a second thought. As I have said before, be millions of times more careful than ever. (WND-1, 839)

Here Nichiren Daishonin cautions Kingo against being ruled by his emotions and acting rashly. He instructs him neither to bow to harsh intimidation nor to let an outwardly benign attitude on his lord's part lull him into a false sense of security and cause him to adopt a conciliatory stance. For in either case Kingo would be giving in to Ema's demands and end up discarding his faith. Out of his sincere wish to protect his disciple, Nichiren offers detailed advice on how to wisely handle the situation.

Untempered iron will melt in a blazing fire, but a finely forged sword will not, he says. With this admonition, he seeks to forge Kingo's faith and inner resolve.

We cannot achieve victory in a true sense if we constantly vacillate between hope and fear over what might await us in the future. Buddhism is reason. Only when we approach life with a serene, unclouded state of mind—forged through cultivating inner strength and polishing our faith—can we truly bring forth the wondrous workings of life that put us on a course to victory.

For us of the SGI today, the path of inner self-development entails our regular morning and evening practice and carrying out activities for kosen-rufu. It is through these continued efforts and the progress we make in our own human revolution that we open the door to victory.

Nichiren then provides an unerring road map to guide Kingo to victory, saying: "Buddhism is reason. Reason will win over your lord." Those who live their lives with honesty and integrity based on faith in the Mystic Law will win in all areas as a matter of course. "Win over your lord" here means that even Lord Ema—who wielded power over the lives of Shijo Kingo and his other retainers by administering rewards and punishments—would be no match for the lucid principles of Buddhism.

Depending on how the situation unfolded, however, the need might arise for Shijo Kingo to risk his life and admonish the error of his lord. It was for this purpose that the Daishonin composed a letter of petition on Kingo's behalf, denouncing the priest Ryokan[15] of Gokuraku-ji, a temple in Kamakura, whose teachings Lord Ema esteemed and who was active behind the scenes in persecuting Shijo Kingo following the Kuwagayatsu Debate. In terms of Buddhism, Ryokan was a source of great evil, disseminating erroneous teachings and leading people astray from the correct path to enlightenment. Only by thoroughly repudiating evil can it be subsumed by good.

Nichiren, therefore, to be doubly sure, strongly reemphasizes to Kingo that he must never discard his faith out of a reluctance to part with his estate. Essentially, this represents a solemn admonition to persevere in faith, no matter what happens. Nichiren offers Kingo a clear guideline: When forced to make a life-and-death choice, choose faith, which is the foundation for everything. Such an unfaltering resolve is crucial in times of great adversity.

Of course, if Kingo were to relinquish his estate and retire from his lord's service in a negative or angry frame of mind, it would not constitute a genuine solution. Though on the surface it might seem he was acting based on faith to sever ties with an unjust feudal lord, in reality it would be nothing more than him being defeated by his own weakness.

For Kingo, "winning over his lord" meant remaining steadfast in faith, conducting himself with integrity and sincerity, and eventually awakening Ema to the correct Buddhist teaching.

Realizing Happiness for Oneself and Others

The Mystic Law is a teaching of harmony. It is the ultimate Law that embraces and gives meaning to all things. It is the core and foundation of harmony. The true victory of Nichiren Buddhism is found in transforming misunderstanding into understanding, conflict into trust, and division into unity through the power of the Mystic Law. The certain victory for which he urges his disciples to strive essentially consists of realizing happiness for oneself and others by bringing forth the harmonizing power of the Mystic Law.

For instance, he instructs the Ikegami brothers, whose father opposed their practice of the Daishonin's teaching, to aim for the goal of family harmony by solidly uniting together in faith. As a result of staunchly upholding the correct teaching despite their father's drastic step of disowning one of them in an attempt to persuade both to abandon their faith, they succeeded in achieving a great and dramatic victory. Not only did their father rescind the elder brother's disownment, but he eventually even embraced the Daishonin's teaching himself. Through the brothers' faith, their father was enfolded in the Mystic Law and came to awaken to the correct teaching.

Similarly, Nichiren reminds Shijo Kingo that he owes his lord a great debt of gratitude, despite currently being persecuted by him. During the Tatsunokuchi Persecution and the Sado Exile, he points out, Ema stood by Kingo when virtually everyone in Japan was hostile to the Daishonin and when many of his followers were having their lands confiscated or being banished. If Kingo were to forget this, he says, and bear an unreasonable grudge against his lord, the benevolent forces of the universe would not protect him.[16] In another letter, Nichiren tells Kingo that even though his lord does not currently embrace faith in the Lotus Sutra, he will definitely accumulate good fortune and enjoy prosperity because he has protected Kingo.[17]

In response to this guidance, Kingo continued praying for his lord to take faith in the Lotus Sutra. Eventually, Ema regained his trust in Kingo and his attitude changed. In the end, Kingo showed great actual proof of victory when he received a new estate from his lord. Referring to the cause of this triumph, Nichiren writes in another letter: "It must have happened because of your profound sincerity in trying to lead your lord to faith in the Lotus Sutra. . . . This is solely because of your deep faith in the Lotus Sutra" ("The Farther the Source, the Longer the Stream," WND-1, 940). Through Kingo's faith, the boundless power of the Mystic Law enveloped Ema's life.

Victory in Nichiren Buddhism is victory based on the supreme principle of the Mystic Law. And its greatest victory in a real sense is the harmonious realm of the Mystic Law spreading in the sphere of our daily lives, workplaces, communities, and beyond—on a global scale transcending national borders.

The Mystic Law has the power to create value, transforming negative influences into positive influences. It has the power to change karma, transforming great evil into great good. It has the power of justice, transforming inhumanity into humanity and reason.

Each disciple winning in society constitutes actual proof of human revolution. This means each individual placing utmost importance on the "treasures of the heart" ("The Three Kinds of Treasure," WND-1, 851) and developing greater depth as a person. In terms of the philosophy of the Lotus Sutra, it means always showing respect for others in one's behavior, based on the conviction that all people have the potential for Buddhahood. The individual growth of each practitioner ensures victory in faith.

That's why the Daishonin constantly admonishes his disciples against abandoning their faith. He describes a number of treacherous erstwhile disciples as being "cowardly, unreasoning, greedy, and doubting" ("On Persecutions Befalling the Sage," WND-1, 998). His words are deliberately severe to prevent other disciples from going the same way. If they were to succumb to negative emotions and lose sight of faith, they could easily descend into a way of life oblivious to the "treasures of the heart" and obsessed with status and wealth. Nichiren's effort to dispel any arrogance or complacency in his disciples is an expression of supreme compassion.

Live Wisely

Shijo Kingo faithfully followed Nichiren Daishonin's guidance and conducted himself with integrity. He won in his heart, or "mastered his mind," just as the Daishonin had instructed. This dramatically changed his entire situation.

Actual victory is achieved through meticulous efforts based on careful thought and wisdom, recognizing that even the smallest things matter. Practitioners upholding the Daishonin's teachings and striving to demonstrate clear proof of faith in an evil age rife with negative influences must remain alert and vigilant. Nichiren even warns Kingo

to "be millions of times more careful than ever." It is crucial that he exercise wisdom and prudence. He further points out to Kingo the importance of making firm allies of the people around him as part of his efforts to personally create an environment for victory. He also advises him to be deeply resolved to win and, based on faith, tenaciously endure what must be endured and then press forward with wisdom toward a breakthrough when the time comes.

At this stage of his life's struggle, when the development of kosen-rufu would hinge more and more on the victorious endeavors of his disciples, the Daishonin taught Shijo Kingo the vital cornerstones of the win-or-lose struggle of Buddhism. I'd now like to reaffirm them.

First, we must always make Buddhism our foundation, basing our lives on faith in the Mystic Law. Second, we must challenge our own weakness and develop inner strength, rising above malicious attacks, temptation. and other negative influences. This essentially means battling negativity and evil. Third, we must believe in the limitless power of the Mystic Law and consistently act with integrity and rich humanity. In other words, we must persevere in our struggle for truth in accord with the principles of Buddhism, bringing forth profound wisdom.

Basing our lives on the Mystic Law with the spirit that Buddhism means winning is the key to achieving fundamental victory and genuine happiness that transcends the vicissitudes of society and the times and endures throughout eternity.

"A Person Who Can Inherit the Soul of the Lotus Sutra"

Since childhood, I, Nichiren, have never prayed for the secular things of this life but have single-mindedly sought to become a Buddha. Of late, however, I have been ceaselessly praying for your sake to the Lotus Sutra, Shakyamuni Buddha, and the god of the sun, for I am convinced that you are a person who can inherit the soul of the Lotus Sutra. (WND-1, 839)

Buddhism is about winning. The victory of each individual practitioner demonstrates the victory of Buddhism. In this spirit, Nichiren Daishonin himself resolutely fought against obstacles and vanquished all negative forces. He opened the boundless path to victory for us who are living in the Latter Day of the Law. Through the triumphant actual proof of faith that Nichiren demonstrated, the transmission of the great Law for the enlightenment of all people in the Latter Day began to spread in society.

Nichiren revived the "soul of the Lotus Sutra"—the spirit to widely propagate the Law and lead people to enlightenment. Who will inherit this soul or fundamental spirit? Who will further expand this path and help people realize genuine happiness into the infinite future of the Latter Day? It is none other than disciples who, just like their mentor, challenge and triumph in their endeavors with the conviction that practicing Buddhism means winning.

When both mentor and disciple win, that achievement creates a powerful current of kosen-rufu that will flow into the eternal future of the Latter Day.

In "The Hero of the World," the Daishonin writes that he is constantly praying for Shijo Kingo so that his disciple could be victorious in his struggles. Needless to say, this is an expression of his profoundly compassionate wish for Kingo's happiness. At the same time, he emphasizes that he is praying above all to ensure that kosen-rufu will continue to flow without cease and that the benefit of the Lotus Sutra will be passed on to future generations.

The appearance of disciples who can "inherit the soul of the Lotus Sutra" signifies the victory of the mentor and the victory of Buddhism. It is then up to the disciples to make the mentor's heart their own—to strive and win through faith with the same spirit as their mentor.

Nichiren wholeheartedly wished for the growth and success of his disciples. And his disciples valiantly challenged the various difficulties they faced, rose above their karmic suffering, and demonstrated wonderful actual proof of faith. This was true of Shijo Kingo and his wife; the Ikegami brothers and their wives; Nanjo Tokimitsu and his mother, the lay nun Ueno; Toki Jonin and his wife; Oto Gozen and her mother; the lay nun Myoichi; and many others. In response to Nichiren's encouragement, they each went on to enact a grand drama of victory in life. This became the wellspring of the eternal flow of kosen-rufu into the Latter Day.

The Bonds of Mentor and Disciple in Nichiren Buddhism

"Buddhism is about winning" is not simply a motto or maxim. It is the very heart and essence of the mentor-disciple relationship in Nichiren Buddhism.

In "On Repaying Debts of Gratitude," Nichiren Daishonin writes:

If Nichiren's compassion is truly great and encompassing, Nam-myoho-renge-kyo will spread for ten thousand years and more, for all eternity, for it has the beneficial power to open the blind eyes of every living being in the country of Japan, and it blocks off the road that leads to the hell of incessant suffering. (WND-1, 736)

It was through his selfless struggles, carried out in the spirit that Buddhism is about being victorious, that the Daishonin opened the way for the eternal transmission of the Law into the eternal future of the Latter Day. It was also in this way that he activated the power of the Law to open the eyes of those blinded by delusion and block off the road to the hell of incessant suffering. For that reason, the transmission of the Law can be undertaken only by disciples who struggle with the same selfless dedication as Nichiren.

In the present age, the SGI alone has persisted on the path of faith with the spirit that Buddhism is winning, as taught by the Daishonin. Indeed, it would be no exaggeration to say that, before the Soka Gakkai's appearance, the earnest struggle for inner transformation based on Nichiren Buddhism—what we of the SGI today call human revolution and transforming reality—was nearly completely forgotten.

Tsunesaburo Makiguchi, the first Soka Gakkai president, declared that the life-blood of Nichiren Buddhism is showing actual proof of faith through striving and triumphing with the spirit that Buddhism means winning. He wrote:

[Clear actual proof of faith] is the life-blood of Nichiren Buddhism. As Nichiren Daishonin says, "Buddhism primarily concerns itself with victory or defeat, while secular authority is based on the principle of reward and punishment."[18]

In addition, Mr. Toda asserted: "Faith is a struggle against deadlock—for the individual and for humanity. It is a struggle between devilish functions and the Buddha. That is why Buddhism teaches the importance of winning in any struggle." That was also his spirit when his businesses were in dire straits. He once said to me: "Daisaku, Buddhism is about winning. Let's fight with courage, giving it our all as long as we live. Life is eternal. Proof of our dedicated efforts will definitely appear in some form in this lifetime." I have fought in accord with these words. I have produced proof. I can honestly say that in life and in my struggles for kosen-rufu, I have not the slightest regret.

Mr. Toda often used to say: "We are practicing Nichiren Buddhism in order to achieve absolute victory. It is crucial that we win in our jobs and in all areas of our life with this resolve." He also said: "Buddhism means being victorious. If we're going to engage in a struggle, we must do so with thoroughgoing preparation, determination, and passion and win without fail."

And he composed the following poem—the very last one I received from him:

> *Winning and losing are both*
> *part of life,*
> *but I pray to the Buddha for final victory.*

Embracing the spirit that Buddhism means winning, the first three Soka Gakkai presidents have triumphed over every obstacle.

Everyone faces the fundamental inner struggle between positive and negative impulses—expressed in Buddhism as the struggle between the Buddha and devilish functions. Buddhism is the teaching for winning in this elemental battle. Our victory ensures that truth and justice prevail and attests to the correctness and validity of Buddhism.

Today, SGI members are emerging in ever-increasing numbers around the world. Each of them—as a person "inheriting the soul of the Lotus Sutra"—is striving with the spirit that Buddhism is about winning.

Disciples are standing up, taking vibrant action, and achieving great victories. We have truly entered an age when the brilliant achievements of the mentors and disciples of Soka encompass the entire globe. Our fellow members' victorious smiles are a bright source of hope for people everywhere. Their actual proof of happiness is creating ripple effects that will change the world.

As we embark on a renewed effort to reach out to young people and foster the development of an ever-youthful SGI organization, I would like to pass on the spiritual baton for eternal victory to each one of my beloved fellow members.

This lecture was originally published in the September 2010 issue of the Daibyakurenge, *the Soka Gakkai's monthly study journal.*

NOTES

1. The Hero of the World: An honorific title of the Buddha, so called because he valiantly confronts all sufferings and leads all people to enlightenment.

2. Land of the Moon (Chn Yüeh-chih): A name for India used in China and Japan. In the late third century BCE, there was a tribe called Yüeh-chih (literally, "moon tribe") who ruled a part of India. Since Buddhism was brought from India to China via this territory, the Chinese seem to have regarded the land of the Yüeh-chih as India itself.

3. "The moon appears in the west" refers to the fact that the new moon is first seen in the west just after sunset. Of course, the moon rises in the east and sets in the west each day just as the sun and stars do, but because its orbital motion is from west to east, it appears to move incrementally in retrograde, from west to east, each day.

4. According to the Nirvana Sutra, the ivory plant is said to grow with the sound of thunder.

5. The Kuwagayatsu Debate: A debate held between Nichiren Daishonin's priest-disciple Sammi-bo and a Tendai priest named Ryuzo-bo, a protégé of Ryokan, the chief priest of Gokuraku-ji, a temple in Kamakura, who was hostile toward the Daishonin. Ryuzo-bo was soundly defeated by Sammi-bo in front of a large audience, which included Shijo Kingo. Fellow samurai retainers who were followers of Ryokan and jealous of Kingo saw a chance to disgrace him in the eyes of his lord, Ema. They falsely reported to Lord Ema that Kingo had forcibly disrupted the debate and had shown contempt not only for Ryuzo-bo but also Ryokan, whom Lord Ema highly esteemed. These reports led Lord Ema to threaten to confiscate Kingo's fief unless he abandoned his faith in the Lotus Sutra.

6. WND-1, 823–25.

7. WND-1, 803–13. (Yorimoto is part of Shijo Kingo's full name.)

8. The Daishonin writes: "If the opportunity arises, submit to your lord the petition I have written on your behalf. Since it contains matters of great import, it will certainly create a stir" (WND-1, 839).

9. King of the Law: Also, Dharma king. Another title of the Buddha.

10. The Annotated Vimalakirti Sutra says: "A secular king commands the people at will. The Dharma king commands the Law at will." A passage in the Immeasurable Meanings Sutra also states, "He [the king of the Law] can exercise his powers freely, free in command of the Law" (LSOC, 10).

11. As described in *The Chronicles of Japan*, the pro-Buddhist Soga clan were led by the father and son, Iname (d. 570) and Umako (d. 626). Iname, the senior minister to Emperor Kimmei, argued in favor of the acceptance of Buddhism. Umako, the senior minister during the reign of Emperor Bidatsu, destroyed the anti-Buddhist Mononobe no Moriya and built a Buddhist temple. The anti-Buddhist Mononobe clan were led by the father and son, Okoshi (n.d.) and Moriya (d. 587). Okoshi, the chief minister of Emperor Kimmei, opposed the Soga clan. Moriya, the chief minister to the two emperors Bidatsu and Yomei, opposed the acceptance of Buddhism but was killed by Umako.

12. In "Letter to Ben," the Daishonin discusses the situations of a number of followers who had abandoned their faith. He writes: "Noto-bo was actually a supporter of mine, but out of fear of what the world might do to him, or out of greed, he not only abandoned me but in fact became my enemy. And Sho-bo has done likewise" (WND-2, 661).

13. Three obstacles and four devils: Various obstacles and hindrances to the practice of Buddhism. The three obstacles are (1) the obstacle of earthly desires, (2) the obstacle of karma, and (3) the obstacle of retribution. The four devils are (1) the hindrance of the five components, (2) the hindrance of earthly desires, (3) the hindrance of death, and (4) the hindrance of the devil king.

14. Three powerful enemies: Three types of arrogant people who persecute those who propagate the Lotus Sutra in the evil age after Shakyamuni Buddha's death, described in the concluding verse section of "Encouraging Devotion," the thirteenth chapter of the Lotus Sutra. The Great Teacher Miao-lo (711–82) of China summarizes them as arrogant lay people, arrogant priests, and arrogant false sages.

15. Ryokan (1217–1303): Also known as Ninsho. A priest of the True Word Precepts school in Japan. With the patronage of the Hojo clan, Ryokan became chief priest of Gokuraku-ji, a temple in Kamakura, and commanded enormous influence both among government officials and among the people. He was hostile to the Daishonin and actively conspired with the authorities to have him and his followers persecuted. Lord Ema and the Ikegami brothers' father were among his devout followers.

16. In "The Eight Winds," Nichiren writes: "Moreover, he showed you great clemency by taking no action against your clan when I incurred the wrath of the government and the entire nation hated me. Many of my disciples had their land seized by the government and were then disowned or driven from their lords' estates. Even if he never shows you the slightest further consideration, you should not hold a grudge against your lord. . . . But if you nurse an unreasonable grudge against your lord, [the heavenly gods] will not protect you, not for all your prayers" (WND-1, 794).

17. In "The Three Kinds of Treasure," Nichiren writes: "Although he has not professed faith in the Lotus Sutra, you are a member of his clan, and it is thanks to his consideration that you are able to make offerings to the sutra. Thus, these [offerings] may become prayers solely for your lord's recovery. Think of a small tree under a large one, or grass by a great river. Though they do not receive rain or water directly, they nonetheless thrive, partaking of dew from the large tree or drawing moisture from the river. The same holds true with the relationship between you and your lord" (WND-1, 848).

18. Translated from Japanese. Tsunesaburo Makiguchi, *Makiguchi Tsunesaburo zenshu* (Collected Writings of Tsunesaburo Makiguchi) (Tokyo: Daisanbunmei-sha, 1987), 10:47.

6

"THE BLESSINGS OF THE LOTUS SUTRA"

PERSONAL INITIATIVE IS THE
SOKA GAKKAI'S FOUNDING SPIRIT

The Passage of Study for This Lecture

The first of the five precepts[1] is not to take life, and the first of the six paramitas[2] is that of almsgiving. The ten good precepts,[3] the two hundred and fifty precepts,[4] the ten major precepts,[5] and all the other rules of conduct begin with the prohibition against the taking of life.

Every being, from the highest sage on down to the smallest mosquito or gnat, holds life to be its most precious possession. To deprive a being of life is to commit the gravest kind of sin.

When the Thus Come One appeared in this world, he made compassion for living things his basis. And as an expression of compassion for life, to refrain from taking life and to provide sustenance for living beings are the most important precepts.

In providing another with sustenance, one obtains three kinds of benefit. First, one sustains one's own life. Second, one brings color to one's face. Third, one gains strength. (WND-1, 667)

If we inquire into the origin of Mount Sumeru,[6] we find that it began with a single speck of dust; and likewise, the great ocean began with a single drop of dew. One added to one becomes two, two becomes three, and so on to make ten, a hundred, a thousand, ten thousand, a hundred thousand, or an asamkhya.[7] Yet "one" is the mother of all. (WND-1, 667)

Bodhisattva Superior Practices,[8] who is entrusted with the daimoku, the core of the essential teaching, had not yet appeared in the world.

But now he will appear in the Latter Day of the Law and propagate the five characters of Myoho-renge-kyo[9] to all the nations and people throughout Jambudvipa. Surely it will spread just as the invocation of Amida's name has spread throughout Japan at the present time.

I, Nichiren, am not the founder of any school, nor am I a latter-day follower of any older school. I am a priest without precepts, neither keeping the precepts nor breaking them. I am an ordinary creature like an ox or a sheep, who is neither particularly wise nor ignorant.

Why did I first begin to chant as I do? Bodhisattva Superior Practices is the one destined to make his advent in this world to propagate the five characters of Myoho-renge-kyo. But before he had even appeared, I began, as though speaking in a dream, hardly aware of what I was doing, to utter the words Nam-myoho-renge-kyo, and so I chant them now. (WND-1, 669)

But I am different from such persons. I firmly uphold the teaching that the Lotus Sutra is supreme among the sutras the Buddha has preached, now preaches, and will preach.[10] Moreover, I chant the daimoku, which is the heart and core of the entire sutra, and I urge others to do likewise. Although the mugwort growing in a hemp field or wood marked for cutting with an inked line may not be straight to begin with, they will as a matter of course become so.

In the same way, one who chants the daimoku as the Lotus Sutra teaches will never have a twisted mind. For one should know that, unless the mind of the Buddha enters into our bodies, we cannot in fact chant the daimoku. (WND-1, 670)

In this entire country of Japan, I am the only one who has been chanting Nam-myoho-renge-kyo. I am like the single speck of dust that marks the beginning of Mount Sumeru or the single drop of dew that spells the start of the great ocean. Probably two people, three people, ten people, a hundred people will join in chanting it, until it spreads to one province, two provinces, and all the sixty-six provinces of Japan,[11] and reaches even to the two islands of Iki and Tsushima. Those persons who have spoken slanderously of me will in time chant in the same way; and everyone from the ruler on down to the multitude of common people will, as described in the "Supernatural Powers" chapter of the Lotus Sutra,[12] chant Nam-myoho-renge-kyo with a single voice. Though the trees may desire to be still, the wind will not cease to blow; though we may wish for spring to linger, it must give way to summer. (WND-1, 672)

In view of all this, your sincerity in sending a gift of five strings of blue-duck coins[13] whenever the opportunity arises truly entitles you to be known as one who propagates the daimoku of the Lotus Sutra in Japan. As first one person, then two persons, then a thousand, ten thousand, a hundred thousand, and then all the people throughout the country come to chant the daimoku, before you know it, their blessings will accrue to you. Those blessings will be like the drops of dew that gather to form the great ocean, or the specks of dust that pile up to become Mount Sumeru. (WND-1, 672)

The more gold is heated in the flames, the brighter will be its color; the more a sword is whetted, the sharper it will become. And the more one praises the blessings of the Lotus Sutra, the more one's own blessings will increase. Bear in mind that the twenty-eight chapters of the Lotus Sutra contain only a few passages elucidating the truth, but a great many words of praise. (WND-1, 673)

LECTURE

My mentor, second Soka Gakkai President Josei Toda, said with deep determination, "I will strive for kosen-rufu, even if no one else does, even if I am all alone." As his disciple, I have exerted myself with this same stand-alone spirit, firmly resolved to work for kosen-rufu and open the way forward, no matter what the situation.

"It starts with me! It starts from now!"—as long as we have this courageous, self-motivated spirit of a lion king in faith, we can definitely triumph over all adversity. The noble undertaking of kosen-rufu in the Latter Day of the Law began with the solitary, selfless struggle of Nichiren Daishonin, who pledged to lead all people to enlightenment. Similarly, the present flow of worldwide kosen-rufu we see today also began with Tsunesaburo Makiguchi and Josei Toda, our first and second presidents, standing up to correctly practice the Daishonin's teachings and establish the Soka Gakkai. Personal initiative—self-motivation—is the very essence of the Soka Gakkai's founding spirit.

With this point in mind, I would like to discuss "The Blessings of the Lotus Sutra," a writing that vividly captures the spirit of Nichiren Daishonin in his passionate commitment to strive for the happiness of humanity in the evil age of the Latter Day.

In 1276, he wrote this letter to a lay follower named Myomitsu,[14] who—as it would appear from the letter's content—regularly sent him sincere offerings.

In this writing, Nichiren explains that the struggle to open the way for all people to attain Buddhahood based on the Mystic Law throughout the ten thousand years and more of the Latter Day began with his lone, trailblazing efforts. He also declares that the time of kosen-rufu will eventually arrive—a time when people far and wide will chant Nam-myoho-renge-kyo. In addition, Nichiren confidently assures Myomitsu that he and his wife will definitely receive boundless benefit for their unstinting support of him and the nascent movement to widely propagate the Mystic Law.

The Benefit of Supporting the Votary of the Lotus Sutra

The first of the five precepts is not to take life, and the first of the six paramitas is that of almsgiving. The ten good precepts, the two hundred and fifty precepts, the ten major precepts, and all the other rules of conduct begin with the prohibition against the taking of life.

Every being, from the highest sage on down to the smallest mosquito or gnat, holds life to be its most precious possession. To deprive a being of life is to commit the gravest kind of sin.

When the Thus Come One appeared in this world, he made compassion for living things his basis. And as an expression of compassion for life, to refrain from taking

life and to provide sustenance for living beings are the most important precepts.

In providing another with sustenance, one obtains three kinds of benefit. First, one sustains one's own life. Second, one brings color to one's face. Third, one gains strength. (WND-1, 667)

Nichiren Buddhism teaches that all people can manifest the sublime power of the Mystic Law within their lives. It is a teaching that elucidates the fundamental dignity and sanctity of all life.

Nichiren Daishonin begins this writing by stating that life is the most precious of all treasures. All living beings, even mosquitoes and gnats, he observes, prize their lives. Shakyamuni Buddha himself especially valued all living things and had immense compassion for them. Nichiren points out that for these reasons, the prohibition against taking life appears first in various different lists of precepts and rules of conduct set forth in the Buddhist canon, including the five precepts. Regarded as equally important, he adds, is making offerings of sustenance, which support life.

By starting his letter in this way, he seeks to lavish the highest praise on Myomitsu for his invaluable offerings that sustain the life of the votary of the Lotus Sutra, an act that will bring the giver unimaginably great benefit.

Nichiren notes that because such offerings benefit the recipient by sustaining his life, brightening his complexion, and

increasing his strength, the same benefits are also gained by the giver.

The Daishonin explains that the givers of such offerings are assured of receiving three kinds of wondrous karmic reward. First of all, in the human and heavenly realms, the benefit of having sustained another's life will manifest as gaining long life; the benefit of having given strength to another will manifest as possessing virtue and influence and winning the trust and respect of many people; and the benefit of bringing color to another's face will manifest as being endowed with the thirty-two features[15] and being as graceful and dignified as a lotus flower (see WND-1, 667). Nichiren also describes the karmic rewards of such offerings in the realm of Buddhahood, which appear as the "three bodies of the Buddha."[16] These benefits respectively consist of manifesting oneself as a Buddha of the Dharma body, a body that is as vast and boundless as space; manifesting oneself as a Buddha of the reward body, emanating the pure and brilliant light of supreme wisdom; and manifesting oneself as a Buddha of the manifested body, overflowing with compassion like Shakyamuni (see WND-1, 667).

Thus, because actions that support and nurture life are the very heart of Buddhist practice, the benefit of providing another with sustenance manifests not only as immense good fortune for the giver in the human and heavenly realms but also manifests in the realm of Buddhahood by one's life becoming perfectly endowed with the three bodies of the Buddha in a single body.

Making offerings enables one to achieve good—the highest expression of which is the supreme good of attaining Buddhahood. In Nichiren Buddhism, especially, the person or teaching to whom the offering is made is also very important. The Hinayana sutras teach that if one makes offerings to a sage one will be reborn in the human and heavenly realms. But by making offerings to the Lotus Sutra, the teaching for attaining Buddhahood, one can manifest the three bodies of the Buddha in one's own life. Accordingly, supporting and protecting a votary of the Lotus Sutra, who expounds and spreads the ultimate teaching for gaining enlightenment, is particularly praiseworthy.

In the next section of this writing, Nichiren discusses his solitary struggle as the first person in the Latter Day to proclaim Nam-myoho-renge-kyo, the teaching that opens the way for all people to attain enlightenment.

The Mission of Bodhisattva Superior Practices

If we inquire into the origin of Mount Sumeru, we find that it began with a single speck of dust; and likewise, the great ocean began with a single drop of dew. One added to one becomes two, two becomes three, and so on to make ten, a hundred, a thousand, ten thousand, a hundred thousand, or an asamkhya. Yet "one" is the mother of all. (WND-1, 667)

Bodhisattva Superior Practices, who is entrusted with the daimoku, the core of the essential teaching, had not yet appeared in the world.

But now he will appear in the Latter Day of the Law and propagate the five characters of Myoho-renge-kyo to all the nations and people throughout Jambudvipa. Surely it will spread just as the invocation of Amida's name has spread throughout Japan at the present time.

I, Nichiren, am not the founder of any school, nor am I a latter-day follower of any older school. I am a priest without precepts, neither keeping the precepts nor breaking them. I am an ordinary creature like an ox or a sheep, who is neither particularly wise nor ignorant.

Why did I first begin to chant as I do? Bodhisattva Superior Practices is the one destined to make his advent in this world to propagate the five characters of Myoho-renge-kyo. But before he had even appeared, I began, as though speaking in a dream, hardly aware of what I was doing, to utter the words Nam-myoho-renge-kyo, and so I chant them now. (WND-1, 669)

Even towering Mount Sumeru began from a single speck of dust, and the vast ocean began from a single drop of dew. All things start from small steps or beginnings. This is the central theme of "The Blessings of the Lotus Sutra." As an old proverb says, "One is the mother of ten thousand" ("A Sage and an Unenlightened Man," WND-1, 131). In this writing, we also find the words: "One added to one becomes two, two becomes three, and so on to make ten, a hundred, a thousand, ten thousand, a hundred thousand, or an asamkhya. Yet 'one' is the mother of all." In the same way, the widespread propagation of the Mystic Law in the Latter Day began with a single person, Nichiren Daishonin.

To clarify this point, the Daishonin first offers a brief outline of the history of Buddhism in Japan, highlighting the propagation of the Lotus Sutra. By Nichiren's time, seven hundred years had passed since Buddhism was first introduced to the country. Over that period, various Buddhist teachers had highly esteemed the Lotus Sutra, but none had spread the *daimoku*, or title, of the Lotus Sutra, Nam-myoho-renge-kyo. While the practice of calling on the names of Amida Buddha,[17] Mahavairochana Buddha,[18] or Shakyamuni Buddha[19] had become widespread, Nichiren asserts that "there has never been anyone who urged them to chant Nam-myoho-renge-kyo, the daimoku, or title, of the Lotus Sutra" (WND-1, 668).

This indicated that many people had placed their faith in gaining rebirth in the Pure Land through the benevolent power of the vow of Amida Buddha. Or they had sought salvation by Mahavairochana Buddha or even had revered Shakyamuni Buddha.

But few had shown the same kind of faith, veneration, or devotion toward the Lotus Sutra. The Lotus Sutra had been prized and studied as a teaching for the protection of the nation and as a sutra that elucidated the profound doctrine of the single vehicle of Buddhahood.[20] But it had never truly become a central focus of faith for ordinary people.

Nichiren refers to the history of Buddhism in India and China, citing the existence of such great teachers as T'ien-t'ai, Miao-lo, and others, who clarified the profound principles of the Lotus Sutra. He notes that while some of them may have chanted the title of the Lotus Sutra themselves, they did not share or spread this practice with the general populace (see WND-1, 668). Even during the two millennia of the Former and Middle Days of the Law after the Buddha's passing, people placed their faith in chanting the names of various Buddhas and bodhisattvas appearing in different sutras. These included Amida Buddha, Mahavairochana Buddha, Shakyamuni Buddha, Bodhisattva Perceiver of the World's Sounds,[21] and Medicine Master Buddha.[22]

Why was it, then, that the daimoku of the Lotus Sutra was not spread in the Former and Middle Days of the Law? In this writing, Nichiren attributes it to two main reasons: The time had not yet come and the person entrusted with propagating the daimoku had not yet appeared in the world.

Nichiren observes that during these earlier periods, the "sickness of delusion" affecting people had not yet become critical

(WND-1, 669). Therefore, even chanting the names of Buddhas or bodhisattvas of the provisional, pre-Lotus Sutra teachings and the theoretical teachings (the first half of the Lotus Sutra)—such as Amida, Mahavairochana, and Perceiver of the World's Sounds—could serve to relieve this spiritual affliction. This is the first reason why the Daishonin asserts that the time had not yet come for the daimoku of the Lotus Sutra to spread. However, he declares that the "grave illness" of slandering the Law that afflicts the people of the Latter Day can be fundamentally cured only by the great beneficial medicine of the five characters of Myoho-renge-kyo (the title of the Lotus Sutra) (see WND-1, 669).

The people of the Latter Day are powerfully driven by deluded impulses arising from the three poisons of greed, anger, and foolishness.[23] No matter how much they called on the names of various Buddhas, doing so would only increase their dependence on those Buddhas for their salvation, which would prevent them from carrying out their own spiritual transformation. No matter how they called on the name of some external Buddha, they would neither be able to realize inner change nor attain Buddhahood.

In contrast, Nam-myoho-renge-kyo is the ultimate Law that is the seed or cause for the enlightenment of all Buddhas, including Shakyamuni. This Law alone has the power to fundamentally relieve the sufferings of the people in the Latter Day. Accordingly, Nichiren teaches that chanting Nam-myoho-renge-kyo alone, not the names of provisional

Buddhas or bodhisattvas, will open the path to Buddhahood in this defiled age.

Next is the question of the entrustment of the Law. In the Lotus Sutra, Shakyamuni Buddha entrusts Bodhisattva Superior Practices, the leader of the Bodhisattvas of the Earth, with the future propagation of the Law in the Latter Day. The people of this evil age—who are deemed to have an adverse capacity to understand the Buddha's teachings—can gain enlightenment only by embracing the five characters of Myoho-renge-kyo, the fundamental seed of Buddhahood. The Bodhisattvas of the Earth are disciples of Shakyamuni from the distant past and are the ones, together with Superior Practices, who are actually "entrusted with the supreme Law" ("The Object of Devotion for Observing the Mind," WND-1, 372). They make their appearance already possessing the Law of Nam-myoho-renge-kyo, the "teaching of sowing."[24] Although in their actions and practice they are bodhisattvas, they possess the ultimate Law by which all Buddhas attain enlightenment. That is why they are able to correctly guide all people in this evil age of the Latter Day.

Many people throughout the centuries had read the Lotus Sutra, but Nichiren Daishonin was the only person who understood the role to be fulfilled by Bodhisattva Superior Practices, and he rose to action to propagate the daimoku of the Lotus Sutra among the populace.

In this writing, he explains his own position, saying, "I, Nichiren, am not the founder of any school, nor am I a latter-day follower of any older school." He makes it very clear that he does not belong to any of the established streams of Buddhism that arose during the two thousand years of the Former and Middle Days of the Law. This passage honestly describes his position as an ordinary individual living in the Latter Day who, without relying on the authority of any existing Buddhist school and without the patronage of any powerful secular figure, read the Lotus Sutra true to the Buddha's intent and embarked on the struggle of Bodhisattva Superior Practices to propagate the Mystic Law.

Nichiren further states that he is "a priest without precepts, neither keeping the precepts nor breaking them" and is "neither particularly wise nor ignorant." He is essentially saying that he is a person who does not fit into any pre-established category of the Buddhist schools of his day.

Nichiren always stood free from the confines and constraints of existing religious convention or authority. As an ordinary individual living in the defiled age of the Latter Day, he focused his full attention on the Lotus Sutra and Shakyamuni Buddha, working tirelessly to establish a people-centered Buddhism in the Latter Day of the Law, as taught in the Lotus Sutra. We can also infer that the Daishonin consistently stressed his ordinariness as a human being to demonstrate how brilliantly the human spirit can shine when one strives unflaggingly in accord with the Buddha's intent to lead all people to enlightenment. For it is only through such dedicated efforts that a Buddhism accessible to ordinary people can be realized.

In Nichiren Buddhism, action is key. In an early Buddhist text, we find these immortal words of Shakyamuni: "Not by birth does one become an outcaste, not by birth does one become a Brahman. By action one becomes an outcaste, by action one becomes a Brahman."[25] This statement that people are defined not by the circumstances of their birth but by their actions is a declaration of human equality that shines with brilliance in the present age.

Nichiren personally achieved the great undertaking that Bodhisattva Superior Practices had been destined to carry out. He encountered many challenging obstacles and persecutions along the way, just as the Lotus Sutra predicted. Given that his efforts validate the sutra's assertions, the Daishonin declares that he surely "must equal the sages T'ien-t'ai and Dengyo"[26] (WND-1, 672). He proclaims that his own struggles are themselves equivalent to the struggles of genuine sages. In other words, he wanted to show us, ordinary people of the Latter Day, that when awakened individuals stand up with a personal commitment to fulfill their true mission, they can actualize the immeasurably noble goal of enabling all people to attain Buddhahood.

Practicing Based on the Lotus Sutra

But I am different from such persons. I firmly uphold the teaching that the Lotus Sutra is supreme among the sutras the Buddha has preached, now preaches, and will preach. Moreover, I chant the daimoku, which is the heart and core of the entire sutra, and I urge others to do likewise. Although the mugwort growing in a hemp field or wood marked for cutting with an inked line may not be straight to begin with, they will as a matter of course become so.

In the same way, one who chants the daimoku as the Lotus Sutra teaches will never have a twisted mind. For one should know that, unless the mind of the Buddha enters into our bodies, we cannot in fact chant the daimoku. (WND-1, 670)

How did Nichiren come to be the first person in the Latter Day to recognize the time and begin spreading the daimoku of the Lotus Sutra of his own volition? He offers an answer in this passage, in which he underscores the importance of faithfully practicing just as the Buddha teaches.

The Daishonin exemplified this commitment in his own actions, always basing himself on the Lotus Sutra and not the interpretations of various teachers and scholars of Buddhism. In contrast, the founders of the different Buddhist schools—apart from the Great Teachers T'ien-t'ai and Dengyo,

who upheld the Lotus Sutra—had all diverged from the true spirit of the Lotus Sutra, having only read its text in reference to the particular sutras on which they based their own doctrines. Because they attempted to understand the Lotus Sutra from the viewpoint of the pre-Lotus Sutra teachings, they failed to comprehend the essence of the Lotus Sutra as a teaching of universal enlightenment grounded in the doctrines of "mutual possession of the Ten Worlds"[27] and "three thousand realms in a single moment of life."[28] For that reason, it was as if they hadn't read the Lotus Sutra at all.

Stating that he is different from these founders of other Buddhist schools, the Daishonin writes, "I firmly uphold the teaching that the Lotus Sutra is supreme among the sutras the Buddha has preached, now preaches, and will preach." He indicates that he has been chanting Nam-myoho-renge-kyo on his own and teaching others to do the same, in exact accord with the Lotus Sutra, which encompasses the very essence of the Buddha's lifetime of teachings.

Here, he emphasizes believing and following the teachings of the Lotus Sutra. Just as the winding stems of mugwort grow straight in a field of hemp or as wood is cut in straight lines by using a stringed inking device, when we chant the daimoku as the Lotus Sutra teaches, our minds will not turn to twisting or distorting the true intent of Shakyamuni Buddha. Nichiren further says, "For one should know that, unless the mind of the Buddha enters into our bodies, we cannot in fact chant the daimoku." This is an extremely important passage.

In "Expedient Means," the second chapter of the Lotus Sutra, we find the words, "honestly discarding expedient means" (LSOC, 79).[29] The Lotus Sutra is thus a teaching in which Shakyamuni honestly discards expedient teachings and directly preaches the true way for attaining Buddhahood. And in "Life Span," the sixteenth chapter of the Lotus Sutra, Shakyamuni speaks of people who are "honest and upright, gentle in intent, single-mindedly desiring to see the Buddha, not hesitating even if it costs them their lives" (LSOC, 271).[30] Accordingly, even in the Latter Day of the Law, the "mind of the Buddha" will come to function in the lives of those who believe in the Lotus Sutra—having cast aside their attachments to arbitrary views and erroneous wisdom, sincerely accepting the Buddha's teaching with gentle hearts and single-mindedly seeking the Buddha with ungrudging devotion.

Nichiren fully and wholeheartedly accepted the Lotus Sutra, which directly elucidates the heart and intent of the Buddha. As a result, on his own he quite naturally realized the significance of the teaching of the five characters of Myoho-renge-kyo and the significance of the Latter Day as being the time for widely spreading the Mystic Law. It was the same kind of recognition Bodhisattva Superior Practices had when he heard the "wonderful teaching preached directly from the golden mouth of Shakyamuni Buddha" (WND-1, 670) during the Ceremony in the

Air[31] and was entrusted with the mission of propagating this teaching in the evil latter age after the Buddha's passing.

The Lotus Sutra forewarns that those who practice exactly as it teaches will invariably encounter great obstacles and persecutions. "Teacher of the Law," the tenth chapter, states, "Since hatred and jealousy toward this sutra abound even when the Thus Come One is in the world, how much more will this be so after his passing?" (LSOC, 203). "Peaceful Practices," the fourteenth chapter, says, the sutra "will face much hostility in the world and be difficult to believe" (LSOC, 246). And "Encouraging Devotion," the thirteenth chapter, describes in detail the three powerful enemies[32] who will assail the practitioners of the Lotus Sutra in the Latter Day (see LSOC, 232–34).

Nichiren experienced hardships and persecutions just as the sutra describes, thereby proving the truth of Shakyamuni's teaching. In this connection, he writes, "If I, Nichiren, had not been born in the land of Japan, then these passages of the sutra would have been mere words on the Buddha's part—empty of all significance" (WND-1, 671).

And it is the Soka Gakkai that has carried on in the direct lineage of Nichiren Daishonin and proven the validity of his teachings. Over the past eight decades since its founding, the Soka Gakkai has steadfastly fought and won through faith that is directly connected to the Daishonin and is based on his writings. As a result, we can share the correct teaching of Nichiren Buddhism with people around the world and develop our organization to encompass a total of 192 countries and territories.

Mr. Makiguchi was determined not to let Nichiren Buddhism remain buried away as a religion to which people paid only token homage at temples; this was the situation that grew out of the compulsory *danka* or parish system[33] introduced in Japan from around the mid-seventeenth century. Returning to the original spirit of the Daishonin, he vowed to make Nichiren's teachings accessible to ordinary people the world over. He not only revitalized Buddhism as a practical philosophy for leading a value-creating life, but he also revived Buddhist practice aimed at the realization of kosen-rufu, stressing that it is important to show actual proof of the beneficial power of faith in the Mystic Law. Moreover, Mr. Makiguchi himself practiced Nichiren Buddhism with an attitude of great strictness toward slander of the Law. When the Nichiren Shoshu priesthood demanded that members of the Soka Gakkai accept the Shinto talisman in line with the directive of the wartime militarist authorities, he adamantly refused to comply. His dignified and decisive stance was that of a true heir to the lineage of faith in Nichiren Buddhism.

Mr. Toda also engraved the Daishonin's writings in his life. Awakening to his mission as a Bodhisattva of the Earth, he vowed to realize kosen-rufu and worked tirelessly to lead people to genuine happiness.

As Mr. Toda's disciple, I, too, have taken full responsibility for kosen-rufu, working together with my sincere and noble fellow members throughout Japan and the world. We have battled the three obstacles and four devils[34]—including the insidious workings of the devil king of the sixth heaven[35]—and have triumphed over the three powerful enemies. We have won in every sphere and struggle.

It is we of the Soka Gakkai who are living the writings of Nichiren Daishonin and proving their relevance and validity in the present age. Our organization alone has inherited the true spirit of Nichiren Buddhism and is faithfully carrying out the Buddha's decree. Our eighty-year history—a history of practicing in accord with the Buddha's teachings without begrudging our lives—is an unequivocal testimony to the Soka Gakkai's legitimacy as the organization of kosen-rufu.

The Beginning of All Things

In this entire country of Japan, I am the only one who has been chanting Nam-myoho-renge-kyo. I am like the single speck of dust that marks the beginning of Mount Sumeru or the single drop of dew that spells the start of the great ocean. Probably two people, three people, ten people, a hundred people will join in chanting it, until it spreads to one province, two provinces, and all the sixty-six provinces of Japan, and reaches even to the two islands of Iki and Tsushima. Those persons who have spoken slanderously of me will in time chant in the

same way; and everyone from the ruler on down to the multitude of common people will, as described in the "Supernatural Powers" chapter of the Lotus Sutra, chant Nam-myoho-renge-kyo with a single voice. Though the trees may desire to be still, the wind will not cease to blow; though we may wish for spring to linger, it must give way to summer. (WND-1, 672)

Nichiren Daishonin rose up alone and set in motion the propagation of the Mystic Law in the Latter Day. In this respect, he says, he is "like the single speck of dust that marks the beginning of Mount Sumeru or the single drop of dew that spells the start of the great ocean." Through his struggles since proclaiming the establishment of his teaching in 1253, the numbers of those chanting Nam-myoho-renge-kyo had steadily grown to two, three, ten, a hundred, and countless more. The groundswell of propagation had spread from one province to another and then eventually throughout all the sixty-six provinces of Japan and even to Iki and Tsushima, two islands in southern Japan that bore the brunt of the Mongol attack in 1274.

Apparently, when Nichiren's prediction of the two calamities of foreign invasion and internal strife came to pass,[36] even those who had originally criticized and maligned him came to change their attitude toward him. He declares, "Though the trees may desire to be still, the wind will not cease to blow; though we may wish for spring to linger, it must give way to summer." No matter how much we try to resist, nature and the seasons continue to move and change. It is the Daishonin's firm conviction that with the same unceasing power, kosen-rufu of the Mystic Law will definitely be achieved.

An important lesson of this writing is the fact that kosen-rufu is realized through one person reaching out and sharing the correct teaching with another—as indicated by the passage "two people, three people, ten people, a hundred people will join in chanting [Nam-myoho-renge-kyo]." This is because kosen-rufu is a movement to awaken the lives of one person after another.

In exact accord with Nichiren's words, we of the Soka Gakkai have spread the correct teaching by talking with others and telling them about our Buddhist practice. The cornerstones of our movement are one-to-one dialogue and discussion meetings.

It was Mr. Makiguchi who began this tradition of dialogue and discussion meetings. To a youth who suggested that holding large-scale lectures might be more effective than discussion meetings, Mr. Makiguchi said with keen insight: "No, it wouldn't. Dialogue is the only way to communicate with another about life's problems. At a lecture, listeners inevitably feel uninvolved. Even Nichiren Daishonin's treatise 'On Establishing the Correct Teaching for the Peace of the Land' was written in the form of a dialogue, you know."

Mr. Toda often said, "Kosen-rufu will be realized through one-to-one, face-to-face dialogue." With this same conviction, I have made constant efforts to engage in one-to-one dialogue.

The important thing is encouraging each person one to one with genuine warmth and humanity and inspiring them in faith. As long as this tradition stays alive, the Soka Gakkai's continued development is assured.

Praising Those Who Uphold the Mystic Law

In view of all this, your sincerity in sending a gift of five strings of blue-duck coins whenever the opportunity arises truly entitles you to be known as one who propagates the daimoku of the Lotus Sutra in Japan. As first one person, then two persons, then a thousand, ten thousand, a hundred thousand, and then all the people throughout the country come to chant the daimoku, before you know it, their blessings will accrue to you. Those blessings will be like the drops of dew that gather to form the great ocean, or the specks of dust that pile up to become Mount Sumeru. (WND-1, 672)

The more gold is heated in the flames, the brighter will be its color; the more a sword is whetted, the sharper it will become. And the more one praises the blessings of the Lotus Sutra, the more one's own blessings will increase. Bear in mind that the twenty-eight chapters of the Lotus Sutra contain only a few passages elucidating

the truth, but a great many words of praise. (WND-1, 673)

In this closing section, Nichiren Daishonin warmly encourages Myomitsu and his wife, who have supported his efforts for kosen-rufu by sending him gifts of "five strings of blue-duck coins" on numerous occasions. He says that Myomitsu's act of making sincere offerings is the same as propagating the daimoku of the Lotus Sutra in Japan. Thus, when people throughout the land chant Nam-myoho-renge-kyo, their blessings will all accrue to Myomitsu. Not only will he enjoy immense benefit as vast as the great ocean or Mount Sumeru, but he will also receive the absolute protection of the heavenly deities.

Nichiren further encourages Myomitsu's wife, who supported her husband. Persevering in faith in the Mystic Law in the Latter Day is a truly commendable achievement. The Daishonin always deeply treasured his followers who strove alongside him for kosen-rufu. We can easily imagine how his sincere encouragement would have inspired the couple to redouble their efforts with fresh resolve.

"The more gold is heated in the flames, the brighter will be its color; the more a sword is whetted, the sharper it will become," he says. The more gold is purified by fire, the more luminous it becomes. The more a sword is sharpened, the finer its edge. The more one praises the benefits of the Lotus Sutra, the more one's own benefits will increase.

In the Lotus Sutra itself, there are only a few pages elucidating the essence of the

Law. Overall, the twenty-eight chapters of the Lotus Sutra could be said to be dedicated almost entirely to describing multitudes of living beings unanimously lauding the blessings of the Law of universal enlightenment. They praise Shakyamuni Buddha, Many Treasures Buddha, and the Buddhas throughout the ten directions; they urge living beings everywhere to accept and uphold the Mystic Law. When read in terms of the meaning hidden in the depths of its text, the entire Lotus Sutra extols the beneficial power of Nam-myoho-renge-kyo.

Praise for the Mystic Law fills one's life with blessings, and praise for those who uphold and propagate the Mystic Law increases those blessings exponentially.

Our Infinitely Noble Potential

We who uphold the Mystic Law believe that all people—both ourselves and others—innately possess the supreme life state of Buddhahood. When we strive as emissaries and disciples of the Buddha—chanting the daimoku of the Lotus Sutra ourselves and encouraging others to do the same—we can spread the philosophy of genuine respect for the sanctity of life far and wide and enrich the world through the workings of Buddhist compassion.

What our world needs today are more and more genuinely committed people who embody the life-affirming ideals of the Lotus Sutra. That is, the world needs individuals who can teach others through their personal experiences and actions that all people alike are endowed with infinitely noble potential. By awakening to that inner potential, we can defeat the discrimination that is the fundamental source of all evil, which arises from the darkness or ignorance in human life. Also, only when we deeply recognize the inherent dignity of all human beings can we triumph in the struggle to fundamentally overcome the perennial problem of war that plagues humanity.

Nichiren lived some seven hundred years after Buddhism was first introduced to Japan. In a dark time when the pure Law of Shakyamuni was on the brink of perishing, the Daishonin made his appearance and established the Buddhism of the sun to illuminate all humanity. And as he chronicles in this writing, he embarked on spreading the daimoku of the Lotus Sutra throughout the entire country.

By some mystic working of destiny, the Soka Gakkai appeared seven hundred years after Nichiren's passing, at a time when the pure flow of Nichiren Buddhism was in danger of being lost. Mr. Makiguchi and Mr. Toda strove to enable as many people as possible to embrace faith in the Gohonzon—the embodiment of Nam-myoho-renge-kyo—so that each person would awaken to the supreme dignity of their own life. Showing actual proof of the beneficial power of faith in the Gohonzon and wishing to share the joy of faith with others, Soka Gakkai members actively spread Nichiren Buddhism and helped countless people receive the Gohonzon. Propagation of the Gohonzon truly began in earnest only through the efforts of the Soka Gakkai.

Today, we of the SGI have secured the foundations for worldwide kosen-rufu and the westward transmission of Buddhism, and veritably "all the nations and people throughout [the entire world]" are voicing high aspirations for the humanism of Nichiren Buddhism. Praise and recognition for the activities of SGI members, who embody the Lotus Sutra's life-affirming ideals, increase with each passing day. The time for us to embark on the full-fledged development of worldwide kosen-rufu has arrived.

Most important are all of you, my precious fellow members, who are polishing your lives day in and day out through participating in SGI activities. The Daishonin's spirit of kosen-rufu and the eighty-year history and tradition of the Soka Gakkai all pulse vibrantly in your hearts. Nichiren would surely praise you. My wife and I are also praying for the good health and vigorous endeavors of each of you, who is an irreplaceable treasure.

Now is the time for us to make a fresh departure. On the grand stage of worldwide kosen-rufu that encompasses all humanity, let us challenge ourselves afresh, each determined to be the single speck of dust that marks the beginning of a new towering Mount Sumeru or the single drop of dew that spells the start of a new great ocean.

The founding spirit of the Soka Gakkai lies in mentor and disciple advancing together with the self-motivated spirit of "It starts with me! It starts from now!"

This lecture was originally published in the November 2010 issue of the Daibyakurenge, *the Soka Gakkai's monthly study journal.*

NOTES

1. Five precepts: The basic precepts to be observed by laypersons. They are (1) not to kill, (2) not to steal, (3) not to engage in sexual misconduct (such as adultery), (4) not to lie, and (5) not to consume intoxicants. These precepts are regarded as the most fundamental of Buddhist precepts; in addition, Buddhism views them as "preventing error and putting an end to evil."
2. Six paramitas: Six practices required of Mahayana bodhisattvas in order to attain Buddhahood. The Sanskrit word *paramita* is interpreted as "perfection" or "having reached the opposite shore," as in, to cross from the shore of delusion to the shore of enlightenment. The six paramitas are (1) almsgiving, (2) keeping the precepts, (3) forbearance, (4) assiduousness, (5) meditation, and (6) the obtaining of wisdom, which enables one to perceive the true nature of all things.
3. Ten good precepts: The precepts prohibiting commission of the ten evil acts, which are (1) killing, (2) stealing, (3) sexual misconduct, (4) lying, (5) flattery or indiscriminate and irresponsible speech, (6) defamation, (7) duplicity, (8) greed, (9) anger, and (10) foolishness, or the holding of mistaken views.
4. Two hundred and fifty precepts: Rules of discipline to be observed by fully ordained monks of Hinayana Buddhism. They are set forth in *The Fourfold Rules of Discipline*, a text of the Indian Dharmagupta school.
5. Ten major precepts: The ten most important among the fifty-eight rules of discipline for Mahayana bodhisattvas set forth in the Brahma Net Sutra. (The others are called the forty-eight minor precepts.) The ten major precepts are (1) not to kill, (2) not to steal, (3) not to engage in any sexual relations, (4) not to lie, (5) not to sell liquor, (6) not to speak ill of the past misdeeds of other Buddhists, (7) not to praise oneself or disparage others, (8) not to begrudge offerings or spare one's efforts for the sake of Buddhism, (9) not to give way to anger, and (10) not to speak ill of the three treasures (the Buddha, his teachings, and the Buddhist Order).
6. Mount Sumeru: In ancient Indian cosmology, the mountain that stands at the center of the world.

7. Asamkhya: A numerical unit of ancient India used to indicate an exceedingly large number.

8. Bodhisattva Superior Practices: One of the four leaders of the Bodhisattvas of the Earth. Shakyamuni entrusts Superior Practices with propagating the Lotus Sutra during the evil age of the Latter Day of the Law. In his writings, Nichiren Daishonin associates himself with Bodhisattva Superior Practices, saying that he is fulfilling the mission entrusted to the bodhisattva by Shakyamuni, and he refers to his propagation efforts as the work of Bodhisattva Superior Practices. Nichikan, the twenty-sixth chief priest of Taiseki-ji, regarded the Daishonin as the reincarnation of Bodhisattva Superior Practices in terms of his outward behavior and as the Buddha of the Latter Day of the Law in terms of his inner enlightenment.

9. Myoho-renge-kyo is written with five Chinese characters, while Nam-myoho-renge-kyo is written with seven (*nam*, or *namu*, being comprised of two characters). The Daishonin often uses Myoho-renge-kyo synonymously with Nam-myoho-renge-kyo in his writings.

10. In "Teacher of the Law," the tenth chapter of the Lotus Sutra, Shakyamuni explains: "The sutras I have preached number immeasurable thousands, ten thousands, millions. Among the sutras I have preached, now preach, and will preach, this Lotus Sutra is the most difficult to believe and the most difficult to understand" (LSOC, 203). This means that compared to all other sutras—that is, the sutras preached before and after the Lotus Sutra, including also the Immeasurable Meanings Sutra and the Nirvana Sutra—the Lotus Sutra is the supreme teaching and is the most difficult to believe and understand.

11. The sixty-six provinces refer to the entire country of ancient Japan. This division of the country was in force from 813 until the Meiji Restoration in the third quarter of the nineteenth century.

12. In "Supernatural Powers," the twenty-first chapter of the Lotus Sutra, the heavenly gods proclaim in open space that Shakyamuni is now preaching the Lotus Sutra in the saha world. On hearing this, all the beings in the ten directions face the saha world and, joining their palms together in reverence, utter the words "Hail, Shakyamuni Buddha! Hail, Shakyamuni Buddha!" (LSOC, 315).

13. At this time, coins had square holes in the center and were usually strung together in hundreds and thousands to form larger monetary units. Here, Myomitsu's offering of five strings of coins—as indicated in the letter's opening reference to "five thousand blue-duck coins" (WND-1, 667)—comprised five strings each containing a thousand coins. Blue-duck coins were copper coins imported from Sung-dynasty China, with a square hole in the center that caused them to be likened to a duck's eye.

14. Myomitsu: A follower of Nichiren Daishonin who lived in Kuwagayatsu in Kamakura. While little information on Myomitsu is available, it appears that he and his wife were sincere believers in the Daishonin's teachings. In "The Blessings of the Lotus Sutra," the only extant letter addressed to Myomitsu, the Daishonin refers to him as "the Honorable Myomitsu" (WND-1, 673), which suggests that he may have been a lay priest.

15. Thirty-two features: Here, this refers to physical characteristics of wheel-turning kings, though usually the term is used to indicate the remarkable physical features of the Buddha.

16. Three bodies of the Buddha: A concept set forth in Mahayana Buddhism to organize different views of the Buddha appearing in the sutras. The three bodies are: (1) the Dharma body, (2) the reward body, and (3) the manifested body. The Great Teacher T'ien-t'ai maintained that the three bodies are not separate entities but three integral aspects of a single Buddha. From this viewpoint, the Dharma body indicates the essential property of a Buddha, which is the truth or Law to which the Buddha is enlightened. The reward body indicates the wisdom, or the Buddha's spiritual property, that enables the Buddha to perceive the truth. The manifested body indicates compassionate actions, or the physical property of a Buddha used to carry out compassionate actions to lead people to enlightenment.

17. Amida Buddha: Amida Buddha is revered by the followers of the Pure Land, or Nembutsu, school. Belief in Amida Buddha spread from India to China. After its introduction to Japan, Honen (1133–1212) was responsible for popularizing it there and establishing the Pure Land school.

18. Mahavairochana Buddha: A Buddha that is described in the Mahavairochana Sutra, which is prized by the True Word school. He is regarded as the Buddha of the Dharma body who personifies the unchanging truth of all phenomena and is the source from which all Buddhas and bodhisattvas spring.

19. This is a reference to Shakyamuni Buddha in terms of the surface or literal meaning of the Lotus Sutra, as opposed to the meaning hidden in the depths of the Lotus Sutra first revealed by Nichiren Daishonin.

20. In contrast to the three vehicles—the teachings expounded for voice-hearers, cause-awakened ones and bodhisattvas, respectively—the single vehicle of Buddhahood, or the one Buddha vehicle, means the teaching that enables all people to attain Buddhahood and corresponds to the Lotus Sutra.

21. Bodhisattva Perceiver of the World's Sounds: Also known as Perceiver of Sounds. Widely known by his Chinese name Kuan-yin, he is one of the most popular bodhisattvas in the Buddhist world and revered as the bodhisattva of infinite compassion. In the Buddha Infinite Life Sutra and the Meditation on the Buddha Infinite Life Sutra, Perceiver of the World's Sounds appears with Bodhisattva Great Power as an attendant of Amida Buddha.

22. Medicine Master Buddha: The Medicine Master Sutra recounts a previous life of the Buddha Medicine Master in which, as a bodhisattva, he made twelve vows to cure all illnesses and lead all people to enlightenment. The great benefit of reciting his name is then described. The sutra also enumerates seven disasters that making offerings to this Buddha can avert and how by doing so one can restore peace to the land.

23. Three poisons of greed, anger, and foolishness: The fundamental evils inherent in life that give rise to human suffering. In Nagarjuna's *Treatise on the Great Perfection of Wisdom,* the three poisons are regarded as the source of all illusions and earthly desires. The three poisons are so called because they pollute people's lives and work to prevent them from turning their hearts and minds to goodness.

24. Teaching of sowing: "Sowing" refers to the process by which the Buddha sows in people's lives the seed or fundamental cause for attaining enlightenment. The entity of the teaching of sowing is Nam-myoho-renge-kyo.

25. *The Group of Discourses (Sutta-nipata),* trans. K. R. Norman (Oxford: The Pali Text Society, 1995), 2:16.

26. T'ien-t'ai (538–97): Also known as Chih-i. The founder of the T'ien-t'ai school in China. His lectures were compiled in such works as *The Profound Meaning of the Lotus Sutra, The Words and Phrases of the Lotus Sutra,* and *Great Concentration and Insight.* He spread the Lotus Sutra in China and established the doctrine of three thousand realms in a single moment of life (see note 28).

   Dengyo (767–822): Also known as Saicho. The founder of the Tendai (T'ien-t'ai) school in Japan. He refuted the errors of the six schools of Nara—the established Buddhist schools of the day—elevated the Lotus Sutra, and dedicated himself to the establishment of a Mahayana ordination center on Mount Hiei.

27. Mutual possession of the Ten Worlds: The principle that each of the Ten Worlds possesses the potential for all ten within itself. "Mutual possession" means that life is not fixed in one or another of the Ten Worlds but can manifest any of the ten—from hell to the state of Buddhahood—at any given moment. The important point of this principle is that all beings in any of the nine worlds possess the Buddha nature. This means that every person has the potential to manifest Buddhahood, while a Buddha also possesses the nine worlds and in this sense is not separate or different from ordinary people.

28. Three thousand realms in a single moment of life: A doctrine developed by the Great Teacher T'ien-t'ai of China based on the Lotus Sutra explaining that all phenomena are contained within a single moment of life and that a single moment of life permeates the three thousand realms of existence, or the entire phenomenal world.

29. In the Lotus Sutra, Shakyamuni declares: "Now I, joyful and fearless, in the midst of the bodhisattvas, honestly discarding expedient means, will preach only the unsurpassed way" (LSOC, 79). With these words, he indicates that the teachings he had preached prior to this time were only expedient and provisional teachings.

30. This passage means that Shakyamuni will appear where there are people who truly believe in the Mystic Law,

have a sincere seeking spirit, and devote themselves unstintingly to their Buddhist practice.

31. Ceremony in the Air: One of the three assemblies described in the Lotus Sutra, in which the entire gathering is suspended in space above the saha world. It extends from "Treasure Tower," the eleventh chapter, to "Entrustment," the twenty-second chapter. The heart of this ceremony is the revelation of the Buddha's original enlightenment in the remote past and the transfer of the essence of the sutra to the Bodhisattvas of the Earth, who are led by Bodhisattva Superior Practices.

32. Three powerful enemies: Three types of arrogant people who persecute those who propagate the Lotus Sutra in the evil age after Shakyamuni Buddha's death. The Great Teacher Miao-lo (711–82) of China summarizes them as arrogant lay people, arrogant priests, and arrogant false sages.

33. Under this system, which was introduced by the Tokugawa military government in the mid-seventeenth century as part of its drive to eradicate Christianity in Japan, Buddhist temples were effectively turned into part of the government bureaucracy and empowered with authority over families living in the assigned district of a temple. It was compulsory for all households to register with a temple. This led to Buddhism becoming increasingly formalistic. Literally, *dan* means "donation" and *ka,* "family." *Danka* means families that support a temple financially. *Danto* means individual members of the danka.

34. Three obstacles and four devils: Various obstacles and hindrances to the practice of Buddhism. The three obstacles are (1) the obstacle of earthly desires, (2) the obstacle of karma, and (3) the obstacle of retribution. The four devils are (1) the hindrance of the five components, (2) the hindrance of earthly desires, (3) the hindrance of death, and (4) the hindrance of the devil king.

35. Devil king of the sixth heaven: He is also named Freely Enjoying Things Conjured by Others, the king who makes free use of the fruits of others' efforts for his own pleasure. Served by innumerable minions, he obstructs Buddhist practice and delights in sapping the life force of other beings. The devil king is a personification of the negative tendency to force others to one's will at any cost.

36. In his treatise "On Establishing the Correct Teaching for the Peace of the Land," the Daishonin predicted that Japan would suffer foreign invasion and internal strife if the government continued to give its support to erroneous teachings. Later these prophecies were fulfilled when Hojo Tokisuke revolted against his younger half brother, Regent Hojo Tokimune, in the second month of 1272, and when the Mongol forces attacked in 1274.

7

"THE SUTRA OF TRUE REQUITAL"

NICHIREN DAISHONIN'S VOW AND TIRELESS STRUGGLE
FOR THE ENLIGHTENMENT OF WOMEN

The Passage of Study for This Lecture

This sutra is superior to all other sutras. It is like the lion king, the monarch of all the creatures that run on the ground, and like the eagle, the king of all the creatures that fly in the sky. Sutras such as the Devotion to Amida Buddha Sutra[1] are like pheasants or rabbits. Seized by the eagle, their tears flow; pursued by the lion, fear grips their bowels. And the same is true of people like the Nembutsu adherents, the Precepts priests, the Zen priests, and the True Word teachers. When they come face to face with the votary of the Lotus Sutra, their color drains away and their spirits fail. (WND-1, 929–30)

For all those who wished to believe the Lotus Sutra and yet could not do so with complete certainty, the fifth volume[2] presents what is the heart and core of the entire sutra, the doctrine of attaining Buddhahood in one's present form. It is as though, for instance, a black object were to become white, black lacquer to become like snow, an unclean thing to become clean and pure, or a wish-granting jewel to be placed into muddy water [to make it transparent]. Here it is told how the dragon girl became a Buddha in her reptilian form. And at that moment there was no longer anyone who doubted that all men can attain Buddhahood. This is why I say that the enlightenment of women is expounded as a model. (WND-1, 930)

Now I, Nichiren, was born as a human being, something difficult to achieve, and I have encountered the Buddha's teachings, which are but rarely to be met with. Moreover, among all the teachings of the Buddha, I was able to meet the Lotus Sutra. When I stop to consider my good fortune, I realize that I am indebted to my parents, indebted to the ruler, and indebted to all living beings.

With regard to the debt of gratitude owed to our parents, our father may be likened to heaven and our mother to the earth, and it would be difficult to say to which parent we are the more indebted. But it is particularly difficult to repay the great kindness of our mother. (WND-1, 930)

Since I have realized that only the Lotus Sutra teaches the attainment of Buddhahood by women, and that only the Lotus is the sutra of true requital for repaying the kindness of our mother, in order to repay my debt to my mother, I have vowed to enable all women to chant the daimoku of this sutra. (WND-1, 931)

Buddhism in Japan today is exactly like this.[3] It is merely plots and rebellions in a different form. The Lotus Sutra represents the supreme ruler, while the True Word school, Pure Land school, Zen school, and the Precepts priests, by upholding such minor sutras as the Mahavairochana Sutra and the Meditation on the Buddha Infinite Life Sutra, have become the deadly enemies of the Lotus Sutra. And yet women throughout Japan, unaware of the ignorance of their own minds, think that Nichiren, who can save them, is their foe, and mistake the Nembutsu, Zen, Precepts, and True Word priests, who are in fact deadly enemies, for good friends and teachers. And because they look upon Nichiren, who is trying to save them, as a deadly enemy, these women all join together to slander him to the ruler of the country, so that, after having been exiled to the province of Izu,[4] he was also exiled to the province of Sado. (WND-1, 932)

Nevertheless, when I was exiled to the province of Sado, the constable of the province and the other officials, following the design of the ruler of the nation, treated me with animosity. . . . Every single steward and Nembutsu believer worthy of the name kept strict watch on my hut day and night, determined to prevent anyone from communicating with me. Never in any lifetime will I forget how in those circumstances you, with Abutsu-bo carrying a wooden container of food on his back, came in the night again and again to bring me aid. It was just as if my deceased mother had suddenly been reborn in the province of Sado! (WND-1, 932–33)

"In order to repay my debt to my mother, I have vowed to enable all women to chant the daimoku of [the Lotus Sutra]." This passage is the crux of "The Sutra of True Requital," the writing of Nichiren Daishonin that we will study in this chapter. It articulates the primary inspiration for the Daishonin's vow to open the way for the enlightenment of all people.

Manifest the Power of the Mystic Law With Sincere Faith

"In order to repay my debt to my mother"— what a beautifully succinct yet profound expression of the humanistic spirit of Nichiren Buddhism! To repay our debt of gratitude to our mothers, who gave birth to us, raised us, and protected us, is an important principle of Buddhism. It could be said that, in a sense, Buddhism seeks to teach us to emulate this spirit of motherly compassion in our interactions with others.

In an early Buddhist scripture, Shakyamuni Buddha instructs, "Just as a mother would protect with her life her own son, her only son, so one should cultivate an unbounded mind toward all beings, and lovingkindness toward all the world."[5] It may be no exaggeration to say that motherly compassion is identical to the heart of the Buddha, which all living beings inherently possess. A mother's compassion or love for her only child is directly linked to the concern or lovingkindness of the Buddha for all living beings. To experience a mother's love and compassion is to experience the heart of the Buddha. All of us are beneficiaries of the great spiritual blessings of motherly love and compassion.

It is an unfortunate reality of our world, however, that many mothers lead lives filled with suffering and sorrow. This is because people's hearts are ruled by self-interest, calculation, and rivalry—polar opposites of compassion. Consequently, as a youth deeply sensitive to the profound debt he owed his mother, Nichiren Daishonin began studying Buddhism in order to fundamentally free his mother from suffering. Referring to the basic aspiration that should be cherished by those who would renounce secular life, he writes, "When a man leaves his parents and home and becomes a monk, he should always have as his goal the salvation of his father and mother" ("The Opening of the Eyes," WND-1, 228).

Further, following his exhaustive study of the Buddhist sutras and commentaries, he came to the clear realization and understanding that the daimoku[6] of the Lotus Sutra—Nam-myoho-renge-kyo—is the Law that enables all living beings to attain Buddhahood. He therefore vowed to "enable all women to chant the daimoku of this sutra."

Of course, the daimoku of the Lotus Sutra is the supreme teaching of Buddhism for all living beings, not only women. However, the first example of the Lotus Sutra's central principle that all living beings can attain Buddhahood in their present form is that of the dragon king's daughter[7]—in other words, a female practitioner becoming a Buddha. This also illustrates that deep sincerity in faith, which women are particularly noted for, is the key to manifesting the power of the Mystic Law in one's own life.

I do indeed feel that women possess a natural inclination to cherish and nurture life, as symbolized by a mother's love and compassion. Thus, when women awaken to the Mystic Law, they can readily and directly tap into the life state of Buddhahood, in which compassion manifests as wisdom and wisdom manifests as compassion. Because of their pure-hearted spirit, they can embrace sincere and unswerving faith in Nam-myoho-renge-kyo, which is the seed for Buddhahood.

The lay nun Sennichi, the recipient of "The Sutra of True Requital," exemplified such faith. Nichiren wrote this letter on July 28, 1278, and had it delivered to her by her husband, the lay priest Abutsu-bo, who had traveled all the way from Sado Island to visit him at Mount Minobu. It is a reply to Sennichi's letter to Nichiren that Abutsu-bo had brought with him. In his response, the Daishonin begins by restating briefly what she had written to him, "In the letter she says that, though she had been concerned about the faults and impediments that prevent women from gaining enlightenment, since according to my teaching the Lotus Sutra puts the attainment of Buddhahood by women first, she relies upon [the Lotus Sutra] in all matters" (see WND-1, 928).

From the sentiments expressed by Sennichi, we can surmise that Nichiren's confident assurances about the enlightenment of women based on the Lotus Sutra must have been a source of immense hope and inspiration for women of his day.

In this writing, wishing to strengthen Sennichi's conviction in her capacity to gain enlightenment, the Daishonin explains that the dragon girl's attainment of Buddhahood in her present form is the heart and core of the Lotus Sutra. He also explains that the enlightenment of women in particular is the foundation of his own vow to propagate the Law, and he outlines the great struggle he has been waging toward that end.

I can vividly picture Sennichi, with this letter in hand, joyfully sharing its inspiring message with her fellow practitioners on Sado.

Let us study "The Sutra of True Requital" while reflecting on the significance of the tremendous efforts Nichiren made to fulfill his vow to enable all women to attain Buddhahood.

The Lotus Sutra Is Foremost Among All the Buddha's Teachings

This sutra is superior to all other sutras. It is like the lion king, the monarch of all the creatures that run on the ground, and like the eagle, the king of all the creatures that fly in the sky. Sutras such as the Devotion to Amida Buddha Sutra are like pheasants or rabbits. Seized by the eagle, their tears flow; pursued by the lion, fear grips their bowels. And the same is true of people like the Nembutsu adherents, the Precepts priests, the Zen priests, and the True Word teachers. When they come face to face with the votary of the Lotus Sutra, their color drains away and their spirits fail. (WND-1, 929–30)

❧

For all those who wished to believe the Lotus Sutra and yet could not do so with complete certainty, the fifth volume presents what is the heart and core of the entire sutra, the doctrine of attaining Buddhahood in one's present form. It is as though, for instance, a black object were to become white, black lacquer to become like snow, an unclean thing to become clean and pure, or a wish-granting jewel to be placed into muddy water [to make it transparent]. Here it is told how the dragon girl became a Buddha in her reptilian form. And at that moment there

was no longer anyone who doubted that all men can attain Buddhahood. This is why I say that the enlightenment of women is expounded as a model. (WND-1, 930)

Nichiren Daishonin stresses that of all the many Buddhist scriptures the Lotus Sutra alone contains the Buddha's true teaching. He declares, "It is like the lion king, the monarch of all the creatures that run on the ground, and like the eagle, the king of all the creatures that fly in the sky."

The primary reason the Lotus Sutra is designated as the king of sutras is its teaching of universal enlightenment. This teaching is elucidated in the doctrines of "three thousand realms in a single moment of life"[8] and the "mutual possession of the Ten Worlds."[9] The pre-Lotus Sutra teachings assert that Buddhahood can be attained only after eradicating the earthly desires of the nine worlds, from hell through the world of bodhisattvas. The Lotus Sutra, by contrast, teaches the mutual possession of the Ten Worlds. It explains that all living beings in the nine worlds have the capacity to reveal their inherent Buddhahood as they are, without having to undergo countless eons of austere practices.

The dragon girl—who in the Lotus Sutra's twelfth chapter instantly attains Buddhahood without changing her form—exemplifies this fundamental principle. The Daishonin notes that simply asserting that Buddhahood is a potential for all people and explaining the principle of three thousand realms in a single moment of life is not enough for people to readily accept its truth.

Moreover, it is especially difficult for people living in the evil age after the Buddha's passing to understand and believe in the Lotus Sutra's teachings. However, when the dragon girl showed the gathered assembly actual proof of attaining Buddhahood in her present form, Nichiren says, it convinced everyone that all living beings have the potential to achieve this goal.

The actualization of the enlightenment of women reveals the Lotus Sutra's power to enable all people equally to attain Buddhahood. Hence Nichiren writes in his letter to Sennichi, "This is why I say that the enlightenment of women is expounded as a model."

While a number of sutras expounded before the Lotus Sutra had mentioned the possibility of women attaining Buddhahood, it was conditional upon their first being reborn as men in a future existence. A similar condition was placed on women seeking to be reborn in the Pure Land, as taught in the Nembutsu school; they could not hope to reach that realm directly in their present form. In these cases, attaining Buddhahood required physical transformation.

In contrast, the Daishonin points out that the attainment of Buddhahood by the dragon girl in the Lotus Sutra is instantaneous, achieved by an ordinary being of the nine worlds. He corroborates this by citing a passage from a commentary by the Great Teacher Dengyo[10] relating to this event, "Through the power of the Lotus Sutra of the Wonderful Law, [one can attain Buddhahood in one's] present form" (WND-1, 930).[11]

In another letter, Nichiren also states: "The heart of the Lotus Sutra is the revelation that one may attain supreme enlightenment in one's present form without altering one's status as an ordinary person. This means that without casting aside one's karmic impediments one can still attain the Buddha way" ("Reply to Hakiri Saburo," WND-1, 410). We can instantly attain perfect enlightenment,[12] the highest stage of practice, as an ordinary person at the initial stage of embracing and practicing the Lotus Sutra. Attaining Buddhahood in one's present form—in which ordinary people manifest the life state of Buddhahood just as they are—is the true substance of enlightenment expounded in the Lotus Sutra.

Again, in "Devadatta," the twelfth chapter, as actual proof of her having attained Buddhahood in her present form, the dragon girl strongly vows to expound the "doctrines [of the Lotus Sutra] to rescue living beings from suffering" (LSOC, 227). This statement truly overflows with joyous resolve.

The portrayal of women in the Lotus Sutra, epitomized by the dragon girl, is in stark contrast to that of earlier provisional sutras expounded by the Buddha. Reflecting the prevailing attitudes in ancient Indian society, these scriptures went out of their way to stress the faults and karmic impediments of women. This in effect robbed women of both hope and dignity. During Nichiren's time, such teachings were widespread in Japan while the Lotus Sutra was all but ignored. Buddhism had turned into a source of oppression and suffering for women. Because the Daishonin wanted to put an end to this, he sought to draw attention to the dragon girl's attainment of enlightenment in her present form. He was driven by a fervent desire to establish a teaching for the happiness of women and mothers and for the inner transformation of all humanity.

Nichiren Buddhism is a transformative teaching that enables us to develop and expand our state of life through the power of faith and the power of practice based on the Mystic Law. The power of faith derives from believing that we ourselves are inherently entities of the Mystic Law, that we are Buddhas. The power of practice, meanwhile, derives from chanting the fundamental Law for attaining Buddhahood, Nam-myoho-renge-kyo, and bringing forth our Buddha nature.

The Daishonin's vow "to enable all women to chant the daimoku of this sutra" might also be described as a vow to realize a reformation in Buddhism that would promote the independence and human revolution of women.

In another writing, he states, "In the case of the Lotus Sutra . . . women who receive and uphold it in body, mouth, and mind, and in particular chant Nam-myoho-renge-kyo with their mouths, will be able to attain Buddhahood readily, as did the dragon king's daughter, Gautami,[13] and Yashodhara,[14] who lived at the same time as the Buddha" ("Those Initially Aspiring to the Way," WND-1, 884). Note the use of the word *readily* here. Women who uphold the great Law for women's enlightenment have nothing to fear.

In a letter addressed to Sennichi a few months later, the Daishonin writes, "A woman who embraces the lion king of the Lotus Sutra never fears any of the beasts of hell or of the realms of hungry spirits and animals" ("The Drum at the Gate of Thunder," WND-1, 949). Women who awaken to and uphold the supreme philosophy of the Lotus Sutra, enabling them to bring forth their own innate dignity, are assured of leading the most noble and honorable of lives.

Nichiren continually strove to impart hope to his female followers, writing such words of encouragement as: "There is nothing to lament when we consider that we will surely become Buddhas" ("The Bow and Arrow," WND-1, 657); "Only in the Lotus Sutra do we read that a woman who embraces this sutra not only excels all other women, but also surpasses all men" ("The Unity of Husband and Wife," WND-1, 464); and "Among all the 2,994,830 women of Japan, you should think of yourself as number one" ("The Buddha Statue Fashioned by Nichigen-nyo," WND-2, 813).

Further, in "The Sutra of True Requital," he confidently replies to the letter received from Sennichi, assuring her, "Though the women of Japan may be condemned in all sutras other than the Lotus as incapable of attaining Buddhahood, as long as the Lotus guarantees their enlightenment, what reason have they to be downcast?" (WND-1, 930).

The actualization of the enlightenment of women opens the way for all people to realize enlightenment. The irrefutable evidence in the Lotus Sutra of a woman attaining Buddhahood secures the hope that all people can do likewise. Accordingly, the Lotus Sutra is the starting point of a truly people-oriented Buddhism.

The Lotus Sutra Is the "Sutra of True Requital"

Now I, Nichiren, was born as a human being, something difficult to achieve, and I have encountered the Buddha's teachings, which are but rarely to be met with. Moreover, among all the teachings of the Buddha, I was able to meet the Lotus Sutra. When I stop to consider my good fortune, I realize that I am indebted to my parents, indebted to the ruler, and indebted to all living beings.

With regard to the debt of gratitude owed to our parents, our father may be likened to heaven and our mother to the earth, and it would be difficult to say to which parent we are the more indebted. But it is particularly difficult to repay the great kindness of our mother. (WND-1, 930)

Since I have realized that only the Lotus Sutra teaches the attainment of Buddhahood by women, and that only the Lotus is the sutra of true requital for repaying

the kindness of our mother, in order to repay my debt to my mother, I have vowed to enable all women to chant the daimoku of this sutra. (WND-1, 931)

Nichiren Daishonin keenly felt the debt of gratitude he owed to his parents, who had loved and raised him—likening his father to heaven and his mother to the earth. And he says, "It is particularly difficult to repay the great kindness of our mother." So immense is the debt we owe our mothers that we can never hope to fully repay it. In another letter, too, he writes: "There is no need at this late date to emphasize how great is the debt one owes to one's father and mother. But I would like to stress that the debt to one's mother is particularly important and worthy to be taken to heart" ("Reply to the Wife of Gyobu Saemon-no-jo," WND-2, 895).

Furthermore, he says his studies of the Buddhist scriptures led him to conclude that only the Lotus Sutra would allow him to repay his debt of gratitude to his mother. For this reason, he says, he vowed to teach all mothers, all women, the daimoku of the Lotus Sutra—Nam-myoho-renge-kyo.

A vow or commitment gives us the strength to persevere and keep forging ahead in our lives. It gives us the power to repel adversity. For example, in his treatise "The Opening of the Eyes," Nichiren pledges never to falter in his efforts to lead people to enlightenment, regardless of the great obstacles and persecutions he may encounter. He writes that the trials he has faced during his exile on Sado Island,[15] far from extinguishing the flame of his commitment, have only strengthened it, making him all the more determined to become the pillar of Japan and to never forsake this vow.[16]

At the heart of his pledge for the salvation of all people expressed in "The Opening of the Eyes" is Nichiren's wish to repay his debt of gratitude to his mother and enable all women to attain enlightenment. Indeed, we can see in "The Sutra of True Requital" that the enlightenment of his mother was a fundamental goal driving him.

Buddhism should be the ally of those experiencing the greatest suffering. Because it opens the doors to enlightenment for women, who had long been rejected and repudiated by traditional Buddhism, Nichiren Buddhism is a teaching that can genuinely help free all people from suffering in the Latter Day of the Law.

Kosen-rufu is a struggle to build an age in which women can truly savor the joy of living; it is the actualization of the Buddha's vow to strive so that mothers throughout the world can experience supreme happiness.

The Daishonin believed that only by making it possible for his own mother to attain enlightenment would he be able to lead all women to enlightenment. Viewed from the Buddhist principle of dependent origination,[17] each person we come in contact with is connected to the rest of humanity.

The Buddhist scriptures offer the beautiful metaphor of Indra's net to explain this interconnectedness of all life. The heavenly palace of the god Indra is adorned with a magnificent net of jewels. A brilliant jewel is attached to each knot of the net, with each jewel reflecting all the others. When one jewel moves in the breeze, all the other jewels sparkle in many different colors. In the same way, each of us is like a knot in an infinite web of mutual interrelationships. When one knot moves, everything begins to move in a great ripple effect. It is indeed true that everything begins with one individual. This is none other than the transformational principle of three thousand realms in a single moment of life.

Returning to the Daishonin's vow, another important point is that it arose from the natural human sentiment of wanting to repay his debt of gratitude to his mother. My mentor, Josei Toda, often taught that showing love and care for our parents is vital for gaining the compassionate state of mind of the Buddha. He was always urging the youth to treasure their parents. He once scolded a youth who acted without thought of his parents, "Are you oblivious to your mother's tears?"

I recall one time when Mr. Toda asked about my mother. When I told him she was doing fine, he said with a tender expression: "Our mother's smiling face stays with us as long as we live. It's that way for me. And I'm sure it will be the same for you." Mr. Toda fondly remembered the love and warm concern his mother had for him. Until his dying day, he treasured the hand-sewn *hanten* (a traditional lined robe from Hokkaido) that she had made for him to take to Tokyo. Handing it to him as he was preparing to leave his hometown to seek his fortune in the big city, his mother told him:

"If you wear this as you work, no matter how difficult things may be, you can accomplish anything." Many years later, when he returned home from his wartime imprisonment by the militarist government and found his robe safe, he said, "Since this *hanten* has survived, I know I'll be all right." He always cherished his mother's prayers.

In a well-known piece of guidance addressed to the youth, Mr. Toda wrote: "There are so many young people who are incapable of having compassion for their own parents. How can they be expected to care about perfect strangers? The effort to overcome the coldness and indifference in our own lives and attain the same state of compassion as the Buddha is the essence of human revolution."[18]

I have constantly called on young people to have compassion for their parents and to be good sons and daughters. It is my belief that youth who have this spirit will grow into people who can positively contribute to the welfare of society and their fellow human beings. Having compassion for one's parents is an important guideline for human revolution.

Remaining Steadfast in One's Commitment

Buddhism in Japan today is exactly like this. It is merely plots and rebellions in a different form. The Lotus Sutra represents the supreme ruler, while the True Word school, Pure Land school, Zen school, and the Precepts priests, by upholding such minor sutras as the Mahavairochana Sutra and the Meditation on the Buddha Infinite Life Sutra, have become the deadly enemies of the Lotus Sutra. And yet women throughout Japan, unaware of the ignorance of their own minds, think that Nichiren, who can save them, is their foe, and mistake the Nembutsu, Zen, Precepts, and True Word priests, who are in fact deadly enemies, for good friends and teachers. And because they look upon Nichiren, who is trying to save them, as a deadly enemy, these women all join together to slander him to the ruler of the country, so that, after having been exiled to the province of Izu, he was also exiled to the province of Sado. (WND-1, 932)

When Nichiren Daishonin embarked on his struggle to propagate the Mystic Law, arrogant false sages,[19] the third and most formidable of the three powerful enemies, attacked him unrelentingly, just as predicted in the Lotus Sutra. Through their scheming, he was persecuted and exiled by the ruling authorities. Disturbingly, women played a key role in his harassment. Misled by these corrupt, self-serving priests, they actively sought to have him discredited. Though Nichiren was the greatest champion of women's enlightenment and strove tirelessly for women's happiness, women throughout the land regarded him with hostility. This was truly a perverse and ridiculous state of affairs, starkly illustrating the frightening nature of slandering the Law.

At the time, faith in the teaching of the Nembutsu school was widespread, and its adherents dismissed the Lotus Sutra. Therefore, motivated by his ardent wish to save the women of Japan, the Daishonin firmly refuted the Nembutsu practice of chanting the name of Amida Buddha, saying, "Since it is not the seed of Buddhahood, they will never become Buddhas" (WND-1, 931). His arguments were based on solid documentary and theoretical proof. However, women who had been deceived by the words of the Nembutsu priests saw Nichiren's criticism as only a personal attack. They eventually came to regard him as a deadly enemy of the Buddha.

In this letter, he indicates that among the driving forces behind his exiles to Izu and Sado were slanderous rumors that high-ranking women had told the ruling authorities. During his exile to Sado in particular, the influential True Word Precepts priest Ryokan of Gokuraku-ji, a temple in Kamakura, and his cohorts colluded to incite the mother of the current regent Hojo Tokimune[20] and other well-connected women to urge action against Nichiren. These women lobbied powerful government officials, who stealthily set about repressing his activities.[21]

This was a case of slanderous priests taking advantage of the sincere faith of women to instigate a crackdown on the Daishonin, a champion of the correct teaching. Such priests can only be described as enemies of the Lotus Sutra—or, expressed another way, enemies of a people-centered Buddhism and enemies of all women.

Nichiren also deplored the behavior of these women, who were being manipulated to speak out against him, when he was the very one committed to helping women attain enlightenment. He describes them as being "unaware of the ignorance of their own minds." The ignorance that allows one to be blinded by slander of the Law and prevents one from believing in the correct teaching is truly frightening.

The Daishonin had stood up with an infinite spirit of compassion to widely communicate the Buddha's true teaching, seeking to dispel the ignorance shrouding people's lives and to lead them to enlightenment—including even those who attacked and persecuted him. He therefore worked tirelessly to help women attain Buddhahood, irrespective of the storms of obstacles he encountered.

The Lotus Sutra teaches that men and women are equally noble and respectworthy. In "Teacher of the Law," the sutra's tenth chapter, the Buddha instructs good men and women to expound the Law in his stead after his passing.[22] And in "Bodhisattva Never Disparaging," its twentieth chapter, Bodhisattva Never Disparaging[23] shows equal reverence to all of the four kinds of believers—monks, nuns, laymen, and laywomen—eloquently attesting to the fact that women of every sphere, too, possess the Buddha nature and are worthy of praise and veneration.

For a long time in the history of Buddhism, however, this precious truth was forgotten and, as a result, women were caused great suffering. For that reason, by Nichiren dedicating his life to realizing the enlightenment of women, it can be said that he severed that misguided legacy and enacted a great transformation that revived Buddhism as a religion of true equality.

"There should be no discrimination among those who propagate the five characters of Myoho-renge-kyo[24] in the Latter Day of the Law, be they men or women" ("The True Aspect of All Phenomena," WND-1, 385). As these words indicate, the mission and the practice of Bodhisattvas of the Earth, who strive to lead all humanity to genuine happiness based on the Mystic Law, are firmly grounded in a view of humanity and the world in which both men and women are equal—that is, a philosophy of complete gender equality.

Our efforts for kosen-rufu today exactly accord with the spiritual struggle waged by Nichiren based on his vow to lead all people to enlightenment. There is no doubt that the development of our grass-roots people's movement, which inherits the original Buddhist spirit of respect for all human beings, will shine brightly in the future annals of history.

Appreciation for the Noble Struggles of Women Practitioners

Nevertheless, when I was exiled to the province of Sado, the constable of the province and the other officials, following the design of the ruler of the nation, treated me with animosity. . . . Every single steward and Nembutsu believer worthy of the name kept strict watch on my hut day and night, determined to prevent anyone from communicating with me. Never in any lifetime will I forget how in those circumstances you, with Abutsu-bo carrying a wooden container of food on his back, came in the night again and again to bring me aid. It was just as if my deceased mother had suddenly been reborn in the province of Sado! (WND-1, 932–33)

Here Nichiren reiterates his appreciation to Sennichi. While he was experiencing the extreme conditions of exile on Sado, she came to his aid and assistance despite great personal risk, based on a spirit of selfless dedication to her faith. So extraordinary were her efforts and devotion that he exclaims: "It was just as if my deceased mother had suddenly been reborn in the province of Sado!" And he further praises her, saying, "You . . . must be a woman who has made offerings to a hundred thousand million Buddhas" (WND-1, 933). He further lauds her constant devotion and support, which has remained unchanged

117

even after he moved far away from Sado, writing: "How great is your sincerity! It is firmer that the great earth, deeper than the great sea!" (WND-1, 933).

The dedicated faith and practice of the Daishonin's female disciples provided him with a strong source of support and protection as he conducted his activities as a votary of the Lotus Sutra. He genuinely valued and appreciated women's sensitivity, resourcefulness, consideration, care, and concern for others. It could be said that the noble wisdom and compassion of mothers manifest in the faith of women practitioners who strive to uphold and protect the Law.

So, in Nichiren's day, while there were women who, regardless of their social standing, clearly misinterpreted and distorted the Buddha's teaching and attacked the Daishonin out of ignorance, there were also a growing number of women who earnestly practiced Nichiren's teaching and took part in the struggle to share it widely with others. These practitioners were surely the greatest proof that steady progress was being made in efforts to propagate the Mystic Law in this evil age. They were proof that people dominated by the three poisons of greed, anger, and foolishness[25] were being guided to the path of Buddhahood and striving to elevate the life state of the entire nation.

The widespread propagation of the Mystic Law in the Latter Day is also a tenacious struggle to awaken one person after another to the mission of the Bodhisattvas of the Earth—a mission ultimately shared by all people.

The female followers striving alongside Nichiren were truly trailblazers of women's attainment of Buddhahood in the Latter Day; they could perhaps be regarded as pioneers of women's liberation.

Among them were young widows, bereaved mothers, childless women, wives who were caring for sick husbands or who were ill themselves, daughters-in-law who were nursing aged mothers-in-law, women who were worried about their husbands' inconsistent Buddhist practice, and the list goes on. All of them were valiantly challenging their own problems and karma as they continued to make efforts to share the Mystic Law with those around them. They waged a great struggle to show actual proof of the enlightenment of women as taught in Nichiren Buddhism. They changed from women who wept over their fate to women who brimmed with a sense of purpose and mission—women who proudly upheld the Mystic Law and displayed great wisdom and compassion through courage. As disciples, they believed wholeheartedly in the sincerity and integrity of the Daishonin and his wish for the happiness of all women, and they proudly walked the path of mission and true fulfillment that he taught.

As long as such a noble realm of mentor and disciple exists, genuine lasting happiness is certain to spread among women throughout the world.

❧

Caring for the Safety and Welfare of His Disciples

At the end of "The Sutra of True Requital," Nichiren Daishonin describes how concerned he has been for the welfare of his disciples. Not only were epidemics raging throughout the land and claiming many lives, but fear and uncertainty reigned due to the prospect of a second Mongol invasion.

The Daishonin especially was especially worried about the safety and welfare of his followers on distant Sado, who had risked their lives to support him during his exile there. Perhaps as a consequence of the widespread epidemics, the number of messengers bringing news to and from Sado may have decreased, for his correspondence with people on the island appears to have almost come to a complete halt. There are in fact no extant letters by Nichiren sent to followers on Sado during the previous year (1277). While praying for the well-being of his followers, he must nevertheless have felt a mounting sense of concern. Just at that time, Abutsu-bo unexpectedly visited the Daishonin's hermitage at Minobu. The first thing Nichiren did was ask about all his followers on Sado. Abutsu-bo replied that fortunately no one had fallen ill in the epidemic and that everyone was fine. Part of their exchange regarding the welfare of various individuals on Sado is recorded in this letter (see WND-1, 933–34).

The Daishonin was overjoyed to learn that everyone was safe and sound, writing, "When I heard all this, I felt as if I were a blind man who had recovered his sight, or as

if my deceased father and mother had come to me in a dream from the palace of King Yama,[26] and in that dream I had felt great joy" (WND-1, 934).

How moved Sennichi must have been to receive this letter overflowing with the Daishonin's warmth and thoughtful concern! I picture Nichiren writing about his conversation with Abutsu-bo and, while doing so, fondly calling to mind the smiling face of Sennichi, his "mother" on Sado Island, who would read his words.

A genuine mentor is constantly concerned about the health and safety of each disciple and always prays wholeheartedly for their development and growth.

I am convinced that the community of believers on Sado had developed to the extent it had because, through separated from the Daishonin by mountains and sea, their hearts were perfectly aligned and united with his. They thought only of their mentor and sought him single-mindedly.

Today, in an age that has seen the vibrant rebirth of Nichiren Buddhism through the efforts of the SGI, there are countless women like Sennichi—mothers of kosen-rufu—in Japan and around the world, who are supporting their fellow members with care and compassion and wisely fostering the development of the youth. They are noble and respectworthy without compare. I, too, offer my deepest appreciation for them with my palms pressed together in reverence.

The women of Soka, the mothers of kosen-rufu, could also be described as "mothers of the local community," who have helped pave the way to happiness for many women, and as "mothers of humanism," who have opened up the path for the enlightenment of women into the eternal future.

When the compassion of mothers everywhere illuminates all humanity, and when all humanity respects the wish for peace cherished by mothers everywhere, the very tenor of modern civilization will undergo a momentous change.

Today, our women's division members are drawing wide praise around the globe, and the members of our young women's Ikeda Kayo-kai are following brightly in their footsteps. They represent hope for humankind.

The sun of great hope has risen. My mentor, Mr. Toda, who declared that kosen-rufu would be achieved through the power of women, must be overjoyed. I can proudly report to him that a solid foundation has been laid for a century of respect for life, a century of women, and a century of peace.

"In order to repay my debt to my mother"— this vibrant pledge of the Daishonin to open the way for the enlightenment of all women is our pledge as members of Soka. It is our wish—no, it is our vow.

"We will build a society in which all mothers and children can live in happiness and peace!"—this is the purpose of kosen-rufu and the focus of establishing the correct teaching for the peace of the land. Now I wish to pass on to all of you the baton of our struggle to fulfill this great vow.

This lecture was originally published in the December 2010 issue of the Daibyakurenge, *the Soka Gakkai's monthly study journal.*

NOTES

1. Devotion to Amida Buddha Sutra: This is a reference to the Amida Sutra, which is not usually known by this name. The Daishonin may have referred to it this way to indicate its association with the Nembutsu, the chanting of Amida Buddha's name, a widespread practice in his day.

2. The fifth volume of the Lotus Sutra: It contains the "Devadatta" through the "Emerging from the Earth" chapters, the twelfth through fifteenth chapters.

3. Nichiren, here, is referring to Taira no Masakado (d. 940) and Abe no Sadato (1019–62). Masakado was a warrior who wielded power in eastern Japan. In 939, he rebelled against the imperial court by proclaiming himself the new emperor. He was killed and his rebellion crushed, however. Sadato headed a powerful family in eastern Japan. He sought independence from imperial rule but was defeated and killed in battle. The Daishonin writes: "Because these men caused a division between the people of their region and the sovereign, they were declared enemies of the imperial court and in the end were destroyed. Their plots and rebellions were worse than the five cardinal sins" (WND-1, 932).

4. Izu Exile: The Daishonin was exiled to Ito in Izu Province, from May 1261 through February 1263. In August 1260, a group of Nembutsu believers, infuriated at the Daishonin's criticism of the Pure Land school, attacked his dwelling at Matsubagayatsu in Kamakura in an attempt to assassinate him. The Daishonin narrowly escaped and fled to Toki Jonin's house in Shimosa Province. When he reappeared in Kamakura in the spring of 1261 and resumed his propagation activities, the government arrested him and, without due investigation, ordered him exiled to Ito. About two years after arriving in Izu, Nichiren was pardoned and returned to Kamakura.

5. *The Group of Discourses (Suttanipata),* trans. K. R. Norman (Oxford: The Pali Text Society, 1995), 2:17.

6. *Daimoku*: 1) The title of a sutra, in particular the title of the Lotus Sutra of the Wonderful Law (Jpn *Myoho-renge-kyo*). The title of a sutra represents the essence of the sutra. Miao-lo (711–82) says in *The Annotations on "The Words and Phrases of the Lotus Sutra,"* "When for the sake of brevity one mentions only the daimoku, or title, the entire sutra is by implication included therein." (2) The invocation of Nam-myoho-renge-kyo in Nichiren's teachings.

7. Dragon king's daughter: According to "Devadatta," the twelfth chapter of the Lotus Sutra, the dragon girl conceives the desire for enlightenment upon hearing Bodhisattva Manjushri preach the Lotus Sutra in the dragon king's palace. She then appears in front of the assembly of the Lotus Sutra and instantaneously attains Buddhahood in her present form.

8. Three thousand realms in a single moment of life: A doctrine the Great Teacher T'ien-t'ai derived from the Lotus Sutra. The principle that all phenomena

are contained within a single moment of life and that a single moment of life permeates the three thousand realms of existence, the entire phenomenal world.

9. Mutual possession of the Ten Worlds: The principle that each of the Ten Worlds possesses the potential for all ten within itself. "Mutual possession" means that life is not fixed in one or another of the Ten Worlds but can manifest any of the ten—from hell to Buddhahood—at any given moment. The important point of this principle is that all beings in any of the nine worlds possess the Buddha nature. This means that every person has the potential to manifest Buddhahood while a Buddha also possesses the nine worlds and in this sense is not separate or different from ordinary people.

10. Dengyo (767–822): The founder of the Tendai (T'ient'ai) school in Japan.

11. In *The Outstanding Principles of the Lotus Sutra,* Dengyo lists ten characteristics of the Lotus Sutra, in light of which he argues its supremacy over all other sutras. One of these characteristics is that the Lotus Sutra enables people to attain Buddhahood in their present form.

12. Perfect enlightenment: Also, supreme perfect enlightenment. The enlightenment of a Buddha. "Perfect enlightenment" also refers to the last and highest of the fifty-two stages of bodhisattva practice, or Buddhahood.

13. Gautami: Also known as Mahaprajapati. A younger sister of Maya, Shakyamuni's mother. When Maya died seven days after Shakyamuni's birth, Mahaprajapati became the consort of King Shuddhodana, Shakyamuni's father, and raised Shakyamuni. After Shuddhodana's death, Mahaprajapati renounced secular life, becoming the first nun to be admitted to the Buddhist Order.

14. Yashodhara: The wife of Shakyamuni before he renounced secular life. She was later converted to Buddhism by Shakyamuni and became a nun in the Buddhist Order.

15. Sado Exile: The Daishonin's exile to Sado Island in the Sea of Japan from October 1271 through March 1274. After Nichiren defeated the priest Ryokan of Gokuraku-ji, a temple in Kamakura, in a contest to pray for rain, Ryokan spread false rumors about Nichiren, using his influence with the wives and widows of high government officials. This led to the Daishonin's confrontation with Hei no Saemon, deputy chief of the Office of Military and Police Affairs, who arrested him and maneuvered to have him executed at Tatsunokuchi in September 1271. When the execution attempt failed, the authorities sentenced him to exile on Sado, which was tantamount to a death sentence. After Nichiren's predictions of internal strife and foreign invasion were fulfilled, however, the government issued a pardon in March 1274, and he returned to Kamakura.

16. In "The Opening of the Eyes," which he wrote while on Sado in February 1272, the Daishonin says: "I vowed to summon up a powerful and unconquerable desire for the salvation of all beings and never to falter in my efforts" (WND-1, 240); and "I will be the pillar of Japan. I will be the eyes of Japan. I will be the great ship of Japan. This is my vow, and I will never forsake it!" (WND-1, 280–81).

17. Dependent origination: Also, dependent causation or conditioned co-arising. A Buddhist doctrine expressing the interdependence of all things. It teaches that no beings or phenomena exist on their own; they exist or occur because of their relationship with other beings and phenomena. Everything in the world comes into existence in response to causes and conditions. That is, nothing can exist independent of other things or arise in isolation. The doctrine of the twelve-linked chain of causation is a well-known illustration of this idea.

18. Translated from Japanese: Josei Toda, *Toda Josei zenshu* (Collected Writings of Josei Toda) (Tokyo: Seikyo Shimbunsha, 1981), 1:60.

19. Arrogant false sages: One of the three powerful enemies who will persecute those who propagate the Lotus Sutra in the evil age after Shakyamuni's passing, as described in the Great Teacher Miao-lo's *Annotations on "The Words and Phrases of the Lotus Sutra."* Arrogant false sages are described as priests who pretend to be sages and who are revered as such, but when encountering the practitioners of the Lotus Sutra become fearful of losing fame or profit and induce secular authorities to persecute them.

20. This woman was also the widow of the regent Hojo Tokiyori and the daughter of the deceased Hojo Shigetoki. As such she wielded immense power behind the scenes.

21. See "On Repaying Debts of Gratitude," WND-1, 728.

22. The passage states, "Good men and good women should enter the Thus Come One's room, put on the Thus Come One's robe, sit in the Thus Come One's seat, and then for the sake of the four kinds of believers broadly expound this sutra" (LSOC, 205). There are also numerous passages elsewhere in the chapter that refer to men and women equally taking responsibility for propagating the Law.

23. Bodhisattva Never Disparaging: Said to be Shakyamuni in a previous lifetime. He deeply respected everyone, and his practice consisted of equally expressing respect to all he met, addressing the four kinds of believers in the following manner: "I have profound reverence for you, I would never dare treat you with disparagement or arrogance. Why? Because you will all practice the bodhisattva way and will then be able to attain Buddhahood" (LSOC, 308).

24. Myoho-renge-kyo is written with five Chinese characters, while Nam-myoho-renge-kyo is written with seven (*nam,* or *namu,* comprising two characters). The Daishonin often uses Myoho-renge-kyo synonymously with Nam-myoho-renge-kyo in his writings.

25. Three poisons of greed, anger, and foolishness: The fundamental evils inherent in life that give rise to human suffering. In the renowned Mahayana scholar Nagarjuna's *Treatise on the Great Perfection of Wisdom,* the three poisons are regarded as the source of all illusions and earthly desires. The three poisons are so called because they pollute people's lives and work to prevent them from turning their hearts and minds to goodness.

26. King Yama: In Chinese and Japanese Buddhism, Yama is regarded as the king of hell who judges and determines the rewards and punishments of the dead.

"KING RINDA"

VIBRANT CHANTING OPENS THE GREAT PATH
TO ABSOLUTE VICTORY

The Passage of Study for This Lecture

If we employ these five flavors[1] as similes for the various Buddhist teachings . . . the Agama sutras may be compared to the flavor of milk; the Meditation and the other sutras of the Correct and Equal period may be compared to the flavor of cream; the Wisdom sutras may be compared to the flavor of curdled milk; the Flower Garland Sutra may be compared to the flavor of butter; and the Immeasurable Meanings, Lotus, and Nirvana sutras may be compared to the flavor of ghee.

Again, if the Nirvana Sutra is compared to the flavor of ghee, then the Lotus Sutra may be compared to a lord who rules over the five flavors. Thus the Great Teacher Miao-lo[2] stated: "If we discuss the matter from the point of view of the doctrines taught, then the Lotus Sutra stands as the true lord of all the teachings, since it alone preaches 'opening the provisional and revealing the distant.'[3] This is the reason that it alone is permitted the word *myo,* or 'wonderful'[4] [in its title]."[5] He also said, "Therefore, we understand that the Lotus Sutra is the true lord of the ghee."

These passages of commentary point out quite rightly that the Lotus Sutra is not to be included among the five flavors. The main import of these passages is that the five flavors serve to nourish life, but life itself is lord over all the five flavors. (WND-1, 983)

The view that the various sutras . . . correspond to the five flavors, while the Lotus Sutra represents the lord of the five flavors—this is a doctrine that reflects the essential teaching. This doctrine was touched upon by T'ien-t'ai[6] and Miao-lo in their writings, but it was not clearly enunciated. This is why there are few scholars who are aware of it.

In the passage of commentary by Miao-lo quoted above, the words "If we discuss the matter from the point of view of the doctrines taught" refer to the daimoku,[7] or title, of the Lotus Sutra, which is what is meant by "the doctrines taught." The words "opening the provisional" correspond to the character *ge* in the five-character daimoku, Myoho-renge-kyo. The words "revealing the distant" correspond to the character *ren* in the five-character daimoku. The words "it alone is permitted the word *myo*" correspond to the character *myo*. And the words "This is the reason" refer to the fact that, when we speak of the Lotus Sutra as the essence of the lifetime teachings of the Buddha, we have in mind the daimoku of the Lotus Sutra. Therefore, one should understand that the daimoku of the Lotus Sutra represents the soul of all the sutras; it represents the eye of all the sutras. (WND-1, 984)

Bodhisattva Ashvaghosha addressed prayers to the Buddhas of the three existences and the ten directions, whereupon a white swan immediately appeared. When the white horses caught sight of the white swan, they whinnied in a single voice. No sooner had the king heard the single neigh of the horses than he opened his eyes. As two white swans, and then hundreds and thousands of them appeared, the hundreds and thousands of white horses were instantly filled with joy and began neighing. The king's complexion was restored to its original state, like the sun reemerging from an eclipse, and the strength of his body and the perceptive powers of his mind became many hundreds and thousands of times greater than they had been before. The consort was overjoyed, the great ministers and high officials took courage, the common people pressed their palms together in reverence, and the other countries bowed their heads. (WND-1, 986)

In a country where the three poisons [of greed, anger, and fool-ishness][8] prevail to such a degree, how can there be peace and stability?

In the kalpa of decline,[9] the three major calamities will occur, namely, the calamities of fire, water, and wind. And in the kalpa of decrease,[10] the three minor calamities will occur, namely, famine, pestilence, and warfare. Famine occurs as a result of greed, pestilence as a result of foolishness, and warfare as a result of anger.

At present the people of Japan number 4,994,828 men and women, all of them different persons but all alike infected by the three poisons. And these three poisons occur because of their relationship with Nam-myoho-renge-kyo. So all of these people at the same moment set out to curse, attack, banish, and do away with Shakyamuni, Many Treasures, and the Buddhas of the ten directions. This is what leads to the appearance of the three minor calamities.

And now I wonder what karma from past existences has caused Nichiren and his associates to become the proponents of the daimoku of the Lotus Sutra? It seems to me that at present Brahma, Shakra, the gods of the sun and moon, the four heavenly kings, the Sun Goddess, Great Bodhisattva Hachiman, and all the major and minor gods of the 3,132 shrines throughout Japan are like King Rinda of past times, that the white horses are Nichiren, and the white swans are my followers. The neighing of the white horses is the sound of our voices chanting Nam-myoho-renge-kyo. When Brahma, Shakra, the gods of the sun and moon, the four heavenly kings, and the others hear this sound, how could they fail to take on a healthy color and shine with a brilliant light? How could they fail to guard and protect us? We should be firmly convinced of this! (WND-1, 989–90)

LECTURE

"The daimoku of the Lotus Sutra represents the soul of all the sutras; it represents the eye of all the sutras," declares Nichiren Daishonin. The title of the Lotus Sutra—Nam-myoho-renge-kyo—is the heart of the entire body of the Buddha's teachings. It is the "essential Law"[11] of Nichiren Buddhism, which has the power to liberate all people from suffering on the most profound level.

Nam-myoho-renge-kyo is the ultimate law of the universe, the fundamental rhythm of life itself. Through the practice of chanting, we can bring forth our inner Buddhahood and increase the splendor and power of our lives.

Chanting Nam-myoho-renge-kyo with deep faith, even if just a single recitation, has infinitely vast and immeasurable power to revitalize our lives. Thus, amazing benefit is bound to manifest when we continue chanting day after day, assiduously summoning forth the power of faith and the power of practice. In light of the Daishonin's teachings, there is no doubt that our lives will be filled with limitless and inexhaustible good fortune and blessings.

In this chapter, we will study "King Rinda," in which Nichiren discusses the profound significance of the daimoku of the Lotus Sutra.

This letter, dated August 1279, is thought to have been addressed to Soya Doso. He, along with his father, Soya Kyoshin, was a dedicated follower of Nichiren in Shimosa Province (part of present-day Chiba Prefecture).

In this writing, the Daishonin emphasizes the tremendous mission and honor he and his followers share in chanting and propagating Nam-myoho-renge-kyo—the source of fundamental life force—at a time when the country is filled with great anxiety and turmoil at the prospect of a second Mongol invasion.

The Lotus Sutra Is the "Lord of the Five Flavors"

If we employ these five flavors as similes for the various Buddhist teachings . . . the Agama sutras may be compared to the flavor of milk; the Meditation and the other sutras of the Correct and Equal period may be compared to the flavor of cream; the Wisdom sutras may be compared to the flavor of curdled milk; the Flower Garland Sutra may be compared to the flavor of butter; and the Immeasurable Meanings, Lotus, and Nirvana sutras may be compared to the flavor of ghee.

Again, if the Nirvana Sutra is compared to the flavor of ghee, then the Lotus Sutra may be compared to a lord who rules over the five flavors. Thus the Great Teacher Miao-lo stated: "If we discuss the matter from the point of view of the doctrines taught, then the Lotus Sutra stands as the true lord of all the teachings, since it alone preaches 'opening the provisional and revealing the distant.' This is the reason

that it alone is permitted the word *myo,* or 'wonderful' [in its title]." He also said, "Therefore, we understand that the Lotus Sutra is the true lord of the ghee."

These passages of commentary point out quite rightly that the Lotus Sutra is not to be included among the five flavors. The main import of these passages is that the five flavors serve to nourish life, but life itself is lord over all the five flavors. (WND-1, 983)

✤

The view that the various sutras . . . correspond to the five flavors, while the Lotus Sutra represents the lord of the five flavors—this is a doctrine that reflects the essential teaching. This doctrine was touched upon by T'ien-t'ai and Miao-lo in their writings, but it was not clearly enunciated. This is why there are few scholars who are aware of it.

In the passage of commentary by Miao-lo quoted above, the words "If we discuss the matter from the point of view of the doctrines taught" refer to the daimoku, or title, of the Lotus Sutra, which is what is meant by "the doctrines taught." The words "opening the provisional" correspond to the character *ge* in the five-character daimoku, Myoho-renge-kyo. The words "revealing the distant" correspond to the character *ren* in the five-character daimoku. The words "it alone is permitted

the word *myo*" correspond to the character *myo.* And the words "This is the reason" refer to the fact that, when we speak of the Lotus Sutra as the essence of the lifetime teachings of the Buddha, we have in mind the daimoku of the Lotus Sutra. Therefore, one should understand that the daimoku of the Lotus Sutra represents the soul of all the sutras; it represents the eye of all the sutras. (WND-1, 984)

Wishing to clarify the beneficial power of chanting Nam-myoho-renge-kyo, Nichiren Daishonin begins this writing by demonstrating that the Lotus Sutra is supreme among all the sutras. He does this by presenting two views of the "five flavors," a metaphor used by T'ien-t'ai to rank the Buddha's teachings in terms of their relative merit or superiority.

According to the first view, the entire body of the sutras is categorized into five flavors, with the Immeasurable Meanings Sutra, the Lotus Sutra, and the Nirvana Sutra corresponding to ghee, the supreme flavor. The other, more profound, view is that the Lotus Sutra surpasses the category of ghee and is the "lord of the five flavors."

The five flavors are produced in the process of refining cow's milk—that is, fresh milk, cream, curdled milk, butter, and ghee. Though each of these products has a different flavor, variety of nutrients, and medicinal value, they all "serve to nourish life." In contrast to this, the "lord of the five flavors" refers to life itself—in other words, that which is nourished by the five flavors.

When it is ranked side by side with the other sutras, the Lotus Sutra is likened to ghee, the most refined form of cow's milk, because it has the unsurpassed power to lead all living beings to enlightenment. This indicates the aspect of bringing benefit to living beings by nourishing their lives. But when it is defined as the "lord of the five flavors," the Lotus Sutra represents the life of the Buddha, or Buddhahood, inherent in the lives of all living beings, which are nourished by the five flavors. In this sense it is viewed as being superior to all other sutras.

Nam-myoho-renge-kyo, which is the heart of the Lotus Sutra, is the ultimate Law of life by which all Buddhas attain enlightenment; it is the life of Buddhahood itself.

In various writings, Nichiren proclaims:

The daimoku of the Lotus Sutra represents the soul of all the sutras; it represents the eye of all the sutras.

The daimoku of the Lotus Sutra . . . is the very heart of all the eighty thousand sacred teachings of Buddhism and the eye of all the Buddhas. ("The Daimoku of the Lotus Sutra," WND-1, 141)

Nam-myoho-renge-kyo, the heart of the "Life Span" chapter, is the mother of all Buddhas throughout the ten directions and the three existences. ("The Essence of the 'Life Span' Chapter," WND-1, 184)

All the Buddhas of the three existences and the ten directions have invariably attained Buddhahood through the seeds represented by the five characters of Myoho-renge-kyo.[12] ("Letter to Akimoto," WND-1, 1015)

Nam-myoho-renge-kyo is not only the core of the Buddha's lifetime teachings, but also the heart, essence, and ultimate principle of the Lotus Sutra. ("'This Is What I Heard,'" WND-1, 860)

As we see in the above passages and other writings, Nam-myoho-renge-kyo is "the eye of all the Buddhas," "the mother of all Buddhas throughout the ten directions and the three existences," "the eye of all the sutras." It is "the core of the Buddha's lifetime teachings," "the heart of the Lotus Sutra" ("The Actions of the Votary of the Lotus Sutra," WND-1, 765), "the heart of the 'Life Span' chapter of the essential teaching" ("Letter to Shimoyana," WND-2, 688), and "the crux of the 'Life Span' chapter" (WND-2, 705). And it is the seed of Buddhahood, the great beneficial medicine for all humankind and the substance or reality of the Law.

Nichiren Daishonin was the first person in the Latter Day of the Law to awaken to and propagate the teaching of the Mystic Law, Nam-myoho-renge-kyo, which he embraced and embodied in his own life. Having fully awakened to the Mystic Law, he gave himself unstintingly to the struggle to widely spread Nam-myoho-renge-kyo into the eternal future of the Latter Day; and he triumphed over every obstacle he encountered along the way. In addition, he inscribed his own life, his enlightened life state of Buddhahood, in the form of a mandala that is the Gohonzon, the fundamental object of devotion for our Buddhist practice.

By centering our lives on the Gohonzon and chanting Nam-myoho-renge-kyo, which is the life of the Daishonin and the eye of all Buddhas, we can call forth the Nam-myoho-renge-kyo that exists within us and manifest the fundamental power of the Mystic Law.

In his commentary on Nichiren's treatise "The Object of Devotion for Observing the Mind," Nichikan, a great restorer of Nichiren Buddhism, writes: "When one embraces faith in this Gohonzon and chants Nam-myoho-renge-kyo, one's life itself at that moment becomes the object of devotion [Gohonzon] that embodies the three thousand realms in a single moment of life.[13] It becomes the life of Nichiren Daishonin."[14]

Nam-myoho-renge-kyo is the ultimate teaching that enables us to dispel the darkness of ignorance, bring forth the same boundless, wise, and compassionate life state of Buddhahood as the Daishonin, and develop indestructible happiness, while helping others do the same. Nichiren established this essential teaching for all people's enlightenment in the form of faith in and practice of Nam-myoho-renge-kyo.[15]

The Eye of All the Sutras

In this writing, basing his remarks on a commentary by the Great Teacher Miao-lo, Nichiren Daishonin goes on to explain why the Lotus Sutra is the "lord of the five flavors."

First, he states, the five characters of Myoho-renge-kyo that form the title of the Lotus Sutra constitute "the doctrines taught," or the essence of the sutra.

According to Miao-lo's commentary, the Lotus Sutra contains two of the most important teachings known as "opening the provisional" and "revealing the distant." The first is found in the theoretical teaching (first half) of the Lotus Sutra, and is more fully known as "opening the provisional and revealing the true." The second, meanwhile, is found in the essential teaching (latter half) of the Lotus Sutra and is more fully expressed as "opening the near and revealing the distant."

"Opening the provisional and revealing the true" means clarifying the purpose and limits of the provisional pre-Lotus Sutra teachings, which were expounded as expedient means, and disclosing the true teaching of the one Buddha vehicle, or the Mystic Law, which enables all living beings to attain enlightenment.

The main reason pre-Lotus Sutra teachings are designated as provisional expedients is because they teach that the Ten Worlds exist as distinct and separate realms, with an especially profound chasm separating the nine worlds and Buddhahood. These expedient teachings also deny the possibility of enlightenment for certain categories of individuals, such as the persons of the two vehicles (voice-hearers and cause-awakened ones), evil people (*icchantikas*, or persons of incorrigible disbelief), and women. In the

Lotus Sutra's theoretical teaching, however, the attainment of Buddhahood by people in these groups is elucidated. This demonstrates that the wisdom and benefit of the Buddha can be manifested in the lives of those dwelling in the nine worlds. Here the expedient means of instituting a distinction or separation between each of the Ten Worlds is discarded, and the lives of all living beings are viewed from the truth of the "mutual possession of the Ten Worlds."[16] This is what is meant by "opening the provisional."

The Daishonin states that "opening the provisional" corresponds to the character *ge* (flower) of *renge* (lotus flower) in Myoho-renge-kyo. *Renge* symbolizes the cause and effect of Buddhahood—with the character *ge* representing the cause and the character *ren* representing the effect. In Buddhism, our lives in the nine worlds are viewed as the cause for attaining the effect of Buddhahood. This is why Nichiren says "opening the provisional," which entails discarding the expedient teachings concerning the nine worlds, corresponds to *ge*.

Next, "opening the near and revealing the distant" refers to the fact that pre-Lotus Sutra teachings and the Lotus Sutra's theoretical teaching explain that Shakyamuni first attained enlightenment during his lifetime in India. "Life Span," the sixteenth chapter and part of the essential teaching, however, reveals that this is not so, that the Buddha actually attained enlightenment in the inconceivably remote past.

The Buddha who attained enlightenment in the remote past and was revealed in the essential teaching represents the true effect or fruit of Buddhahood. Even after attaining Buddhahood in the remote past, this Buddha never exists outside the nine realms, appearing in various forms in the nine worlds in order to help others attain Buddhahood.

Consequently, because the words "revealing the distant" refer to disclosing the true effect or fruit of Buddhahood, the Daishonin says that they correspond to the Chinese character *ren*, which symbolizes effect or fruit.

Thus, the two characters *renge* in Myoho-renge-kyo are expressions of two of the Lotus Sutra's most important teachings—namely, "opening the provisional" and "revealing the distant." They clarify that all living beings have the potential to manifest the power of *myo*, or the Mystic Law, that embodies the "mutual possession of the Ten Worlds" and the "simultaneity of cause and effect."[17] Because the Lotus Sutra possesses these mystic principles and functions that are inherent in the lives of all living beings, it alone has the character *myo* (wonderful or mystic) in its title.

In other words, "the doctrines taught" in the entire Lotus Sutra—which reveals that the lives of all living beings are entities of the Mystic Law—are contained within the five characters Myoho-renge-kyo. When we understand the Lotus Sutra in this way, the Daishonin says, we can see that the five characters of Myoho-renge-kyo are not only the essence of the Lotus Sutra but the "essence of the lifetime teachings of the Buddha," the very heart of Buddhism as a whole.

The Lotus Sutra thus reveals the truth that the lives of all livings beings embody the mystic principles and functions of the mutual possession of the Ten Worlds and the simultaneity of cause and effect. Because it presents this clear and undistorted picture of living beings—nourished by the five flavors—it is designated as the lord of the five flavors.

Myoho-renge-kyo is not simply the title of one particular sutra; it expresses the mystic principles and functions inherent in our lives. It is the Law that corresponds to the Buddha's intent or essence of his teachings directed toward guiding people to enlightenment. This is why Nichiren describes the title of the Lotus Sutra as the "soul of all the sutras" and "the eye of all the sutras."

Our Voices When Chanting Call Forth Our Fundamental Life Force

Bodhisattva Ashvaghosha addressed prayers to the Buddhas of the three existences and the ten directions, whereupon a white swan immediately appeared. When the white horses caught sight of the white swan, they whinnied in a single voice. No sooner had the king heard the single neigh of the horses than he opened his eyes. As two white swans, and then hundreds and thousands of them appeared, the hundreds and thousands of white horses were instantly filled with joy and began

neighing. The king's complexion was restored to its original state, like the sun reemerging from an eclipse, and the strength of his body and the perceptive powers of his mind became many hundreds and thousands of times greater than they had been before. The consort was overjoyed, the great ministers and high officials took courage, the common people pressed their palms together in reverence, and the other countries bowed their heads. (WND-1, 986)

Chanting Nam-myoho-renge-kyo is a joyous declaration that the boundless life state of Buddhahood is inherent in our lives. It is also a call to awaken others to this truth.

When Nam-myoho-renge-kyo is chanted powerfully and pervades everything, then all living beings in the Ten Worlds will be invigorated and society will be peaceful and secure. To illustrate this point, the Daishonin relates the Buddhist parable of King Rinda and the white horses,[18] which I would now like to summarize here.

There was once a wise and worthy ruler named King Rinda. When he heard white horses neighing, his life state was invigorated, and he flourished and thrived. As a result, his realm did too. The people were happy and secure, the weather was mild and seasonable, and the kingdom enjoyed peace with its neighbors. These white horses, however, only neighed when they saw white swans. So when all the white swans disappeared from the kingdom one day, the white horses ceased to neigh. As a result, the king and his people grew weak and listless, unpredictable weather visited the land, famines and epidemics occurred, and neighboring countries began to attack.

First, the king commanded non-Buddhist teachers to offer prayers, but the white swans did not return. Then, Bodhisattva Ashvaghosha came forth and prayed to the Buddhas of the three existences and the ten directions, whereupon the white swans immediately appeared, and the white horses began to neigh joyfully. King Rinda recovered from his feeble state, gaining countless times the physical strength and mental acuity he had before. The people were also revived, and peace and prosperity were restored to the kingdom.

The Daishonin employs this famous parable to illustrate the power of Nam-myoho-renge-kyo in easily accessible terms.

Later in this same writing, he declares: "The white horses are Nichiren, and the white swans are my followers. The neighing of the white horses is the sound of our voices chanting Nam-myoho-renge-kyo." And in another writing in which he refers to the story of King Rinda, "White Horses and White Swans," he says, "The white swans are the Lotus Sutra, the white horses are Nichiren, and the neighing of the white horses is the sound of Nam-myoho-renge-kyo" (WND-1, 1068). Though these two passages differ in the interpretation of the white swans that cause the horses to neigh, both clearly express the principle that the voices of practitioners of the Lotus Sutra chanting Nam-myoho-renge-kyo have the

innate power to awaken the fundamental life force of all living beings—that is, their Buddhahood, or Buddha nature.

In the letter "White Horses and White Swans," the Daishonin also writes that when King Rinda heard the white horses neighing, "his complexion became as bright as the sun, his skin as fresh-looking as the moon, his strength as powerful as the god Narayana,[19] and his plans for government as sagacious as those of the god Brahma" (WND-1, 1065). And in this writing, "King Rinda," Nichiren says, "The strength of his body and the perceptive powers of his mind became many hundreds and thousands of times greater than they had been before."

Our vibrant voices chanting Nam-myoho-renge-kyo give power and strength not only to the main tutelary gods of Buddhism, Brahma, and Shakra, but to all heavenly deities—the benevolent forces of the universe—activating and strengthening their protective functions. Chanting also moves all the Buddhas and bodhisattvas of the ten directions and three existences into action, and the functions of harmony and value creation will flourish in our communities and throughout the land.

We must remember the words "The voice does the Buddha's work" (see OTT, 4). Had the neighing of the white horses been weak and hesitant, King Rinda would probably not have regained his powers to the extent he did. Similarly, when it comes to chanting, it's important that we constantly strive to strengthen our faith and deepen our practice. Our conviction in faith and persistence in practice are the cornerstones of chanting.

Our invincible prayer—overflowing with the power of faith and the power of practice—can break through the darkness that shrouds our lives and the lives of others and call forth the magnificent dignity and strength of the Buddha nature that is inherent in all living beings. Through chanting, we can expand the realm of happiness and joy and bring forth a world filled ever more with the positive energy and peace of mind that is a reflection of Buddhahood.

Vibrantly Chanting Nam-myoho-renge-kyo to Our Heart's Content

The image of the neighing of the white horses, though just a metaphor, has something deeply significant to say about how we should chant. In other words, our chanting Nam-myoho-renge-kyo should be light, refreshing, and vibrant, like a noble steed galloping freely across the vast open plains.

It's also important that we chant honestly and openly, just as we are. All of us face times of worry, anguish, or sadness in our lives. When we do, we can feel free to go straight to the Gohonzon with our suffering and chant about it wholeheartedly, just like a child seeking its mother's warm embrace.

My mentor, second Soka Gakkai President Josei Toda, often said that there's no need for us to stand on ceremony when chanting about our problems; we just need to chant honestly to the Gohonzon, to truly look at what is in our hearts. The practice of chanting, he said, is the practice of manifesting the same life state as the Daishonin within us, so we should chant with the resolve to embody his state of life.

For example, if we've done something we regret, we can chant with a determination never to repeat the same mistake, making our prayer the first step toward a new and better future. When we face a decisive challenge, we can chant strongly and courageously with the firm resolve to win. When battling the three obstacles and the four devils,[20] we can chant with the heart of a lion king, filled with confidence that we'll vanquish those negative functions. When we're faced with the opportunity to transform our karma, we can infuse our prayer with an unwavering resolve not to be defeated. When we're happy about something, we can chant with a deep spirit of appreciation and gratitude. What matters is that we continue chanting Nam-myoho-renge-kyo throughout all, "regarding both suffering and joy as facts of life" (see "Happiness in This World," WND-1, 681), as the Daishonin teaches.

Chanting Nam-myoho-renge-kyo is the only way to truly polish our lives at the deepest level. Those who put chanting first can thoroughly polish their lives that have been clouded by darkness and make them shine like a bright mirror, reflecting the Dharma nature.[21] Chanting is a process of polishing and forging our lives, which is why our faith is so important.

Consequently, the benefit of chanting Nam-myoho-renge-kyo is absolutely not dependent on the amount we chant. What matters is that we chant to our own heart's content, the amount that feels right and satisfying for us. Nowhere in his writings does the Daishonin say we should chant a specific quantity. The efficacy of our prayers is influenced by the strength and depth of our faith and by our determination and attitude.

At the same time, sincerely resolving to chant a specific amount is also an expression of faith. We can chant the amount we've decided on each day, while continually renewing and deepening our resolve. Victory will undoubtedly come to those who persevere in the practice of chanting Nam-myoho-renge-kyo, diligently polishing their mirror day and night (see "On Attaining Buddhahood in This Lifetime," WND-1, 4),[22] just as the Daishonin urges.

Faith that ignores the importance of self-transformation; faith that lacks clear focus and determination, merely waiting for salvation from some external source; faith that abandons all striving and challenge out of fear and a desire to escape reality; faith that expects benefits to magically appear without making any personal effort—such faith is completely contrary to that which is taught in Nichiren Buddhism.

Chanting Nam-myoho-renge-kyo is our fundamental Buddhist practice for carrying out our human revolution, or inner transformation. To chant with a strong vow or commitment—thereby deepening our own determination and conviction, activating the protective functions of the universe and achieving absolute victory—is the essence of chanting in Nichiren Buddhism.

The Daishonin writes, "There is no true happiness for human beings other than chanting Nam-myoho-renge-kyo" ("Happiness in This World," WND-1, 681). Chanting brings us the infinitely profound and vast benefit of inner transformation. This is the greatest happiness—something that countless members of the SGI around the world today deeply recognize and savor. Just being able to chant Nam-myoho-renge-kyo—the supreme form of Buddhist practice and the source of unsurpassed joy—is in itself the greatest good fortune and benefit. There is no deeper joy or happiness in life.

The parable of King Rinda and the white horses teaches us that chanting has the power to unlock our innate life force and invigorate society with dynamism.

This latter function is related to the principle of "establishing the correct teaching for the peace of the land." Let us, therefore, now turn to a passage in the second half of this writing and examine the relationship between chanting and the realization of a peaceful and prosperous society.

The Three Poisons Intensify the Three Calamities

In a country where the three poisons [of greed, anger, and foolishness] prevail to such a degree, how can there be peace and stability?

In the kalpa of decline, the three major calamities will occur, namely, the calamities of fire, water, and wind. And in the kalpa of decrease, the three minor calamities will occur, namely, famine, pestilence, and warfare. Famine occurs as a result of greed, pestilence as a result of foolishness, and warfare as a result of anger.

At present the people of Japan number 4,994,828 men and women, all of them different persons but all alike infected by the three poisons. And these three poisons occur because of their relationship with Nam-myoho-renge-kyo. So all of these people at the same moment set out to curse, attack, banish, and do away with Shakyamuni, Many Treasures, and the Buddhas of the ten directions. This is what leads to the appearance of the three minor calamities. (WND-1, 989)

In a kalpa of decrease, when people's life force wanes, the three calamities of famine, pestilence, and warfare occur, and Nichiren Daishonin notes that there is a close connection between such calamities and the three poisons of greed, anger, and foolishness, which pollute people's lives. He writes,

"Famine occurs as a result of greed, pestilence as a result of foolishness, and warfare as a result of anger."

T'ien-t'ai says to the same effect in his *Words and Phrases of the Lotus Sutra:* "Because anger increases in intensity, strife of arms occurs. Because greed increases in intensity, famine arises. Because foolishness increases in intensity, pestilence breaks out" (OTT, 33). He also refers to how the three calamities arise owing to the prevalence of the three poisons and how these calamities then go on to intensify the three poisons in people's lives, thereby creating a vicious, never-ending cycle that leads to the age itself becoming polluted and degenerate. This, he says, describes the impurity of the age, one of the five impurities.[23]

In the Great Collection Sutra, the calamity of famine is expressed as "high grain prices" ("On Establishing the Correct Teaching for the Peace of the Land," WND-1, 10). This calamity is particularly caused by intensified greed in people's hearts, which eventually comes to dominate society as a whole. The Great Collection Sutra gives the example of powerful landowners with large agricultural estates who, during times of bad weather, think only of their own profits and, motivated by greed, monopolize resources such as water. This causes poor harvests for other small-scale farmers, which in turn leads to high grain prices and eventually high prices for all goods.

Unfortunately, even today in the twenty-first century—so far removed in time from the age when Shakyamuni expounded his teachings—this phenomenon of disaster caused by human greed remains. If anything, it now occurs on a global scale and has become an even more serious threat. And it is the ordinary people, the weak and unprotected, who suffer the most from famine, poverty, discrimination, and economic distress.

Epidemics, meanwhile, are said to be caused by the poison of foolishness. It's certainly true that even today, in spite of remarkable advances in scientific knowledge, many illnesses still spread because of our ignorance of their causes. Others spread because, though their causes have been identified, no effective treatment has been found. And in still other cases, the cause may be known and proven ways of preventing and treating the disease may exist, but disasters in the form of epidemics nevertheless occur because the proper steps cannot be taken due to economic or cultural reasons. In some instances, the scope of an epidemic is exacerbated by the folly of people thinking of profit first and failing to work together to swiftly deal with the problem at hand.

Warfare, lastly, is ascribed to the poison of anger. Anger, here, refers to the deep and intense feeling of rage and burning resentment that can arise from thwarted desires. There is a terrible destructive force in the fiery magma of anger that wells up at frustration, discrimination, betrayal, insult, or exploitation by others. When that suppressed negative energy explodes, it can manifest as violence or aggression and even escalate into warfare. These eruptions of hatred and malice in the forms of nationalism or of economic, ideological, or religious conflict are often the cause of war and armed conflict in our present age.

Nichiren Daishonin says that the entire population of Japan in his day has been infected by the three poisons arising from their hostility to the teaching of Nam-myoho-renge-kyo, and this is the cause of the three calamities.

In other words, the people of his time were guilty of "religious ignorance" (foolishness), because they failed to realize that through practicing erroneous Buddhist teachings they were slandering the Lotus Sutra, the teaching that reveals the Buddha's true intent. While they believed that they were practicing the teachings in earnest, in fact, they were disregarding the Buddha's fundamental spirit. And even when Nichiren pointed out this slander as he spread the correct teaching, they exhibited a kind of "religious greed," clinging even more persistently to the erroneous teachings in which they had placed their faith. On top of that, they were filled with a "religious anger," hating and despising the Daishonin as a foe and attacker, though in fact he was the votary of the Lotus Sutra propagating Nam-myoho-renge-kyo for the enlightenment of all people.

In the age Nichiren lived the three calamities were constantly occurring in various forms. Nam-myoho-renge-kyo is the source of the life force of the universe and the seed for attaining Buddhahood. The Daishonin declares that the increased confusion of the times was being caused by slander of the Mystic Law, which was polluting the lives of the Japanese people with the three poisons of greed, anger, and foolishness.

The Driving Force for Establishing the Correct Teaching for the Peace of the Land

And now I wonder what karma from past existences has caused Nichiren and his associates to become the proponents of the daimoku of the Lotus Sutra? It seems to me that at present Brahma, Shakra, the gods of the sun and moon, the four heavenly kings, the Sun Goddess, Great Bodhisattva Hachiman, and all the major and minor gods of the 3,132 shrines throughout Japan are like King Rinda of past times, that the white horses are Nichiren, and the white swans are my followers. The neighing of the white horses is the sound of our voices chanting Nam-myoho-renge-kyo. When Brahma, Shakra, the gods of the sun and moon, the four heavenly kings, and the others hear this sound, how could they fail to take on a healthy color and shine with a brilliant light? How could they fail to guard and protect us? We should be firmly convinced of this! (WND-1, 989–90)

Nichiren Daishonin notes that the country and the people have fallen into a negative cycle of the three poisons fueling the three calamities that threatens their very existence—a cycle set in motion through the error of misguidedly upholding erroneous teachings while slandering the correct teaching. To save Japan from this destructive course, the Daishonin called on people to chant and propagate Nam-myoho-renge-kyo—the Mystic Law that is the fundamental source of life force and the heart of the Lotus Sutra, the "lord of the five flavors."

Nichiren returns to the story of King Rinda, mentioned earlier. He asserts that just as the neighing of the white horses, sustained by the white swans, revived King Rinda and restored vigor and prosperity to his kingdom and its people, the sound of Nichiren and his followers chanting Nam-myoho-renge-kyo will increase the strength and brilliance of the benevolent forces of the universe and definitely activate their protective functions.

Even when the very survival of the country and its people is in question, those who confidently chant and propagate the Mystic Law can tap the fundamental life force of the universe in their own lives and stand up as agents of positive change in such a time of peril.

In this passage, the followers who are likened to white swans are none other than a gathering of disciples who are just such agents of change. Following the lead of their teacher, the Daishonin, who embodied the fundamental transformative power of the Mystic Law and stood up to open the way to enlightenment for all people, they chanted Nam-myoho-renge-kyo with the same strong conviction as he and taught others to do the same.

Our mission as practitioners of the Lotus Sutra in the Latter Day who chant Nam-myoho-renge-kyo is to employ this great beneficial medicine of the Mystic Law to win a decisive victory in the battle against the ever-intensifying maladies caused by the three poisons. As the Daishonin writes, "In the final analysis, unless we succeed in demonstrating that this teaching is supreme, these disasters will continue unabated" ("The Treatment of Illness," WND-1, 1114).

The more troubled and confused the times, the more powerful the unity of the oneness of mentor and disciple becomes. When mentor and disciple are united in chanting Nam-myoho-renge-kyo, it becomes the most powerful means for overcoming negative karma, dispelling the dark clouds looming over society and achieving the ideal of "establishing the correct teaching for the peace of the land." Chanting is the fundamental force for transforming karma. No matter how heavy the chains of karma, we can break free of them through the mystic function of chanting Nam-myoho-renge-kyo, which brings forth the inherent power of our life.

Nam-myoho-renge-kyo is the power source for human revolution. When we activate our innate Buddhahood through chanting and fully experience that free and uplifting state of life, we can realize the most expansive life condition in which we savor the "greatest of all joys" (OTT, 212).

Chanting Nam-myoho-renge-kyo is the driving force for "establishing the correct teaching for the peace of the land." The ripples of joy stirred in our lives through chanting instantly spread out to encompass the entire universe. Consequently, they cannot fail to create ripples of joy in the hearts of all living beings and to bring joy to our families, communities, and societies.

We who chant based on the shared vow of mentor and disciple and dedicate our lives to kosen-rufu have absolutely nothing to fear. Let's boldly and vigorously stride forward on the great path of absolute victory, filled with self-confidence and vitality, as we chant vibrantly day after day and year after year.

This lecture was originally published in the January 2011 issue of the Daibyakurenge, *the Soka Gakkai's monthly study journal.*

NOTES

1. Five flavors: The flavors of fresh milk, cream, curdled milk, butter, and ghee. In the Mahaparinirvana Sutra, Shakyamuni says: "Good man, milk comes from the cow, cream is made from milk, curdled milk is made from cream, butter is made from curdled milk, and ghee is made from butter. Ghee is the finest of all. One who eats it will be cured of all illnesses, just as if all kinds of medicinal properties were contained in it." The Great Teacher T'ien-t'ai of China used these five flavors as a metaphor for his doctrine of the five periods. The "five periods" is a classification of Shakyamuni's entire body of teachings according to the order in which T'ien-t'ai believed they were expounded. They are the Flower Garland period, the Agama period, the Correct and Equal period, the Wisdom period, and the Lotus and Nirvana period. T'ien-t'ai compared this process by which Shakyamuni instructed his disciples and elevated their understanding to the process of converting milk into ghee.
2. Miao-lo (711–82): A patriarch of the T'ien-t'ai school in China. He is revered as the school's restorer.
3. "Opening the provisional and revealing the distant" are the abbreviated forms of the two doctrines of "opening the provisional and revealing the true" and "opening the near and revealing the distant," respectively.
4. The Japanese title of the Lotus Sutra is *Myoho-renge-kyo,* which literally translates as the Lotus Sutra of the Wonderful Law. The Chinese character *myo* means not only wonderful but also mystic and unfathomable.
5. From Miao-lo's *The Annotations on "Great Concentration and Insight."*
6. T'ien-t'ai (538–97): The founder of the T'ien-t'ai school in China. Commonly referred to as the Great Teacher

T'ien-t'ai. His lectures were compiled in such works as *The Profound Meaning of the Lotus Sutra, The Words and Phrases of the Lotus Sutra,* and *Great Concentration and Insight.* He spread the Lotus Sutra in China and established the doctrine of three thousand realms in a single moment of life.

7. Daimoku: 1) The title of a sutra, in particular the title of the Lotus Sutra of the Wonderful Law (Jpn *Myoho-renge-kyo*). The title of a sutra represents the essence of the sutra. Miao-lo (711–82) says in *The Annotations on "The Words and Phrases of the Lotus Sutra,"* "When for the sake of brevity one mentions only the daimoku, or title, the entire sutra is by implication included therein." (2) The invocation of Nam-myoho-renge-kyo in Nichiren's teachings.

8. Three poisons of greed, anger, and foolishness: The fundamental evils inherent in life that give rise to human suffering. In the renowned Mahayana scholar Nagarjuna's *Treatise on the Great Perfection of Wisdom,* the three poisons are regarded as the source of all illusions and earthly desires. The three poisons are so called because they pollute people's lives and work to prevent them from turning their hearts and minds to goodness.

9. Kalpa of decline: The period of time during which a world decays; one of the four stages in the cycle of formation, continuance, decline, and disintegration. A kalpa is an immeasurably long period of time.

10. Kalpa of decrease: A period in which the human life span diminishes. In the kalpa of continuance, the life span of human beings is said to repeatedly undergo a pattern of decrease and increase. Any period of diminution is called a kalpa of decrease.

11. See OTT, 242–43.

12. Myoho-renge-kyo is written with five Chinese characters, while Nam-myoho-renge-kyo is written with seven (*nam*, or *namu*, comprising two characters). The Daishonin often uses Myoho-renge-kyo synonymously with Nam-myoho-renge-kyo in his writings.

13. Three thousand realms in a single moment of life: A doctrine developed by T'ien-t'ai based on the Lotus Sutra. The principle that all phenomena are contained within a single moment of life and that a single moment of life permeates the three thousand realms of existence, or the entire phenomenal world.

14. Translated from Japanese. *Commentary on "The Object of Devotion for Observing the Mind,"* in *Nichikan Shonin mondanshu* [Commentaries of Nichikan Shonin] (Tokyo: Seikyo Shimbunsha, 1980), 548.

15. The daimoku of the essential teaching (i.e., Nam-myoho-renge-kyo) has two aspects: the daimoku of faith and the daimoku of practice. The former means to believe in the Gohonzon, and the latter means to chant Nam-myoho-renge-kyo and spread it.

16. Mutual possession of the Ten Worlds: The principle that each of the Ten Worlds possesses the potential for all ten within itself. "Mutual possession" means that life is not fixed in one of the Ten Worlds but can manifest any of the ten—from hell to the state of Buddhahood—at any given moment. The important point of this principle is that all beings in any of the nine worlds possess the Buddha nature.

17. Simultaneity of cause and effect: This means that cause (the nine worlds) and effect (Buddhahood) simultaneously exist in one's life. See *The Soka Gakkai Dictionary of Buddhism* for more detail.

18. Recounted in Nagarjuna's *Commentary on the Mahayana Treatise.* The story is supposedly set in a previous lifetime of Ashvaghosha, a Mahayana scholar and poet.

19. Narayana: Originally the god Vishnu in Hindu mythology. He was incorporated into Buddhism as a protective deity said to possess great physical strength, and thus he appears as a symbol of strength in Buddhist scriptures.

20. Three types of obstacles that obstruct Buddhist practice and four types of devils. The three obstacles are (1) the obstacle of earthly desires, (2) the obstacle of karma, and (3) the obstacle of retribution. The four devils are (1) the hindrance of the five components, (2) the hindrance of earthly desires, (3) the hindrance of death, and (4) the hindrance of the devil king.

21. Dharma nature: Also, fundamental nature of enlightenment: The unchanging nature inherent in all things and phenomena. It is identified with the fundamental Law itself, the essence of the Buddha's enlightenment, or ultimate truth.

22. In "On Attaining Buddhahood in This Lifetime," the Daishonin writes: "A mind now clouded by the illusions of the innate darkness of life is like a tarnished mirror, but when polished, it is sure to become like a clear mirror, reflecting the essential nature of phenomena and the true aspect of reality. Arouse deep faith, and diligently polish your mirror day and night. How should you polish it? Only by chanting Nam-myoho-renge-kyo" (WND-1, 4).

23. Five impurities: Also, five defilements. Impurity of the age, of desire, of living beings, of thought (or view), and of life span. This term appears in the "Expedient Means," the second chapter of the Lotus Sutra. (1) Impurity of the age includes repeated disruptions of the social or natural environment. (2) Impurity of desire is the tendency to be ruled by the five delusive inclinations, i.e., greed, anger, foolishness, arrogance, and doubt. (3) Impurity of living beings is the physical and spiritual decline of human beings. (4) Impurity of thought, or impurity of view, is the prevalence of wrong views such as the five false views. (5) Impurity of life span is the shortening of the life spans of living beings.

9

"THE KALPA OF DECREASE"

NICHIREN DAISHONIN'S BUDDHISM: WISDOM FOR REALIZING HAPPINESS FOR ALL HUMANITY

The Passage for Study in This Lecture

The present age is such that neither the non-Buddhist scriptures, the Hinayana sutras, the Mahayana sutras, nor the one vehicle of the Lotus Sutra has any effect. The reason is that the enormity of the greed, anger, and foolishness in people's hearts is equal to the superiority of the World-Honored One of Great Enlightenment in great good. . . . The extremity of greed, anger, and foolishness in people's hearts in the impure world of the latter age makes it difficult for any worthy or sage to control.

This is because, though the Buddha cured greed with the medicine of the meditation on the vileness of the body,[1] healed anger with the meditation on compassion for all,[2] and treated foolishness with the meditation on the twelve-linked chain of causation,[3] teaching these doctrines now makes people worse and compounds their greed, anger, and foolishness. . . .

Now in this latter, evil age, great evil arises less from secular wrongdoing than in connection with the doctrines of the religious world. When people today, who are unaware of this, endeavor to cultivate roots of good, events that lead to the ruin of the world occur all the more. Although superficially it may seem to be an act of good to provide support to the priests of the Tendai, True Word, and other schools of the present age, in reality it is a great evil surpassing even the five cardinal sins[4] and the ten evil acts.[5]

For this reason, in order that peace reign in the age, if a wise man existed in the world with wisdom like that of the World-Honored One of Great Enlightenment, and if he met with a worthy ruler like King Sen'yo[6]; and if together they devoted themselves to putting an end to these acts of good and committed the great evil of censuring, banishing, cutting off alms to, or even beheading those persons of the eight schools[7] who are thought to be men of wisdom, then the age may be pacified to some extent.

This is explained in the first volume of the Lotus Sutra where it says, "The true aspect of all phenomena can only be understood and shared between Buddhas." In the phrase "consistency from beginning to end," "beginning" indicates the root of evil and the root of good, and "end" indicates the outcome of evil and the outcome of good. One who is thoroughly awakened to the nature of good and evil from their roots to their branches and leaves is called a Buddha. . . . The Lotus Sutra states, "[The doctrines that they preach . . .] will never be contrary to the true [aspect]."[8] T'ien-t'ai commented on this, saying that "no worldly affairs of life or work are ever contrary to the true [aspect]." A person of wisdom is not one who practices Buddhism apart from worldly affairs but, rather, one who thoroughly understands the principles by which the world is governed.

When the Yin dynasty became corrupt and the people were suffering, T'ai-kung Wang[9] appeared in the world and beheaded King Chou of the Yin, bringing an end to the people's misery. When the Second Emperor of the Ch'in dynasty[10] caused the people to taste bitterness, Chang Liang[11] appeared and restored order to the world, enabling them to know sweetness. Though these men lived before the introduction of Buddhism, they helped the people as emissaries of Shakyamuni Buddha, the lord of teachings. And though the adherents of the non-Buddhist scriptures were unaware of it, the wisdom of such men contained at heart the wisdom of Buddhism. . . .

Great evil portends the arrival of great good. If all of Jambudvipa were to be thrown into chaos, there could be no doubt that [this sutra would] "be widely propagated throughout Jambudvipa."[12] (WND-1, 1120–22)

LECTURE

One day, my mentor, Josei Toda, and I were talking about the Soka Gakkai's mission to widely propagate the Mystic Law, and I asked him why it was important to strive in faith with the spirit of "not begrudging one's life"[13] taught in the Lotus Sutra. He replied to the effect:

On our planet, people kill each other in wars; our economies are based on the survival of the fittest, and do not necessarily lead to human happiness; and many of society's leaders, who by rights ought to help others, instead often look down on and exploit people. And the same kind of thing is found in such spheres as politics, science, and religion. Call it humanity's karma, but society is complex and full of contradictions. Nowhere there can we find the fundamental path to happiness for all people.

Only Nichiren Daishonin's Buddhism sets forth the means for fundamentally transforming our karma. It teaches the path of eternity, happiness, true self, and purity,[14] the path of lasting fulfillment and satisfaction. There is no higher path in life than this. That is why, if you give your all for the sake of faith, you will never regret it.

Deeply moved by Mr. Toda's words, I renewed my determination to give my all in pursuing this unparalleled path in life just as he taught.

There is no more exciting, satisfying, or meaningful way to spend one's life than dedicating it to the noble cause of realizing happiness for all humanity.

"The Kalpa of Decrease," the writing we will study in this chapter, affirms that putting into practice the teachings of Nichiren Buddhism constitutes the "fundamental path to happiness for all people."

A "kalpa of decrease"[15] refers to a period when people's vitality or life force wanes both spiritually and physically, owing to the three poisons of greed, anger, and foolishness[16] intensifying in their lives. The present era in which we find ourselves is regarded as belonging to a kalpa of decrease.

In such an age, the wisdom of Nichiren

Buddhism is indispensable if we are to live with strength and integrity, unaffected by the three poisons, and achieve true happiness. This is because Nichiren Buddhism offers profound and perceptive insights into how we can overcome the inner delusions—characterized by the three poisons—that are the root cause of unhappiness.

This writing titled "The Kalpa of Decrease" is thought to have been composed after the death of the lay priest Takahashi Rokuro Hyoe,[17] a follower of the Daishonin who lived in Suruga Province,[18] and addressed to someone close to him. Some scholars have suggested that it was sent to a family member or relative of Takahashi's who was a fellow practitioner in Suruga (someone like the lay priest of Nishiyama,[19] for instance). In any case, from the content of the letter, which frankly lays out the essence of the problems then facing the country, it seems most likely that the recipient was a member of the warrior class.

The letter's date has been placed around 1276, sometime after the first Mongol invasion (of 1274). The lay priest Takahashi had been a follower of strong faith who sincerely sought out the Daishonin's teaching. In the letter, the Daishonin says that he had personally wanted to go and perform a memorial service at Takahashi's grave after his passing. But during the Kamakura period, Suruga Province was directly controlled by the Hojo clan [many of whose members, as followers of existing Buddhist schools, were hostile toward the Daishonin's teachings]. If he were to travel there, he notes, it would most certainly cause trouble for his followers in the region; so, instead, he decided to send a disciple to recite the verse section[20] of "Life Span," the sixteenth chapter of the Lotus Sutra at Takahashi's grave on his behalf (see WND-1, 1122).[21] The Daishonin always showed the utmost concern for the safety and well-being of his followers.

At that time, a sense of impending crisis filled the land, as fears spread that another attack by the Mongol forces would bring about the destruction of Japan. People felt immense anxiety and didn't know where to turn.

The Kamakura military government had ordered the True Word and other established Buddhist schools of the day to conduct prayers for the defeat of the enemy, and the general populace was also placing great faith in these prayers. The various schools all complied with the government's directive in the hopes of gaining official reward for their efforts. Even non-Buddhist religious teachers and divination masters were said to have participated.

In other words, the nation's rulers, the religious establishment, and the people were all filled with fear and uncertainty—the epitome of a doomed nation whose populace was controlled by greed, anger, and foolishness.

In this letter, the Daishonin outlines how, in the Latter Day of the Law, the negative influence of the life-sapping three poisons had been strengthened and reinforced as a result of the teachers of various erroneous schools appropriating and misusing the wisdom of great good expounded in the sutras by Shakyamuni Buddha. This grave error of slander—of confusing and corrupting the Buddha's teaching—the Daishonin asserts, was the prime reason why the nation was headed toward ruin.

As a result, he writes, even the wisdom of great good of Shakyamuni taught in the sutras could not withstand the magnitude of greed, anger, and foolishness of the people of the Latter Day. None of the wisdom of the pre-Lotus Sutra teachings—not even the wisdom of the one vehicle[22] of the Lotus Sutra—were effective against it. It was thus also a time of the most urgent crisis for Buddhism itself.

However, the Daishonin conveys the powerful conviction that this was precisely the time for a "wise person," possessing wisdom of great good like that of Shakyamuni Buddha, to appear and work together with a "worthy ruler" to eradicate error and ultimately actualize the widespread propagation of the Law throughout the world.

We can read this as meaning that the wisdom of the correct teaching can, through the efforts of people of wisdom, be manifested in society as a force that benefits all and generates a great wave of positive change. His position is that this is the only way to free humanity from the scourge of greed, anger, and foolishness in the Latter Day of the Law.

In the treatise "The Object of Devotion for Observing the Mind," the Daishonin also discusses how the four leaders of the Bodhisattvas of the Earth[23] appear in the form of wise Buddhist practitioners and worthy rulers.[24]

In "The Kalpa of Decrease," he goes on to state that a true person of wisdom in the realm of Buddhism is one who practices the correct teaching in society in order to realize the happiness of all people (see WND-1, 1121).[25]

In the letter, the Daishonin explains that the correct teaching of Buddhism provides the wisdom for curing the three poisons and actualizing happiness for all people and peace throughout the land, which the Lotus Sutra reveals is the true intent or purpose of the Buddha's preaching. The people of the evil latter age, however, lost sight of the fundamental intent articulated in that sutra. Instead, they embraced partial or expedient provisional teachings of the Buddha, which then turned into harmful influences that only exacerbated the greed, anger, and foolishness in people's hearts. It was at such a time that a person of wisdom appeared and boldly took action to achieve the original aim of Buddhism, which is to enable all people to attain enlightenment. This person possessed the true wisdom of the correct teaching of Buddhism and the power to implement that wisdom in society for the benefit of all.

"The Kalpa of Decrease" identifies Nichiren Daishonin as this true person of wisdom who appears in the Latter Day. He has the dedication, practical ability, and leadership to guide all people to genuine happiness and to actualize the widespread propagation of the Mystic Law.

The Intensity of Three Poisons in the Latter Day of the Law

The present age [of the Latter Day of the Law] is such that neither the non-Buddhist scriptures, the Hinayana sutras, the Mahayana sutras, nor the one vehicle of the Lotus Sutra has any effect. The reason is that the enormity of the greed, anger, and foolishness in people's hearts is equal to the superiority of the World-Honored One of Great Enlightenment [Shakyamuni Buddha] in great good. . . . The extremity of greed, anger, and foolishness in people's hearts in the impure world of the latter age makes it difficult for any worthy or sage to control.

This is because, though the Buddha cured greed with the medicine of the meditation on the vileness of the body, healed anger with the meditation on compassion for all, and treated foolishness with the meditation on the twelve-linked chain of causation, teaching these doctrines now makes people worse and compounds their greed, anger, and foolishness. (WND-1, 1120–21)

In this writing, the Daishonin indicates that the three poisons of greed, anger, and foolishness are the fundamental evil that weakens people's vitality or life force. Because these poisons intensified in the Latter Day of the Law, the influence of people's "evil wisdom" had come to outstrip that of the "good wisdom" of Buddhism (see WND-1, 1120).

Shakyamuni expounded numerous teachings for overcoming the three poisons. The Daishonin explains, however, that in the defiled age of the Latter Day of the Law, the evil in people's hearts arising from these poisons had increased to the extent where it could no longer be subdued by the teachings of any worthy or sage. For example, in earlier times, people followed the Buddha's teaching that greed could be overcome by meditating on the vileness of the body, anger by meditating on universal compassion, and foolishness by meditating on the twelve-linked chain of causation. But the Daishonin explains that in the Latter Day, not only were these practices ineffective, but they also actually had the reverse effect of increasing the intensity of people's greed, anger, and foolishness. In other words, trying to treat harmful ills without understanding their fundamental causes only made them worse.

Nichiren declares that, in the Latter Day, the three poisons could not be controlled even by the wisdom of great good of Shakyamuni expounded in the teachings thus far. This was because, although people followed Shakyamuni's teachings, their attachment to partial or expedient provisional doctrines had caused them to lose sight of the all-important aims of universal enlightenment and overcoming suffering that are the Buddha's true intent. In the Latter Day, the Daishonin notes, these teachings of Shakyamuni no longer had the power to make positive use of and spread the wisdom of Buddhism and revitalize people's lives and society as a whole.

When we come to deeply understand the Buddha's intent of universal enlightenment as articulated in the Lotus Sutra, we realize how important it is for each of us to develop our full potential and take action for kosen-rufu, which carries the struggle of human revolution forward from one person to another.

I've met and spoken with many leading world thinkers, most of who agree that the fundamental solution to the crises facing our world must ultimately start with the inner transformation of human beings themselves. Naturally, we also need to take concrete and speedy measures to effectively deal with the many problems confronting us. In this respect, it is more important than ever for economists, lawmakers, educators, and leaders in every field who are genuinely committed to people's welfare to make concerted efforts to pool their creativity and wisdom toward that end.

On a still more fundamental level, however, humanity is seeking a philosophy and practical means for vanquishing the deep-rooted deluded impulses of greed, anger, and foolishness. It is imperative that we ourselves as human beings change.

A Person of Wisdom and a Worthy Ruler Acting in Tandem for the People's Welfare

Now in this latter, evil age, great evil arises less from secular wrongdoing than in connection with the doctrines of the religious world. When people today, who are unaware of this, endeavor to cultivate roots of good, events that lead to the ruin of the world occur all the more. Although superficially it may seem to be an act of good to provide support to the priests of the Tendai, True Word, and other schools of the present age, in reality it is a great evil surpassing even the five cardinal sins and the ten evil acts.

For this reason, in order that peace reign in the age, if a wise man existed in the world with wisdom like that of the World-Honored One of Great Enlightenment, and if he met with a worthy ruler like King Sen'yo and if together they devoted themselves to putting an end to these acts of good and committed the great evil of censuring, banishing, cutting off alms to, or even beheading those persons of the eight schools [of Buddhism] who are thought to be [persons] of wisdom, then the age may be pacified to some extent. (see WND-1, 1121)

Here, Nichiren asserts that error in the realm of Buddhism causes more harm and suffering to the people than wrongdoing in the secular realm. He denounces the Buddhist schools in Japan of his day for espousing erroneous teachings that contributed to the misfortunes of the people. These schools, he said, were guilty of slandering the Law by going against the Buddha's intent set forth in the Lotus Sutra—that is, discrediting the teaching that all people have the potential to attain enlightenment.

Shakyamuni's basic wish was to enable all human beings to attain Buddhahood, as expressed most succinctly in his great vow in the Lotus Sutra "to make all persons equal to me, without any distinction between us" (LSOC, 70). The essence of this Buddhist ideal is for us to recognize all people can bring forth their infinitely noble Buddha nature and, based on that, to respect each other and build a peaceful society.

Strictly speaking, the pre-Lotus Sutra teachings also elucidated, at least partially, this ideal of respect for human dignity. By rights, the wisdom of Buddhism in its entirety ought to stand as a great bastion of humanistic religion that contributes richly to humanity. Unfortunately, during the Daishonin's day, the existing Buddhist schools had lost sight of the Buddha's true intent and the fundamental ideals of Buddhism. They had become attached to partial or provisional teachings from the sutras expounded prior to the Lotus Sutra. Moreover, in the process of touting the teachings of their own schools as the ultimate truth of Buddhism, they slandered the Lotus Sutra and rejected the Buddhist wisdom that teaches respect for all human beings.

The clergy of these schools displayed the characteristics of "arrogant priests" and "arrogant false sages"—two of the three powerful enemies[26] (the other one being "arrogant lay believers"). They harbored intense enmity toward the Daishonin, the votary of the Lotus Sutra, much like the four kinds of believers (monks, nuns, laymen, and laywomen) who persecuted Bodhisattva Never Disparaging[27] in the Lotus Sutra.

The lay followers of the various Buddhist schools, however, were taken in by the priests' religious authority and appearance of respectability and failed to see the true situation. As a result, though they thought they were accumulating good causes through their Buddhist practice, they were in fact, frighteningly enough, steeping themselves in the poison of slander of the Law. It was as if the healing medicine that people thought they had been prescribed was actually toxic. This is the meaning of "Great evil arises . . . in connection with the doctrines of the religious world."

The Daishonin indicates that the only way for this situation to be remedied was for a wise person possessing the wisdom of the correct teaching and a worthy ruler to join together to put a stop to this great evil.

A wise person with "wisdom like that of the World-Honored One of Great Enlightenment" could recognize slander of the Law committed by the erroneous Buddhist schools of the day. This person could discern the true nature of their priests, combat that evil, and restore the ideal of respect for all people that is the original aim of Buddhism.

This person, joining together with a worthy ruler possessing excellent powers of judgment concerning right and wrong, worked to repudiate misguided teachings and principles that only ultimately cause people suffering. This was the path to genuinely leading people to enlightenment and creating a secure and prosperous society.

A true person of wisdom in the Latter Day of the Law must embody not only the great good wisdom of the correct Buddhist teaching but also be able to detect error, fight against it, and strive earnestly to free people from the hold of false teachings. Nichiren stood up as that person to engage in this struggle without begrudging his life. He was determined to convey the fearful nature of slander of the Law to the people of Japan. Undeterred by any obstacles or persecution, the Daishonin continued his efforts to educate people to the fact that the seemingly devout, self-renouncing priests of the day were actually guilty of the great evil of destroying Buddhism.

But the times only grew darker as even the Tendai school—which was originally based on the Lotus Sutra and should have protected that teaching—succumbed to the influence of the esoteric doctrines and rituals of the True Word school [a school that enjoyed special patronage from the ruling powers]. The Tendai school indulged in magical spells and other True Word practices aimed at securing immediate benefit, completely forgetting the Buddha's intent as taught in the Lotus Sutra.

Such developments prompted the Daishonin to declare the need to fight uncompromisingly and tirelessly against those who sought to destroy the Lotus Sutra's spirit of respect for all people. In this letter, he goes so far as to call for "censuring, banishing, cutting off alms to, or even beheading those persons." Of course, the Daishonin is speaking figuratively; he isn't calling for the priests to actually be executed. But the reality was that those were the very acts that he himself was experiencing. Though he was taking action at the risk of his life for people's happiness and a peaceful society, he was being attacked, exiled, denied support, and threatened with execution by both the authorities and the general public. Against that backdrop, his call for the use of apparently draconian measures was intended as a stern rebuke to the authorities, who were ready to take harsh action against him while failing to focus on the right target. He was issuing a warning to the nation's leaders, who should have been the mainstay and compass for the people. He was trying to awaken them to the fact that the nation was destined to ruin unless they correctly distinguished between good and evil, true and false. He was remonstrating with the government to behave as a "worthy ruler" who heeded the words of a person of wisdom.

A "worthy ruler" here represents a social entity that acknowledges a person of wisdom. Today, in our democratic society, the "worthy ruler" corresponds to a wise and awakened citizenry. Such a citizenry is vital if a peaceful and prosperous society is to be realized. As people grow wiser and stronger, the ideals of the sanctity of life and the absolute importance of peace will become more widely and deeply accepted and established in society. And this will lead to more people rejecting self-centered ideas that give rise to discrimination and war, which inflict human suffering. In other words, even if corrupt priests go unpunished, if the people become wise and are able to recognize evil for what it is and stop its spread, it will be cut off at its root. Ultimately, people themselves must strive to prevent the negative workings of life from manifesting and holding sway. It could be said that building a network of individuals dedicated to genuine good is the contemporary equivalent of the appearance of a person of wisdom and a worthy ruler. To create such a society, it is crucial to widely spread the philosophical principles of the sanctity of life, respect for all people, and peacebuilding.

We, as practitioners of Nichiren Buddhism, have a personal mission and social responsibility to appeal to others' conscience through the power of words, dialogue, and ideas, and actualize a peaceful and prosperous society. I firmly believe that our unceasing efforts toward this end are deeply consonant with the principle of change based on defeating evil to realize good that is elucidated in this letter, "The Kalpa of Decrease."

To Know the Fundamental Causes and Manifestations of Good and Evil

This is explained in the first volume of the Lotus Sutra where it says, "The true aspect of all phenomena can only be understood and shared between Buddhas. In the phrase "consistency from beginning to end," "beginning" indicates the root of evil and the root of good, and "end" indicates the outcome of evil and the outcome of good. One who is thoroughly awakened to the nature of good and evil from their roots to their branches and leaves is called a Buddha. . . . The Lotus Sutra states, "[The doctrines that they preach . . .] will never be contrary to the true [aspect]" [LSOC, 304]. T'ien-t'ai commented on this, saying that "no worldly affairs of life or work are ever contrary to the true [aspect]." A person of wisdom is not one who practices Buddhism apart from worldly affairs but, rather, one who thoroughly understands the principles by which the world is governed.

When the Yin dynasty became corrupt and the people were suffering, T'ai-kung Wang appeared in the world and beheaded King Chou of the Yin, bringing an end to the people's misery. When the Second Emperor of the Ch'in dynasty caused the people to taste bitterness, Chang Liang appeared and restored order to the world, enabling them to know sweetness. Though these men lived before the introduction of Buddhism, they helped the people as emissaries of Shakyamuni Buddha, the lord of teachings. And though the adherents of the non-Buddhist scriptures were unaware of it, the wisdom of such men contained at heart the wisdom of Buddhism. (WND-1, 1121–22)

Here, the Daishonin indicates that a true person of wisdom in the Latter Day of the Law not only knows the roots, or fundamental causes, of good and evil but also their branches and leaves—that is, their myriad manifestations in the real world. He says that such a person also has a thorough understanding of both the principles of Buddhism and of worldly affairs, along with a strong grasp of the principles by which the world is governed. In other words, from the perspective of the Daishonin's teachings, a person of wisdom is someone who can transform reality based on the wisdom of Buddhism.

In this section of "The Kalpa of Decrease," the Daishonin refers to the doctrines of the "true aspect of all phenomena"[28] and "three thousand realms in a single moment of life"[29] expounded in the Lotus Sutra. The "true aspect of all phenomena" is the reality of the world exactly as the Buddha wisdom perceives it. The Buddha wisdom perceives the true aspect of not only visible external phenomena but also the good and evil life conditions of living beings in the Ten Worlds, as well as the causes behind them.

When meeting people, a Buddha ponders the true reality of their life condition, the

151

goodness or evil in their heart, their suffering and joy, the causes that have led them to unhappiness and misfortune. By doing so, a Buddha can accurately grasp what they need to do to positively transform their state of life, and then compassionately preaches the teaching that will help free each person from suffering—a teaching designed to inspire the particular individual to embark on a path of inner transformation.

Stated another way, a Buddha is one who thoroughly understands the root of good (enlightenment to the essential nature of phenomena) and the root of evil (fundamental darkness or ignorance), as well as the branches and leaves that sprout from those roots (the diverse manifestations of good and evil, suffering and joy, that express themselves in the real world). The correct teaching of Buddhism by its very nature is a teaching of transformation that allows each person to move out of negative cycles and onto a beneficial path of good.

In this section, the Daishonin quotes a passage from "Benefits of the Teacher of the Law," the nineteenth chapter of the Lotus Sutra, "[The doctrines that they preach . . .] will never be contrary to the true [aspect]" [LSOC, 304], and T'ien-t'ai's commentary on this asserting that "no worldly affairs of life or work are ever contrary to the true [aspect]."

In another writing, "The Gift of Rice," in which he cites the same quote from T'ien-t'ai, the Daishonin writes: "The true path lies in the affairs of this world. . . . The Lotus Sutra explains that in the end secular matters are

the entirety of Buddhism" (WND-1, 1126).

The affairs of daily life, all without exception, are in themselves Buddhism. The illuminating light of the wisdom of Buddhism shines in the midst of the darkness of our troubled, tortured world, imparting hope, courage, and reassurance. As the Daishonin clearly states in this section of "The Kalpa of Decrease": "A person of wisdom is not one who practices Buddhism apart from worldly affairs but, rather, one who thoroughly understands the principles by which the world is governed."

Buddhism does not exist apart from human society. A truly wise person is one who takes action to contribute to society and guides it in a positive direction through the power of Buddhist wisdom and compassion. Meanwhile, a society imbued with the wisdom of Buddhism will prosper and thrive.

The SGI has striven steadfastly in its endeavors, following the correct path of "faith equals daily life" and "Buddhism manifests itself in society." Based on the conviction that a religion that is divorced from reality is a dead religion and that a living religion is one that is immersed in the lives of the people, we have consistently emphasized the importance of daily life and society.

Many people, however, still see Buddhism and secular matters as being separate. President Makiguchi wrote:

Even the most eminent scholars— excepting an extremely small number of religious leaders with a proper understanding—fail to grasp the life principle of "consistency from beginning to end" (LSOC, 57), which means that Buddhism encompasses all worldly affairs. Even those who have an intellectual grasp of this principle are usually unable to embody it in their actual lives. Consequently, in the more than a dozen centuries since the transmission of the Buddhist teachings to Japan, Buddhism and secular matters have been treated as being completely unrelated and separate. But when our members demonstrate the validity of this principle by actually putting it into practice, and when the supreme Law of life for which humanity is collectively thirsting—that is, the Mystic Law for attaining Buddhahood—becomes easily accessible to all, then people will naturally want to share its benefit with everyone and help them attain unsurpassed happiness.[30]

An abiding conviction in the principles of "faith equals daily life" and "Buddhism equals society" is the starting point of faith for the Soka Gakkai and the driving force for all our activities. The actual proof of putting the teachings of Buddhism into action in society that Mr. Makiguchi anticipated has been achieved for all to see in the experiences of our members over the past eighty years.

"Unless the human spirit is fundamentally transformed through a religious revolution, the chaos in human affairs will never be remedied,"[31] wrote Mr. Makiguchi as he embarked on a grand challenge to transform society. This is the eternal practice of Nichiren Buddhism, guided by the principle of establishing the correct teaching for the peace of the land.

What we must remember above all is the Daishonin's spirit of great compassion that refuses to overlook people's suffering and distress—a spirit that is eloquently conveyed at the start of his treatise "On Establishing the Correct Teaching for the Peace of the Land" (WND-1, 6–26).

In this section of "The Kalpa of Decrease," the Daishonin's compassionate gaze extends even to the sufferings of the Chinese people before the introduction of Buddhism to China. He refers to the stories of T'ai-kung Wang and Chang Liang, who fought and defeated rulers who caused suffering to their people in the Yin and Chou dynasties, respectively. Of course, since Buddhism had not yet arrived from India, neither of the two was aware of Shakyamuni's teachings. But the Daishonin attributes their efforts on behalf of the welfare of the people to the fact that, taking into account their respective missions, they were "emissaries of Shakyamuni Buddha, the lord of teachings" and that "the wisdom of such men contained at heart the wisdom of Buddhism."

His words indicate that an aspect of the world of Buddhahood is manifested, and the wisdom of Buddhism shines, in any dedicated effort to serve the welfare of others and earnestly find the wisdom to open the way to happiness for all people and establish a peaceful society. Based on a broader interpretation, this means that attacking the root cause of people's suffering is indispensable to the process of building a network of good that can protect the people's welfare. This is the essence of the humanism of Nichiren Buddhism.

The SGI is engaged in wide-ranging activities and exchanges for the promotion of peace, culture, and education. Buddhism is a teaching that exists for people's happiness. That is its very basis. We must, therefore, take a firm stand against authoritarian forces that seek to subvert the humanistic ideals of Nichiren Buddhism and turn it into a religion that exists only for its own sake and exploits people for its own ends.

Great Evil Portends Great Good

Great evil portends the arrival of great good. If all of Jambudvipa [the entire world] were to be thrown into chaos, there could be no doubt that [this sutra would] "be widely propagated throughout Jambudvipa." (WND-1, 1122)

A society's growth and development depend upon the ideals and philosophies valued by the people who make up that society.

The society of the Daishonin's day refused to recognize the truths he presented to it. It condoned slander of the Law that brought suffering down upon the people. It was difficult for such a society to grow and prosper soundly, given that it granted legitimacy to erroneous Buddhist schools that

either ignored or made an empty pretense of working for people's happiness.

But the light of wisdom of the correct teaching of Buddhism shows its true worth in times of great confusion and turmoil. The Daishonin clearly believed that the darkest hour of night was but a prelude to a dawn of people's awakening—an opportunity for change, a turning point. "Great evil portends the arrival of great good," he writes. He is saying in effect: "There's no need for pessimism. I, Nichiren, possessing the sun-like wisdom of the Buddha, have appeared in response to this dark time. Great evil portends the arrival of the great good of kosen-rufu." How inspired and heartened the Daishonin's followers must have been by his resolute conviction.

The Daishonin further writes: "If all of Jambudvipa [the entire world] were to be thrown into chaos, there could be no doubt that [this Lotus Sutra would] 'be widely propagated throughout Jambudvipa.'" Of course, the Daishonin's Buddhism does not by any means advocate a doomsday vision; rather, its aim is to put an end to people's suffering and enable them to attain happiness in the real world. Precisely because the Latter Day of the Law is a time of seemingly insoluble challenges, we can take action to transform things, overturning evil practices of the past, carrying out radical reevaluations, and starting at the source to find solutions for change. Such thoroughgoing transformation will, quite naturally, meet with resistance, but it is the only way to open a new path forward. The Buddhism of Nichiren Daishonin is a teaching of unwavering commitment to the positive transformation of reality—a teaching that makes it possible for us to change this troubled saha world into a realm of peace and happiness without fail.

In other words, the struggle of a person of wisdom is the key to achieving worldwide kosen-rufu.

In his writing "Great Good and Great Evil," Nichiren Daishonin declares:

When great evil occurs, great good follows. Since great slander already exists in our land, the great correct Law will spread without fail. What could any of you have to lament? Even if you are not the Venerable Mahakashyapa,[32] you should all perform a dance. Even if you are not Shariputra,[33] you should leap up and dance. When Bodhisattva Superior Practices emerged from the earth, did he not emerge dancing? (WND-1, 1119).

The Daishonin encourages his followers by saying that now is the time to forge ahead in high spirits, to set forth anew, joyously and dynamically.

The hallmark of a transformative teaching is that it has the power to help people transform great evil into great good—moving forward toward hope, happiness, security, and peace.

Mr. Toda once wrote:

Civilization and scientific progress were supposed to contribute to stronger nations and stronger people, but until now, humanity has been concentrating all its energies on struggles and disputes between nations, taking us in the exact opposite direction of peace. The more technological advances we see in our daily lives, the more high-handed we've become. The more civilized or culturally developed we've become, the more arrogant we've grown. Both advanced technology and civilization, it would seem to me, have contributed to making us not only more high-handed and arrogant but also envious and cowardly. What, then, can serve as the driving force for creating a utopia of peace and happiness on earth? It has to be religion.[34]

The activities of the SGI, following the great path of putting Buddhism into practice in the real world, offer a brilliant light of hope for the spread of the humanistic principles of Buddhism and the realization of peace for people everywhere.

Since Buddhism
is inseparable
from the affairs of society,
we strive with fresh joy,
day after day.

NOTES

1. Meditation on the vileness of the body: A meditation practice aimed at overcoming craving and greed. One of the five meditations or meditative practices for quieting the mind and eliminating delusion. They are (1) meditation on the vileness of the body, (2) meditation on compassion, (3) meditation on dependent origination, (4) meditation on the correct discernment of the phenomenal world, and (5) breath-counting meditation.

2. Meditation on compassion: A meditation practice aimed at eliminating anger and hatred. One of the five meditations.

3. Meditation on the twelve-linked chain of causation: Also, meditation on dependent origination. A meditation practice aimed at eliminating foolishness or ignorance. One of the five meditations. The twelve-linked chain of causation is an early doctrine of Buddhism showing the causal relationship between ignorance and suffering. Shakyamuni is said to have expounded this teaching in answer to the question of why people have to experience the sufferings of aging and death. Each link in the chain is a cause that leads to the next.

4. Five cardinal sins: The five most serious offenses in Buddhism. Explanations vary according to the sutras and treatises. The most common is (1) killing one's father, (2) killing one's mother, (3) killing an arhat, (4) injuring a Buddha, and (5) causing disunity in the Buddhist Order. It is said that those who commit any of the five cardinal sins invariably fall into the hell of incessant suffering.

5. Ten evil acts: Evils enumerated in the Buddhist scriptures. They are the three physical evils of killing, stealing, and sexual misconduct; the four verbal evils of lying, flattery or indiscriminate and irresponsible speech, defamation, and duplicity; and the three mental evils of greed, anger, and foolishness, or the holding of mistaken views.

6. King Sen'yo: The name of Shakyamuni Buddha when he was a king in a previous existence, according to the "Noble Practice" chapter of the Nirvana Sutra. The chapter describes King Sen'yo as the ruler of a great kingdom who had deep reverence for the great vehicle, or Mahayana, sutras. In his heart, he was pure and good, free from evil thoughts, jealousy, or stinginess. He continued to make offerings to Brahmans for twelve years. One day, when he heard Brahmans slander the great vehicle teachings, he put them to death to protect the teachings. Because of this act, the sutra says, he was never thereafter in danger of falling into hell. The Daishonin refers to him here, not to condone the killing of slanderers, but to underscore the importance of a strict attitude toward protecting the correct Law.

7. Eight schools: The eight major schools of Buddhism in Japan before the Kamakura period (1185–1333). They are the Dharma Analysis Treasury, Establishment of Truth, Precepts, Dharma Characteristics, Three Treatises, Flower Garland, Tendai, and True Word schools.

The first six schools flourished in the Nara period (710–794), while the Tendai and True Word schools rose to prominence during the Heian period (794–1185).

8. From *The Profound Meaning of the Lotus Sutra.*

9. T'ai-kung Wang was a general who served as a teacher and adviser to Hsi Po, the Earl of the West (later known as King Wen of the Chou dynasty of China). His strategies are said to have enabled Hsi Po's son, King Wu, to overthrow King Chou of the Yin (Shang) dynasty, who epitomized a bad ruler, and establish the Chou dynasty.

10. The Second Emperor of the Ch'in dynasty of China refers to Hu Hai (229–207 BCE). A puppet ruler, he was controlled by the eunuch official Chao Kao, who in order to advance his own ambitions eventually forced Hu Hai to commit suicide.

11. Chang Liang (d. 168 BCE) was a statesman and strategist who assisted Liu Pang, later known as Emperor Kao-tsu, in the overthrow of the Ch'in dynasty and the establishment of the Former Han dynasty of China.

12. The Daishonin alludes here to the passage from "Encouragements of the Bodhisattva Universal Worthy," the twenty-eighth chapter of the Lotus Sutra: "After the Thus Come One has entered extinction, I will cause it [the Lotus Sutra] to be widely propagated throughout Jambudvipa [the entire world] and will see that it never comes to an end" (LSOC, 363).

13. "Encouraging Devotion," the thirteenth chapter of the Lotus Sutra, speaks of "never begrudging our bodies or lives" (LSOC, 229) in the pursuit of and the propagation of the teaching of Buddhism.

14. Eternity, happiness, true self, and purity are known as the four virtues. Describing the noble qualities of the Buddha's life, the four are explained as follows: "eternity" means unchanging and eternal; "happiness" means tranquillity that transcends all suffering; "true self" means true and intrinsic nature; and "purity" means free of illusion or mistaken conduct.

15. Kalpa of decrease: A period in which the human life span is said to diminish. In the kalpa of continuance—the second of the four kalpas of formation, continuance, decline, and disintegration that a world undergoes—the human life span repeats a cycle of change, alternately decreasing and increasing. Any period of diminution is called a kalpa of decrease. Any of the periods in which the human life span is increasing is called a kalpa of increase. It is said that Shakyamuni appeared in the present kalpa of continuance, in the ninth kalpa of decrease.

16. Three poisons of greed, anger, and foolishness: The fundamental evils inherent in life that give rise to human suffering. In Nagarjuna's *Treatise on the Great Perfection of Wisdom,* the three poisons are regarded as the source of all illusions and earthly desires. The three poisons are so called because they pollute people's lives and work to prevent them from turning their hearts and minds to goodness.

17. Takahashi Rokuro Hyoe (n.d.): Also known as the lay priest Takahashi. A follower of Nichiren Daishonin, he lived in Kajima in Fuji District of Suruga Province

(present-day Fuji City in central Shizuoka Prefecture). He was converted to the Daishonin's teaching by his wife's nephew Nikko Shonin, the Daishonin's disciple and designated successor. A letter to Takahashi from the Daishonin entrusted him with the responsibility of propagation in the area where he was living, which would indicate that he enjoyed the Daishonin's trust and was a leading figure among the lay believers in Fuji District.

18. Suruga Province: Currently, central Shizuoka Prefecture.

19. The lay priest of Nishiyama (n.d.): A follower of Nichiren Daishonin who lived in Nishiyama Village in Fuji District of Suruga Province. He is the recipient of a number of letters from the Daishonin.

20. Verse section: This refers to the verse section of "Life Span," the sixteenth chapter of the Lotus Sutra, which is recited in the second part of gongyo, or the SGI liturgy. It begins with the line, *Ji ga toku burrai* (Since I attained Buddhahood), and ends with the passage, *Mai ji sa ze nen, i ga ryo shujo, toku nyu mujodo, soku joju busshin* (At all times I think to myself: How can I cause living beings to gain entry to the unsurpassed way and quickly acquire the body of a Buddha?) (LSOC, 270–73).

21. The Daishonin writes: "I have decided to send [one of my priest-disciples] Acharya Daishin to pay a visit to the grave of the late lay priest [Takahashi]. In the past, I had thought that, if there were people in the Kanto region who had heard this teaching, I would go to their graves myself and recite the verse section of the 'Life Span' chapter of the Lotus Sutra. If I were to go there under the present circumstances, however, the entire province would hear of it within the day, and it would probably cause an uproar as far away as Kamakura. Even though they have steadfast faith, wherever I go, people must fear the eyes of others" (WND-1, 1122).

22. One vehicle: Also, single vehicle, Buddha vehicle, one Buddha vehicle, one vehicle of Buddhahood, or supreme vehicle. Refers to the Buddha's highest or true teaching that can carry or lead all people to enlightenment; in other words, the Lotus Sutra.

23. Four leaders of the Bodhisattvas of the Earth: Also, the four bodhisattvas or four great bodhisattvas. Their names are Superior Practices, Boundless Practices, Pure Practices, and Firmly Established Practices. They are the leaders of the countless bodhisattvas who appear from the earth in response to Shakyamuni's call in "Emerging from the Earth," the fifteenth chapter of the Lotus Sutra. In "Supernatural Powers of the Thus Come One," the twenty-first chapter, Shakyamuni transfers the essence of the sutra and entrusts its propagation after his passing to these bodhisattvas.

24. For instance, the Daishonin writes: "In the time for the practice of shakubuku [i.e., in the Latter Day of the Law] the four bodhisattvas appear as worthy rulers who rebuke and convert ignorant rulers" ("The Object of Devotion for Observing the Mind," WND-1, 375).

25. The Daishonin writes: "A person of wisdom is not one who practices Buddhism apart from worldly affairs but, rather, one who thoroughly understands the principles by which the world is governed" (WND-1, 1121).

26. Three powerful enemies: Three types of arrogant people who persecute those who propagate the Lotus Sutra in the evil age after Shakyamuni Buddha's passing, described in the concluding verse section of "Encouraging Devotion," the thirteenth chapter of the Lotus Sutra. The Great Teacher Miao-lo (711–82) of China summarizes them as arrogant lay people, arrogant priests, and arrogant false sages.

27. Bodhisattva Never Disparaging: A bodhisattva described in "Bodhisattva Never Disparaging," the twentieth chapter of the Lotus Sutra. This bodhisattva—Shakyamuni in a previous lifetime—would bow in reverence to everyone he met. However, he was attacked by arrogant people, who beat him with sticks and staves and threw stones at him. The sutra explains that his practice of respecting others' Buddha nature became the cause for him to attain Buddhahood. Those who persecuted Never Disparaging fell into the hell of incessant suffering, but due to the connection that they formed with Buddhism through their actions, after they had finished expiating their offenses, they once more encountered Never Disparaging and were able to attain Buddhahood.

28. True aspect of all phenomena: The ultimate truth or reality that permeates all phenomena and is in no way separate from them. Through the explanation of the ten factors, "Expedient Means," the second chapter of the Lotus Sutra, clarifies that all people are inherently endowed with the potential to become Buddhas, and that they can tap and manifest this potential.

29. Three thousand realms in a single moment of life: A doctrine developed by the Great Teacher T'ien-t'ai of China based on the Lotus Sutra. The principle that all phenomena are contained within a single moment of life, and that a single moment of life permeates the three thousand realms of existence, or the entire phenomenal world.

30. Translated from Japanese. Tsunesaburo Makiguchi, *Makiguchi Tsunesaburo zenshu* (Collected Writings of Tsunesaburo Makiguchi) (Tokyo: Daisanbunmei-sha, 1987), 10:27.

31. Translated from Japanese. Tsunesaburo Makiguchi, *Makiguchi Tsunesaburo shingenshu* (Selected Quotes of Tsunesaburo Makiguchi), ed. by Takehisa Tsuji (Tokyo: Daisanbunmei-sha, 1979), 211.

32. Mahakashyapa: One of Shakyamuni's ten major disciples, who was known as the foremost in ascetic practices. After Shakyamuni's death, he served as head of the Buddhist Order, and is said to have been the first of the Buddha's successors.

33. Shariputra: One of Shakyamuni's ten major disciples, who was known as foremost in wisdom for his understanding of the true intent of the Buddha's preaching.

34. Translated from Japanese: Josei Toda, *Toda Josei zenshu* (Collected Writings of Josei Toda) (Tokyo: Seikyo Shimbunsha, 1981), 1:21.

INDEX

A

ability, increased by efforts, 15, 45, 146
Abutsu-bo, 107, 109, 117, 119
achievements, mentor's, 12, 14, 32, 71, 82, 89, 98
action(s), 3, 6, 12, 21, 39, 46, 74, 94, 100, 154
actual proof, 81
adversity, confronting, 75
all vehicles becoming the one Buddha vehicle, 13, 24; misguided stance of, 23
arhats, 6
Aryasimha, 9
Atsuhara Persecution, 60
attainment of Buddhahood in one's present form, 23, 42, 105, 109–11
attitude, 135
authoritarianism, stand against, 154

B

battle between the provisional and true teachings, 8–13, 30–31, 39, 42
beginnings, all things starts from, 91–92, 101
behavior, importance of one's, 32, 79
benefits, 62, 89, 97, 99–100, 118, 127
"Benefits of the Teacher of the Law" chapter (Lotus Sutra), 152
"The Blessings of the Lotus Sutra," 89, 92
blessings to be gained through one instance of belief and understanding in the Lotus Sutra, during Shakyamuni's lifetime, 23,
bodhisattva, spirit of, 10, 21, 23, 30, 40, 46, 66, 93, 97, 116–18
Bodhisattva Ashvaghosha, 125, 132–33
Bodhisattva Never Disparaging, 9, 149

"Bodhisattva Never Disparaging" chapter (Lotus Sutra), 26, 116
Bodhisattva Superior Practices, 86–87, 91, 155
boundless joy of the Law, experiencing, 49. See also happiness
Buddha wisdom, 151
Buddhism, 4, 6, 8, 11–12, 19, 21–22, 25, 28, 31–32, 44, 46, 48–49 63, 66, 69, 72, 74, 78, 81–82, 90–91, 94, 98, 112, 114, 117–19, 127, 131, 141, 144, 146, 149, 153; as a foundation in all matters, 73, 77, 79; enemies of, 116; errors of other schools of, 10, 13, 24–27, 29, 31, 39, 95, 144–45, 148–49, 154; humanism of, 14, 108, 153–55; people-oriented, 113; practitioners of, 73, 146; promoting, 30, 38, 44, 50, 62, 100–101; and reason, 70, 76–77; teaching contrary to, 135; transmission of, 69–70; value of expedient teaching of, 24; victory of, 80
Buddhism and daily life, 152
Buddhism equals society, 152–53, 155
Buddhism is about winning, 73, 81–82
Buddhist, life as a, 61–62; social responsibility as a, 150

C

cause and effect, Buddhist law of, 32, 74
Ceremony in the Air, as described in the Lotus Sutra, 96
challenge, spirit of, 12, 65, 73, 101, 134, 153
Chang-an, 47
Chang Liang, 143, 151, 153
change, opportunity for, 154–55

changing poison into medicine, 56–57, 61–63
character, building, 76
Ch'in dynasty, 143, 151
China, Buddhism in, 74, 92, 153
Chronicles of Japan, The, 74
Chu Tao-sheng, 9
citizenry, awakened, 150
community, building better relations with
        the, 78, 133, 139
compassion, 30, 39, 44–46, 50, 56, 63, 75,
        85, 89–90, 100, 109, 118, 130,
        152–53; and reason, 11, 29
complacency, dispelling, 78–79
confidence, 14, 59, 61, 65, 134
conflict, transforming, 77
consistency from beginning to end, teaching
        of, 142, 151, 153
conviction, 45, 49, 61, 80, 98, 133, 135, 138
correct teaching, establishing the, 4, 6, 10–11,
        13, 23, 25–26, 29, 32, 37, 39, 40–41,
        43–44, 46, 48, 58, 65, 74, 78, 96,
        98, 116, 137, 145–46, 149, 152, 154;
        slandering the, 138. *See also* Lotus
        Sutra
courage, 3, 26, 30, 79, 118, 125, 132
cowardice, 7
crucial moment, for a Buddhist practitioner, 8

D

daimoku (invocation of Nam-myoho-renge-
        kyo), 87–88, 91–92, 95, 124. *See also*
        Nam-myoho-renge-kyo
daimoku of the Lotus Sutra, 95, 108, 113,
        126–27, 138; chanting the, 100;
        promoting the, 99. *See also* Nam-
        myoho-renge-kyo
death, Buddhist perspective on, 48
dedication, selfless, 6, 30, 47–48, 146
Dengyo, 35–36, 43–45, 47, 95, 111
dependent origination, 114
determination, 12, 47, 59, 61–62, 64, 76–77,
        82, 134–35, 144

"Devadatta" chapter (Lotus Sutra), 111
Dharma nature, 134
dialogue, 14, 50, 98
dignity, recognizing, 100
discrimination, defeating, 100, 117, 150
division, transforming, 77

E

Eagle Peak. *See* Land of Tranquil Light
efforts, 47; earnest, 14, 81, 94, 150
eight or ten schools, of Buddhism, 13, 25,
        142, 148
Ema, Lord, 71–72, 77–78
encouragement, importance of, 45, 56, 58–59,
        61, 65, 71–73, 76, 80, 99, 112
"Encouraging Devotion" chapter (Lotus
        Sutra), 40, 96
epidemics, disaster caused by, 137
equality, achieving human, 94; philosophy of
        gender, 117
eradication of one's offenses, by practicing the
        Lotus Sutra, 23
establishing the correct teaching for the peace
        of the land, 10, 13, 62, 120, 138,
        153; achieving the ideal of, 139. *See
        also* society
evil, refuting, 4; transforming, 77–78, 149–50
evil man, 54
"Expedient Means" chapter (Lotus Sutra), 96
experiences, sharing, 100, 153

F

faith equals daily life, 152–53
families, happiness in, 139
Fa-tao, Tripitaka Master, 9
fear, 7
fearless, being, 8, 36, 47, 54, 60–62, 139
February Campaign, of the Soka Gakkai, 21
financial hardships, overcoming, 66
five cardinal sins, 142, 148
five impurities, 28, 136

five precepts, 85, 89
Former Day of Law, 20, 26, 92–94; teachings of, 27–28
fostering, capable individuals, 25, 82
four leaders of the Bodhisattvas of the Earth, 145
four universal sufferings, 60, 65
four virtues, 15, 60, 144
friendship, 14
Fu Hsi, 3, 12, 14

G

Gautami, 112
"The Gift of Rice," 152
Gohonzon (fundamental object of devotion), 28, 32, 61, 65, 100–101, 130; acquiring the power of the, 22; chanting honestly to the, 134
good circumstances, 57, 61–62, 78, 90, 99, 106, 127
gratitude, 65, 106, 117–19, 134
"Great Good and Great Evil," 155
great obstacles lead to enlightenment, building a life state of understanding, 15
greed, disaster caused by human, in the twenty-first century, 136–37

H

happiness, 4, 11, 14–15, 25, 30, 38–39, 41–42, 45–46, 48–49, 55–62, 65–66, 73, 75–76, 79–80, 89, 91, 93–94, 97, 100, 108, 110, 118, 129–30, 132, 134–35, 137, 141, 146, 148, 153, 155; for all humanity, 144, 146, 153–54
hardships, triumphing over, 6, 11, 21, 57–58
health, champion of, 55–56, 63, 65–66
Hero of the World (title of the Buddha), 69, 73
"The Hero of the World," 72, 74, 76, 80
Hilty, Carl, 66
Hinayana teachings, 20, 26, 141, 146; offerings made to, 91

Hojo Tokimune, 116
Hoki-bo. See Nikko Shonin
hope, 15, 82, 155
humanism, 79

I

Ikegami brothers, overcoming obstacles, 80; family harmony achieved by the, 78
illness, facing, 55–56, 58–66
Immeasurable Meanings Sutra, 24
independence, promoting, 112
India, Buddhism in, 69, 72, 92, 153
inhumanity, transforming, 78
initiative, 85, 89, 146
injustice, confronting, 32–33
inner potential, 11, 28, 30, 44, 100, 112, 117, 127; activating, 42, 133–34, 139, 148
inner transformation, 14, 50, 77–79, 81, 93, 112, 115, 135, 147, 152–53
integrity, 77, 118; acting with, 79
interactions, 108
"It starts with me! It starts from now!" self-motivated spirit, 101

J

Japan, Buddhism in, 25, 69, 72, 74, 87, 92, 107, 115, 126; hostility to Buddhism by, 136–37
justice, 82; speaking up for, 46. See also Osaka Incident

K

Kachi ron (Theory of Value) (Makiguchi), 4
kalpa of decline, 125, 136
kalpa of decrease, 125, 136
"The Kalpa of Decrease," 144, 146, 151–53
karma, transforming, 62, 75, 78, 118, 134, 139, 144

King Rinda and the white horses parable, 132–33, 135, 138
King Sen'yo, 142, 148
kosen-rufu, 21, 79; striving for, 1, 5–7, 11–12, 14–15, 23, 33, 46, 49–50, 63, 65–66, 71, 80–81, 89, 97–99, 114, 117, 120, 139, 147; and women, 120; worldwide, 12, 32, 56, 71, 89, 101, 155

L

Land of Tranquil Light, 4, 37, 47–49
Latter Day of the Law, 4, 6–7, 10, 20, 25–26, 29, 31, 39, 53–54, 56–57, 60, 89, 91, 96, 111, 129, 142, 145–48, 154; practice for the, 28, 40, 93–94; practitioners of the, 36, 45; shakubuku practice in the, 35, 38
leaders, 32–33, 55
lessening karmic retribution, 58
"Letter from Sado," 27
"Letter to Misawa," 41
"The Letter of Petition from Yorimoto," 71
life, 124; discovering the beauty and power of, 127, 139; preciousness of 85, 89–90; of victory, 62, 66
life and death, Buddhist perspective of, 49
life force, 137; unlocking innate, 135
"Life Span" chapter (Lotus Sutra), 96, 131, 145
life state, 112, 118, 139
longevity, champion of, 66, 90
Lotus Sutra (true teaching), 1, 3, 5, 10–13, 15, 20, 22–26, 28, 30, 35, 38–43, 49, 53, 59, 62, 73, 75, 78–80, 85, 87–88, 92–96, 99–100, 105–07, 109, 112–13, 115, 131, 138, 142, 146–47, 150–52, 154; as the King of the sutras, 110–11; as the lord of the five flavors, 123–24, 127–28, 130–32; connection with the, 57–58; demonstrating the supremacy of the, 128–29; enemies of the, 29, 116; offerings made to the, 91; practicing the, in modern times, 4; practitioners of the, 6–7, 9–10, 43, 53, 138. See also correct teaching; one vehicle

M

Mahakashyapa, 155
Mahayana teachings, 20, 26, 141, 146
Makiguchi, Tsunesaburo, 3–4, 12–13, 21, 30–32, 49, 61, 65, 81, 89, 98, 100, 152–53; concern for a follower in Shimotsuma by, 65; obstacle charged path of, 32, 46; revitalization of Buddhism by, 97; selfless devotion of, 32, 65
Many Treasures Buddha, in Buddhism, 37, 47, 100, 126, 136
March 16, 1958, meeting, 37
meditation on compassion, 141, 146–47
meditation on the vileness of the body, 141, 146–47
meditation on the twelve-linked chain of causation, 141, 146–47
mentor and disciple relationship, 81
mentor(s), 71–72; behavior of the, 119
Miao-lo, 47, 92, 123–24, 127–28, 130; Annotation on "The Words and Phrases of the Lotus Sutra," 58
Middle Day of the Law, 20, 26, 92–94, 96; practitioners of the, 45; teachings of, 27–28
mission, 25, 55–56, 64, 66, 71, 94, 118, 138, 150, 152
mothers, compassion of, 14–15, 108, 120; gratitude to, 108; happiness of, 112; kindness to, 113–14; repaying debt to gratitude to, 14
Mount Minobu, 71, 109, 119
Mount Sumeru, 86–88, 91, 97, 99, 101
mutual possession of the Ten Worlds, 39, 42, 95, 110, 131–32
myo (wonderful), 3, 123, 128, 131
Myoichi, the lay nun, overcoming obstacles, 80

Myomitsu (lay follower), 89–90, 99

Myoshin, the lay nun, 59

Mystic Law, 3, 8, 10–13, 132, 41, 55, 58, 62, 66, 72, 77–79, 89–90, 109, 112, 115, 117, 130, 153; promoting the, 9, 21, 38, 47–48, 56, 62, 92, 94, 100, 118, 129, 146; workings of the, 14–15, 61. *See also* Nam-myoho-renge-kyo

N

Nagarjuna, 36, 43

Nam-myoho-renge-kyo, 23, 36–37, 81, 85, 91, 109, 131, 137; chanting, 3, 11–14, 26, 28, 44, 47–50, 55, 58, 62, 64, 87–89, 92–93, 95–96, 98–100, 108, 112–13, 117, 123, 126–30, 132–36, 138–39; promoting, 127 138. *See also* daimoku; daimoku of the Lotus Sutra; Mystic Law

Nanjo Tokimitsu, 55, 59, 62, 64, 66; overcoming obstacles, 80; selfless devotion of, 60

Narayana (god), 133

negative functions, 40–41, 54–55, 63; defeating, 4, 11–12, 15, 30, 39, 41–42, 56, 60–61, 64, 74, 81–82, 130, 134, 144, 150

Nembutsu school, 111, 116

Nichikan, 46; commentary on "The Object of Devotion for Observing the Mind," 130

Nichiren Daishonin, 7–9, 11, 13–14, 21–25, 27, 29, 31, 38–39, 41–43, 45, 47, 49, 55, 57, 59–60, 66, 72–74, 76, 77–78, 86, 90–92, 99–101, 105–06, 110–11, 120, 126–28, 130, 135, 137–39, 152, 155; action of, 93; as a role model, 4–5, 15; as a student of Buddhism, 108, 113; as the person of wisdom, 149–50; battling illness, 64; as Bodhisattva Superior Practices, 93–94; compassion of, 79, 116, 119, 144–45; conviction, of, 56, 62, 154;

Izu Exile of, 44, 107, 113, 115–16; female followers of, 118; Komatsubara Persecution of, 36, 43; life state of, 15, 44, 48, 64–65; and the Lotus Sutra, 95–96; manifesting the life state of, 134; nature of slander on, 115–16; obstacle charged path of, 36, 43–45, 48, 94, 96, 109, 115, 117, 150; overcoming obstacles, 129; role of, 146; Sado Exile of, 44, 107, 113, 115–17, 119; selfless devotion of, 71, 75, 81, 89; shakubuku spirit of, 29–30, 35–36; slander of the Mystic Law during the time of, 137–39, 148–49; spirit of, 45, 153; stand-alone spirit of, 98; as the votary of the Lotus Sutra, 63–64; victory as demonstrated by, 80; vow of, 108–09, 112–14, 117; writings of, 3, 15, 49–50

Nichiren Shoshu priesthood, 31–32, 97

Nichiro, 56

Nikko Shonin, 55

nine great persecutions, 36, 43

Nishiyama, the lay priest of, 144

not begrudging one's life, spirit of, 15, 97, 143–44

Noto-bo, 70, 75

O

"The Object of Devotion for Observing the Mind," 5, 145

obstacles, encountering, 39–42, 44–47, 49, 54, 60–61, 76, 96; overcoming, 44, 61, 65–66, 76, 79, 113, 127

"On Curing Karmic Disease," 58

"On Establishing the Correct Teaching for the Peace of the Land" dialogue form, 98

"On Practicing the Buddha's Teachings," 15, 24, 27, 32, 49–50; significance, 5–6, 22–23, 38; translates to, 4

"On Replying Debts of Gratitude," 81

"On the Buddha's Prophecy," significance, 6

one vehicle, 3, 10–12, 14, 19–20, 22–26, 28–29, 92, 130, 141, 145. *See also* Lotus Sutra
oneness of mentor and disciple, the, 1, 3, 5–6, 21–22, 33, 38, 46, 49, 56, 80, 82, 101, 118; unity of, 139
"The Opening of the Eyes," 5, 8, 15, 27, 45, 113–14
opening the provisional and revealing the distant, corresponds to the daimoku, 123–24, 127–28
ordinary people, 53, 57, 60, 92, 137; and Buddhism, 94
Osaka Incident, 46. *See also* justice
Ota, lay priest, 58–59, 66
Ota Gozen, overcoming obstacles, 80

P

parents, gratitude to, 113–115; kindness to, 106
passion, 82
"Peaceful Practices" chapter (Lotus Sutra), 20, 26, 31, 96
perseverance, 133, 135
person of wisdom, 155; in the Latter Day of the Law, 151–52
poison-drum relationship, in Buddhism, 58
positive forces, of the universe, 37, 47–48, 50, 55, 64, 99, 100, 126, 133, 136; activating the, 135, 138
practicing as the Buddha teaches, meaning of, 10, 46–47, 95
praise, era for, 88, 99–100
prayer, 3, 47, 55, 63–64, 80
pre-Lotus teachings, 2, 110, 145, 148; as provisional teaching, 29, 130
priests, corrupted, 31
"The Proof of the Lotus Sutra," 56, 61, 64
prosperity, 14, 78
Pure Land School, of 107, 115
purification of the six sense organs, by practicing the Lotus Sutra, 23

R

Record of the Orally Transmitted Teachings, The, 61
rejecting evil and embracing good are two sides of the same coin, Tsunesaburo Makiguchi's conviction of, 30
religion, 152, 155; for the twenty-first century, 30
respect, winning, 90
role model, Nichiren Daishonin as a, 4–5, 15
Ryokan, 77, 116

S

Sado Island, 5, 109
saha world, 41; transforming, 155
Sairen-bo, 63
secular authority, 69, 72, 81
self-confidence, 3, 6, 76, 79, 139
self-renewal, 66
Sennichi, lay nun, 47, 109, 111–12, 119; selfless dedication of, 117–18
SGI, 5, 46 119, 152; activities of the, 14, 101, 154–55; Buddhist practice of the, 32, 77, 101, 154–55; ever-youthful, 82; facilities of, 14; humanism of the, 30; members of the, 11, 14, 21, 30, 63, 101, 135; path of self-development in the, 77; shakubuku spirit of the, 32; winning spirit of the, 81
shakubuku (refutation of the provisional doctrine), 3, 12–13, 19–20, 28, 30; in modern times, 30; practice of, 26–27, 29, 31, 39–41, 43, 49
Shakyamuni, 6, 9–10, 13, 15, 24, 35–37, 43, 45, 47–48, 53, 57, 73–75, 80, 92, 94–96, 108, 126, 136, 143, 145–46, 151; Buddhism of, 100, 147; intent of, 22–23; spiritual awakening of, 131; vow of, 148
shared commitment of mentor and disciple, 49
Shariputra, 155

Shen Nung, 3, 12, 14

Shijo Kingo, 75, 80; persecutions faced by, 71–74, 76–77; winning over his lord, 77–79

simultaneity of cause and effect, 131–32

sincerity, 77, 88, 109, 118

Sho-bo, 70, 75

shoju, 19; practice of, 26–27, 31

six paramitas, 85, 89

slander, 54–55, 57

society, building a better, 6, 9, 13–15, 115, 120, 132, 135, 139 146, 148–50, 152–54. *See also* establishing the correct teaching for the peace of the land

Soka Gakkai, 3, 21, 37–38, 47, 49–50, 66, 89, 99–101; Buddhist practice of the, 8, 98; inheriting Nichiren Daishonin's legacy, 96–98; members of the, 100–101; presidents of the, 12, 32, 82; shakubuku spirit of the, 32

Soya Doso, 127

Soya Kyoshin, 127

"Supernatural Powers" chapter (Lotus Sutra), 88, 98

Suruga Province, 144

"The Sutra of True Requital," 108–09, 112, 114, 119

sutras, king of all the, 124, 128

T

T'ai-kung Wang, 143, 151, 153

Takahashi Rokuro Hyoe, 144

Tatsunokuchi Persecution, 36, 43–44

"Teacher of the Law" chapter (Lotus Sutra), 96, 116; five practices in the, 26

technology, and civilization, 155

ten demon daughters, 37

ten evil acts, 142, 148

ten good precepts, 85, 89

ten major precepts, 85, 89

Ten Worlds, 132, 151

Tendai School, 31, 142, 148–49

time, as referred in Buddhism, 27

thirty-two features of the Buddha, 90

three bodies of the Buddha, 90–91

three calamities, 138

three carts and the burning house parable, 2

three evil paths, 54, 57

three existences, 55

three kinds of benefit, 86, 90

three major calamities, 125, 136

three minor calamities, 125–26, 136

three obstacles and four devils, 8, 29, 41, 43–44, 60, 65, 75, 97, 134

three poisons, 6–7, 93, 118, 125–26, 136, 137–39, 141, 144–46; overcoming the, 147

three powerful enemies, 1–2, 4, 7–9, 29, 35–36, 38–44, 47, 75, 96–97, 115–16, 149

three thousand realms in a single moment of life, 39, 44, 95, 110, 114, 130, 151

three vehicles, 10, 22

T'ien-t'ai, 28–29, 35–36, 43–45, 47, 92, 95, 124, 128, 142, 151–52; *Great Concentration and Insight*, 58; *The Profound Meaning of the Lotus Sutra*, 13; *"Words and Phrases of the Lotus Sutra,"* 136

Toda, Josei, 4, 7–8, 14, 22, 31–32, 41, 44, 48, 65, 71, 81, 98, 100, 114, 120, 134, 143, 155; declaration of, 37–38; determination of, 89; goal of, 21; mother's concern for, 114; obstacle charged path of, 32, 46; poem of, 82; selfless devotion of, 32; spirit of, 12; spiritual awakening of, 97; support to, 22

Toki (Toki Jonin's wife), the lay nun, 59, 62; overcoming obstacles, 80

Toki Jonin, overcoming obstacles, 80

treasures of the heart, 78–79

"The Treatment of Illness," 43

true aspect of all phenomena, 23, 41, 142, 151

True Word school, 107, 115, 142, 145, 148–49

trust, 30, 77, 90

truth, 2, 31, 82

twenty-first century, as a century of life, 66, 120

two heavenly kings, 37

two sages, 37

U

understanding, 77

Ueno, lay nun, overcoming obstacles, 80

Ueno Shichiro Jiro, 54, 59

unity, 47, 77

uphold the Buddha's golden words, not the opinions of others, standard to, 24–25

V

value, creating, 62–63, 66, 97, 133

victory, 3, 33, 44, 49, 60, 62–63, 69, 71–73, 76, 79, 81, 123, 135, 139; of individual practitioner, 80

vitality, 139

votary of the Lotus Sutra, 44, 56

vow, 6–7, 15, 65, 94, 100, 106, 108, 113–15, 120, 135, 139

W

warfare, disaster caused by, 137; overcoming, 100, 150

"A Warning against Begrudging One's Fief," 71–72

wisdom, 3, 45, 63, 73, 79, 90, 109, 118, 130, 141, 143, 146, 151–53

with the same mind as Nichiren, 6

women, 107; enemies of all, 116; happiness of, 105–06, 109–14, 116–17, 120; harassment of Nichiren Daishonin by, 115–16; and the Mystic Law, 109

women's division, 47, 119–20

workplaces, victory in, 78, 82

world peace, 1–4, 10, 13–15, 49, 120, 150, 155

worthy ruler, in modern times, 150; Nichiren Daishonin as a, 146

Y–Z

Yashodhara, 112

young women's division, 47; Ikeda Kayo-kai of the, 120

youth, 82; fostering the, 119; and parents, 115

youth division, 12, 33, 37, 71; mission of the, 38; and study, 4–5

Zen school, 107, 115